Politics and the American Press
The Rise of Objectivity, 1865–192(

Politics and the American Press takes a fresh look at the origins of modern journalism's ideals and political practices. In particular, Richard Kaplan addresses the professional ethic of political independence and objectivity widely adopted by the US press. He shows how this philosophy emerged from a strikingly different ethic of avid formal partisanship in the early twentieth century.

The book also provides fresh insights into the economics of journalism and uses business papers and personal letters of publishers to explore the influence of competition, advertising, and an explosion in readership on the market strategies of the press. Kaplan documents the changes in political content of the press by a systematic content analysis of newspaper news and editorials over a span of 55 years. The book concludes by exploring the question of what should be the appropriate political role and professional ethics of journalists in a modern democracy.

RICHARD KAPLAN is Lecturer in the Sociology Department at the University of California, Santa Barbara. His work on media history has received the *Catherine Covert Prize* for best published article in Mass Communications History (1996). He has published in *Journalism History; Media, Culture, and Society*; and *American Journalism*.

Politics and the American Press
The Rise of Objectivity, 1865–1920

Richard L. Kaplan

CAMBRIDGE
UNIVERSITY PRESS

PUBLISHED BY THE PRESS SYNDICATE OF THE UNIVERSITY OF CAMBRIDGE
The Pitt Building, Trumpington Street, Cambridge, United Kingdom

CAMBRIDGE UNIVERSITY PRESS
The Edinburgh Building, Cambridge CB2 2RU, UK
40 West 20th Street, New York NY 10011–4211, USA
477 Williamstown Road, Port Melbourne, VIC 3207, Australia
Ruiz de Alarcón 13, 28014 Madrid, Spain
Dock House, The Waterfront, Cape Town 8001, South Africa

http://www.cambridge.org

First published 2002

Printed in the United Kingdom at the University Press, Cambridge

Typeface Plantin 10/12 pt   *System* 3b2   [CE]

A catalogue record for this book is available from the British Library

Library of Congress Cataloguing in Publication data

Kaplan, Richard L. (Richard Lee), 1955–
Politics and the American Press: the rise of objectivity, 1865–1920 / Richard L.
Kaplan.
    p. cm.
Includes bibliographical references and index.
ISBN 0 521 62151 8 (hb.) ISBN 0 521 00602 3 (pb.)
1. Press and politics – United States – History – 19th century. 2. Press and
politics – United States – History – 20th century. 3. Journalism – Objectivity –
United States – History – 19th century. 4. Journalism – Objectivity – United
States – History – 20th century. I. Title.

PN4888.P6 K37 2001
071′.3′09034 – dc21   2001025240 CIP

ISBN 0 521 62151 8 hardback
ISBN 0 521 00602 3 paperback

For my mother and father

Contents

Acknowledgments

Debts, debts, debts. In writing this book, I have accumulated a heavy burden of debts. To the following people I am deeply grateful for their advice and support.

I am beholden to Michael Rogin whose lectures and writings inspired my explorations into American cultural history. To Ann Swidler I owe a special debt of gratitude for her impressive care and guidance as I began this project. She kibitzed and quibbled over many a detail, all the while recalling me to the larger issues at stake in this study. And I thank Kim Voss for her persistent concern with the nuts and bolts of sociology – the logic of argument and the methodology of research – and her always friendly smile.

I am obliged to the following sagacious media scholars for having read and commented on various parts of this book: Thomas Leonard, James W. Carey, Jon Cruz, and Michael Schudson. Colleagues and friends at the University of California, Berkeley spread their own version of moist, enriching fertilizer over this volume. Thanks particularly to Orville Lee, Lyn Spillman, Paul Lichterman, Arlene Stein, and Nina Eliasoph. Finally let me express my appreciation to Simonetta Falasca Zamponi – wife, cook, general caretaker, or should I rather say colleague, taskmaster, critic? Without her love and assistance doubtless this book would still be sitting on the desk a confused pile of notes and computer disks.

To my parents, Netta and Marvin Kaplan, I am permanently indebted for their special combination of caring hearts and critical minds. This book is dedicated to them.

Introduction

On October 15, 1868 the Detroit *Free Press*, a Democratic newspaper, reported:

> The Democracy of Shiawasee county assembled *en masse* at this place to-day and raised a magnificent hickory, something over one hundred feet high, and all pronounced it the handsomest pole that has been raised in this section of the country. After getting it raised and properly secured a magnificent streamer thirty feet long, bearing the names of our glorious standard bearers, [Presidential candidate] Seymour and Blair, was hoisted to the breeze, when cheer after cheer was sent up as the flag unfurled and these names, which are synonyms of liberty and equality, floated at the top of the pole . . .

Political culture in the second half of the nineteenth century was pervasively partisan. Despite hour after hour of political speeches dissecting the issues of the day, election campaigns were more than duty.[1] Notwithstanding the torchlight parades, the raising high of the hickory pole, and the barbecue of whole oxen, campaigns were more than diversion. Election ceremonies offered an opportunity for American voters to display their commitment to a political community, a political party.

The *Free Press*, like other daily newspapers, participated in these rituals of political belonging. As official state paper of the Democratic Party, the *Free Press*'s political advocacy extended well beyond the publication of a list of endorsements on elections day, as our contemporary press is wont to do. Indeed, partisanship was a public and ubiquitous phenomenon that defined the very essence of nineteenth-century American journalism. Endorsements were not for individual candidates, but for entire party slates without exception. And, the paper publicized its choices day upon day for weeks before the election, as a sort of special badge of honor. Editorials naturally rung with the rhetoric of forthright political stands. Indeed, the majority of opinion pieces argued the party's cause, defending its policies from all criticism by unprincipled opponents. News reports too were hardly exempt from partisanship and reflected in important ways journalism's public mission.

The individual journal was the organ of the partisan political community, and charged with the task of articulating the community's ideas and expressing its interests. In their prouder moments such journals could claim to have enriched American democracy. Journals enhanced the public's attention to social issues and people's sense of political involvement. In their darker days, such journals ruthlessly suppressed and distorted the news, letting the interests of politicians ride roughshod over any open reporting of vital issues.

In the early twentieth century, however, journalism in Detroit as in other American cities broke its historical ties with the Republicans and Democrats. No longer "official organs" of the party, they disavowed their past exuberant, political journalism. No longer faithful partisans, Detroit papers cast a cool appraising eye when judging the news value of the speeches of politicians. And then the words were usually discounted, marked down as of limited value, consisting solely of the debased currency of political speech.

At this time, newspapers elaborated a new occupational ethic and reconstructed their political role in the public arena. The press, journalists pledged, would be governed only by a rigorous ethic of impartiality and public service. The daily paper should represent only the general public in reporting and investigating the news, not particular political interests. The press changed from being a strenuous advocate and ally of the parties to a formally neutral and independent medium of public communication for, ideally, a whole range of political voices. In its new impartial guise, the press gave up much of its right to express a political viewpoint, to inject into the news its own sentiments and evaluations. Politics no longer held pride of place in the daily columns, and journalism dispensed with the partisan passions that had imbued its narratives with excitement and drama.

This book explores changes in the political role of the American press from 1865 to 1920. Over the course of these fifty-five years, journalism fundamentally altered how it reported on the words and deeds of politicians. How did this shifting political stance of the press, I ask, affect the way American citizens perceive and participate in politics? What accounts for such transformations? And how can the tools of social science – most particularly political and cultural sociology – help us to understand these dynamics of change? Against specifically economic, cultural, and professional explanations, this book argues for a political interpretation of journalism's permutations. Both press and polity should be understood in tandem as institutions of the "public sphere." Both are contentious partners in America's public debate with all its disputes over what is and what should be the proper ordering to the nation.

Politics of the press

Today's news media assert that they are independent of all direct political ties. Journalism, they say, is quite unencumbered by any guiding political beliefs, obligations, or allegiances; the press selects its news according to autonomous criteria of journalistic importance. Despite this appearance of formal autonomy, however, the media's selections and interpretations are not a matter of a free choice by the free press. The fourth estate of both the nineteenth and twentieth centuries, this book argues, is quite weak and easily overpowered by rival political powers. Indeed, the press is inevitably entangled in the debate of the public arena and influenced by the political powers that be. Contextualizing the press within the public sphere – with its distribution of resources and legitimacy among diverse public speakers – reveals the nature of, and constraints on, reporting.[2] It helps account for the media's relative subordination in defining the news agenda. More generally, it explains the press's public pose, whether it be as avid partisan advocate, effaced neutral recorder, or impartial expert analyst.

For the press always possesses a political dimension. Three main factors account for this inescapable, if subterranean, politicization of the news. First, in constructing its daily quota of news narratives, the press aspires to present a formal, authoritative account of the day's most important words and deeds. The media transform private events into public affairs and suggest these reports are worthy of the nation's attention. Society in some sense accepts the importance and centrality of these news stories. As a "cultural focal point" that in part defines our reality, the news inevitably becomes a crucial "symbolic resource" for politicians: an object warranting their close attention and concern.[3]

Second, political groups may differ with the press over the accuracy of the news. They may deny the validity of the press's descriptions, denounce their analyses, and impugn their motives. Or, at least, the politician, the public relations agent, and the citizen's advocate realize that other news reports with alternative spins would serve their purposes better. They know that more favorable press coverage can be obtained by assertions of injury and unfairness, in sum, by heaving a few criticisms in the direction of the press. Consequently, the interpretations of reporters necessarily come into conflict with other public or political organizations.

Third, journalism lacks any of those special attributes which might shield it from external critics.[4] Unlike other professions, reporters cannot boast of any formal credentialed training, nor specialized technical knowledge, nor an esoteric occupational language. Journalism vends its wares in the public arena and misses all those professional traits which might grant it an exclusive authority to depict our social world. Furthermore, the press confronts other public speakers – most notably the President – who have their own legitimacy, their own mandate to define what is important and true about our social reality.

In sum, journalism confronts rival public authorities and is unable to establish any technocratic justifications that would allow it to report the news free from external criticisms. The news media do not stand above the battles and debates that animate American public discussion. Rather, they are inevitably embroiled in the contentions of the public sphere. Threatened by attacks on its credibility and its centrality, the press responds. To ensure the acceptability of its news reports to both the mass public and elite alike, the media draw upon the norms of the broader political culture and accede to the views and voices of "legitimate" political representatives in the public arena.[5] In this manner, politics fundamentally influences the news – both in the specific selection of events for coverage and in journalism's definition of its highest professional ideals.

The democratic public sphere and the press

The press flourishes and, in fact, survives only in the democratic public arena. What is this "public sphere"? "At the root of all politics," declares E. E. Schattschneider, "is the universal language of conflict."[6] But only in the modern era is conflict accepted as a central part of the definition of politics. Only in the "Democratic Age" is a social space created for the permissible expression of opposed points of view and interests. This arena of conflict, this "public sphere," with its lack of automatic identity among truth, power, and law, involves the articulation of a new normative political project and political identity for society.[7] In this normative project, no prime minister, president, or king is permanently entitled to control political office or to wield the power of government. No social group is considered automatically to hold the truth. Rather, the truth and power of democracy derive from the permanently open and revisable deliberations of public opinion. Ideally, into this open space of democracy, into this public discussion, all citizens can freely enter as equals, propound their perspectives, and participate in the formation of a political consensus. No *a priori* fixed views or privileged speakers establish the correct policy. Instead, the better argument should triumph over mere social power.

The social space in which public opinion forms is the "public sphere." Jürgen Habermas in his classic study, *Structural Transformation of the Public Sphere*, explains that in a crucial, minimal sense the public sphere emerges "in every conversation in which private individuals assemble to form a public body."[8] With this conception, Habermas rooted modern democracy in civil society, below the summits of formal political power. This defining down of politics allows modern representative democracy to escape the restrictions on participation and deliberation that would necessarily ensue if discussion was confined to formal governmental institutions. Such institutions, with their scarce resources and their limited time to reach decisions, necessarily exclude the mass of the population. Instead, in civil society, in the public sphere, these limits do not obtain.

Classical democratic theory proposed that the policies of government should reflect this more general process of deliberation in the public arena. Congress or Parliament's legislation, like public opinion in general, was to follow from the better argument of what was right, and not just from momentary, fluctuating power balances: *Veritas non auctoritas facit legem* – Truth, not the arbitrary authority of the ruler, makes law. Between government and society there was not to be just a top-down, one-way, flow of power and speech. Rather, parliament's deliberations would also be guided and informed by the issues and reasoned perspectives raised in civil society.

This concept of a public sphere – an open, multi-sided, popular discussion aimed at consensus – was institutionalized in the formally democratic state through enumerated rights. Its autonomy was guaranteed by rights of freedom of speech and assembly. Its power over government was ensured by universal suffrage and by rendering governmental decision-making public and open to scrutiny by citizens and their representatives.[9] The politicians charged with implementing the consensus elaborated by public opinion were to exercise power in accordance with the law and in a transparent manner.[10]

The press was supposed to play a crucial role in this ideal model of democracy, and indeed journalism has historically been central to the viability and vitality of public discussion. As Alexis de Tocqueville pointed out a century and a half ago, the press remedies the problems of political communication in modern mass society. When democracy expands from a small polis to a nation-state, the exchange of opinions and information can no longer be encompassed by face-to-face conversation. Instead, the press assumes the crucial role of bearer of political discussion among citizens separated by vast geographical, and also social, distances.[11] Furthermore, Habermas and others have detailed how the press crucially fought for the rights of the public. In the US, as in Europe, journalists contested the secrecy of the national legislature as well as the government's censorship of public discussion.[12]

But we do not need to rely on Habermas or even the earlier de Tocqueville to recognize the press's preeminent place in democracy's deliberations. For in manifold ways the press as an institution of the public sphere is directly inscribed into our legal–constitutional system – from the First Amendment with its mandate for press freedom to economic privileges that are specific to journalism because of its political status, to "shield laws" that permit the news media to keep their sources confidential in judicial proceedings.[13] Society bestows upon the media special rights, and in turn expects them to accomplish a difficult political task: the press should facilitate the citizens' exchange of ideas and information without compromising the public sphere's classical ideals of openness and equality among participants.[14]

Social histories of the American press

This is journalism's public mission. It would of course be naive to accept at face value the press's claim to fulfill these eighteenth or even twentieth-century ideals. Despite all their democratic aspirations, the news media do not respond to the needs of all citizens equally, they do not permit all members of the public to enter the public sphere as represented in their columns and pages. In addition to responding to the public sphere's ethic of equal, open communication, the press is an economic entity, a political resource, and a cultural product. The nightmare forces of power, profit, and ideology often intrude upon journalism's democratic dreams and disturb its commitments to serve the public without fear or favor.[15]

In fact, across time and from country to country, the press has promoted the ideals of the public arena in markedly diverse and contradictory ways. It is the curious trait of past historiography, however, to provide only an extremely limited perspective on the diversity and alterations in the politics of the press. Historians appear to possess only a few crude conceptual tools with which to elucidate media transformations. Change is often taken for granted, turned into a quasi-biological process of natural evolution, or ascribed to one or two inevitable forces such as increasing modernization or commercialization of the media. Overwhelmingly, historians ignore the role of such social variables as power and culture in the constitution of the news. Similarly the outcome of change is conceived in simplified, dichotomous terms of a "free" versus "controlled" media. In this manner, the variable ways in which the media enhance or inhibit democratic discussion are lost, and the actual social construction of the news is neglected.[16]

The case study offered here aims to remedy these defects. Between the nineteenth and the twentieth century, the American press fundamentally refashioned its mode and manner of facilitating democratic discussion. A consideration of this change will reveal the alternative ways in which the press functioned within the public arena, and the principles of their variation. But first it is necessary to reflect upon the insights and inadequacies of past historical accounts of this journalistic revolution.

Progressive historiography

Every historical age creates its own paradigm of historical understanding. In the triumphant reign of each paradigm a new image of the polity and the press is normally produced. In the early twentieth century, Progressive historiography depicted journalism as having evolved through a sequence of stages towards political independence and objectivity. By the early 1900s, the fourth estate supposedly freed itself from the contaminating influence of government, political parties, and "the (commercial) interests."[17] In the typical metaphor of the period, the press was seen as maturing, becoming a machine. The press grew into a bureaucratic corporation. Yet this new, controlling "iron cage" guaranteed the press's freedom, not its servitude. The dictates of the market, a complex division of labor, and professionalism – in sum, modernity – purportedly imposed a sobriety, impersonality, and impartiality upon the journalistic trade. As a manifestation of their new complexity, daily newspapers eliminated the arbitrary authority of individual partisan editors, whether in their pose as political propagandists, moral crusaders, or just plain eccentric characters.

The press thus achieved freedom from both corrupting external powers (political parties, corporations), and capricious internal powers (the partisan editor, the capitalist owner).[18] The press's evolution towards truth and independence presumably culminated in an ideal endpoint – expert news personnel freely pursuing their specific journalistic function in autonomous organizations. Instead of a biased, personal organ serving interests, journalism supposedly became a professional public service assisting American democracy with unbiased information and impartial analysis.[19]

This Progressive account is dismissed by Michael Schudson as a form of "natural history." Typically natural history presents a descriptive chronology of events without thematizing the causal factors that resulted in one specific outcome instead of another.[20] The Progressives portrayed the press as an unfolding organic form that follows its own internal, teleological path of development towards press freedom. Journalism's relationship to its environment – the variable forms of political institutions and culture – is left unquestioned.

Baldasty's economic history of the news

Gerald Baldasty's recent volume effectively inverts the Progressives' natural history of American journalism. Yet, although his *The Commercialization of the News in the Nineteenth Century* is the latest synthetic account of the growth of newspaper independence, it is in many ways a classical account. It merits our attention, beyond its evident insights, because Baldasty largely expresses the conventional wisdom on press changes. He argues that indeed, across the span of the nineteenth century, journals steadily dispensed with their original partisan commitments and advocacy. This advancing movement, according to him, reflected not the purification of the press from political control, but a new brand of corruption. Rather than fulfilling its democratic duties, the Gilded Age press became ever more addicted to the profits offered by a mass audience and advertisers. Baldasty elaborates the familiar theory of transformations in nineteenth-century journalism as the product of increasing "commercialization." His achievement is to turn this received wisdom into a clear, systematic, and thoroughly documented account.

For Baldasty, an early partisan press was supported largely by the patronage payoffs of parties. In the middle decades of the century, propelled by visions of new-found wealth and increasing capital investments, publishers traded in the limited party patronage for the bountiful commercial revenues offered by advertisers. By the waning years of the 1800s, daily sheets "usually eschewed close political affiliation" and were largely autonomous.[21] In Baldasty's theory, news content and indeed "journalistic visions" followed from this funding mechanism. And this commercialization dictated one result: a depoliticized news that addresses its audience as consumers, not citizens.[22]

Baldasty richly details the changed fundamentals of the newspaper business. His is the most substantiated narrative yet of the shifts in managerial strategies, newspaper organization, and market constraints affecting the journalistic enterprise. But in his simple reversal of Progressive history Baldasty largely reproduces its straightforward, deterministic account of the news. Culture and power are largely (if not entirely) missing in his history. [23] His attention remains steadfastly on the sources of funding for the news business. As he succinctly writes,

The intimate connection between finances and content figures prominently in the changing nature of the press during the century and was central to the rise of commercialized news . . . [W]hen advertisers came to replace political parties as the key constituent (and financial angel) of the press, the press came to support them, too. These two constituencies, first political parties and later advertisers, were instrumental in defining the news. Both helped shape the news to reflect their own needs and interests.[24]

Baldasty can blithely ignore culture and politics because he inadequately analyzes how economics influences the conduct of journalism. His assertion of a "simple interplay of money and content" is too simple. He ignores the ambiguities of a market-oriented press and bluntly juxtaposes it to a politically funded journalism. As my chapter 2 argues in more detail, markets do not automatically expel press partisanship. A concern for profits will not necessarily exclude political advocacy. Indeed, in certain market contexts, and given popular attachment to parties, newspapers which publicly proselytize for a party may well gather more subscribers than ostensibly independent papers. This capacity of a profit-driven press to maintain its partisan stance reflects, in part, the different ways that politics and economics affect the content of journalism.

While a concern for either profit maximization or power accumulation may impair the press's service to public deliberation, power and profit inflict their injuries in different ways. Politics, we may say, constitutively enters into cultural works, whereas economics only makes their production and distribution highly dependent. Politics is directly concerned with reshaping journalistic content for persuasive propagandistic purposes. The politician wishes to mold the reader's political convictions. A profit orientation is only secondarily concerned with the message of the news; commercial publishers desire first and foremost to sell the journal to readers and, then, to peddle readers' attention to advertisers. The news is molded to attract the readers' interests and concerns (and with an eye on the bottom-line). This recasting of journalism may entail stories of celebrities and scandals, and even a fictionalization of the news, but not necessarily. *Depending* upon the cultural expectations of readers and the structure of the market, the news may or may not respond to democracy's need for diverse, critical perspectives and reliable information.[25]

In this context, Baldasty's intensified inspection of journalism's commercialization insufficiently captures the social forces shaping American journalism at the end of the twentieth century. It fails to explain the press's continued attention (however diminished) to politics and the particular form this coverage takes. In general, Baldasty's delineation of the growth of commercial concerns provides a forceful, but ultimately inadequate, portrait of press politics in the waning years of the Gilded Age.

Schudson's Consensus history

Michael Schudson's *Discovering the News* endures as the standard social history of the American press, in part because of its succinct overview and probing analyses. Against Progressive historians' description of the press's progress towards independence as a development purely internal to the institutions of journalism, Schudson firmly contextualizes his press history in a description of the changes convulsing American society in the 1830s. Positioned against the historical backdrop of the Jacksonian era, the Progressives' natural chronology of the fourth estate's slow passage to freedom becomes a cultural–historical explanation.

In the 1830s, Schudson explains, the equivalent of a middle-class or "bourgeois" revolution occurred, where both the market and institutions of mass democracy expanded to include all adult, white males. This mass inclusion and accompanying institutional and cultural change were the social background for a new, specifically modern type of newspaper. The change created the (economic) resources and (cultural) demand for the modern press as the purveyor of a distinctive, novel commodity: the news.[26]

Prior to the 1830s, there circulated throughout the new republic more expensive commercial and partisan newspapers with a distribution and an editorial appeal confined to the social elite. The partisan papers consisted largely of opinions and commentary published under the directorship of politicians. These six-penny journals were insulated from the economics and culture of the market both by their circulation to an audience composed exclusively of faithful partisans, and by patronage payoffs from the parties.

The expansion of the market in the 1830s provided the press with the opportunity to free itself from all dependence upon party funding. A cheaper "penny press" with expanded circulation broke from the politicians and relied almost exclusively on the profits to be gained from selling the news to a mass audience and advertising revenues. As Schudson observes, "Sources of income that depended on social ties or political fellow-feeling were replaced by market-based income."[27]

Along with a burgeoning commercial market, the Jacksonian era saw a number of political transformations crucial for the emergence of modern American journalism. For Schudson, the modern idea of the news depends upon a depoliticization of society. Extrapolating from Schudson, we can say that the news, with its claim to present non-controversial, apolitical, factual information about the world, rests on a social consensus.[28] Schudson finds these shared social values in the triumph of liberal individualism in the Jacksonian era. He adopts the perspective of the Consensus School which sees the US as possessing a cultural consensus or "hegemony" of acquisitive individualism.[29] America is not characterized by groups upholding sharply juxtaposed social visions and values. Mundane facts of daily economic life are not subject to emphatically polarized interpretations. What counts in the US is not the battle between classes over resources and the future direction of society, but rather the largely shared culture of economic liberalism.

Furthermore, even the political realm underwent a privatization in the 1830s. Previously, says Schudson, the social elite was organized into political cliques and had battled over rival conceptions of the public good. But in the 1830s this limited elite politics was marginalized by the rise of mass parties. Instead of the common good, the new Democrat and Whig parties, staffed by professional politicians, proposed policies intended to maximize the economic interests of their supporters. Similarly, newspapers reflected this shift from the political to the "social"; news content evolved from public debate over the proper ends of the commonwealth to matters of private interest subject to public scrutiny – that is, from editorials to news.[30]

To summarize, Schudson presents a powerful incisive analysis of the origins of the modern independent press. American journalism's defining ideals and distinctive public posture are not taken for granted, but traced back into innovative features of American society and culture of the 1830s. Contingent cultural and political factors enter into the constitution of American journalism.

Schudson's history parallels that of writers such as Habermas.[31] Schudson depicts the emergence in the 1830s of a popular press that has dispensed with its political function for the sake of potential earnings. While some historians, such as Baldasty, appear to naturalize the press's turn to profits as automatic, Schudson offers a cultural explanation for why a market orientation predominates. Yet, his narrative is largely wrong for the entire nineteenth century. As Schudson now recognizes, partisanship endured until the century's end.[32] Schudson mistakenly projects into the previous century the characteristics of the twentieth-century's pluralist institutions: general citizen apathy, a decayed party system, politics as competing interest groups, and the general predominance of the "social" over the political. Overlooking the sustained popular, partisan attachments of the late 1800s, Schudson also misses the party affiliations of papers.[33] Claiming a depoliticized populace and press, he cannot begin to explain the reconstruction of journalistic ideals after 1900. And the emerging detachment of press from parties at this time necessarily eludes him.

Furthermore, I would suggest, Schudson unfolds his own version of "natural history." He never fully problematizes the cultural and political presuppositions of a modern press. Once the press achieves independence, it is considered free from political entanglements. Nor does Schudson recognize the potentially variable forms of contemporary journalism. He, like his Consensus Theory mentors, slips from viewing the hegemony of liberal individualism as a specific historical construction to considering it a natural, even ideal, aspect of modernity. This naturalization is clear in Schudson's further history of the press. From 1830 to 1920, after the seed of the modern press has been planted in the rich loam of American soil, there occurs only the slow growth, fruition, and then crisis of this same press and society.[34] Political contention over alternative cultural models of American politics and press are nowhere to be found.

Because Consensus Theory always attributed views of acquisitive individualism to the consensual majority in American civil society, its representatives missed the power relations necessary for the continued dominance of this cultural world-view.[35] Eliding power and conflict in society, they necessarily assumed that the polity and press simply reflected liberal society in a power-free manner. Consequently, they could not see how these public institutions (including the news media) were entangled in, and worked to reproduce, the public apathy at the root of economic individualism.[36] The historian Michael McGerr subverts this perspective by delineating a "thick" notion of political life. McGerr reveals how press and polity are permanently involved in the symbolic construction of public life and political identities.

McGerr and the new political history

Michael McGerr's *The Decline of Popular Politics: the American North, 1865–1928* clearly reflects the paradigm shift of the new political history of the 1970s and the studies in political culture of the 1980s.[37] McGerr corrects the omission of parties from Schudson's portrait of nineteenth-century political life. Relying on the revisionism of quantitative political historians such as Walter Dean Burnham, Paul Kleppner, and Richard

Jensen, he recognizes the pervasive partisanship of the post-bellum era. And, once he catches the scent, he can easily track this partisanship into the lair of journalism.

In a review of histories of the Gilded Age, Geoffrey Blodgett has noted that it is typical for historians to pit the nineteenth century's political universe against that of the twentieth. The Third Party System (1856–96) and the Fourth (1896–1928) are placed in stark opposition, and the historian's denigration of politics of one period results in the elevation of the other as an ideal.[38] Progressives and their intellectual progeny denounced the ritual, emotional partisanship of the Gilded Era; McGerr and the new political historians reverse the evaluations of the Progressives. They mourn the lost, actively partisan political world of the nineteenth century as more democratic. However, their tears of grief over the Third Party System's demise, I will argue, cloud their perception of the power and unrepresentativeness of the major parties.[39]

McGerr joins with these political historians to explain the shift in electoral styles, the fall in voter participation, and the decline in political centrality of parties that occurred after the pivotal election of 1896. McGerr's particular project is to reconstruct the causes for the precipitous fall in voter turnout. His explanatory strategy is based on the new cultural history of politics. He complements the new political history's standard statistical analysis of voter behavior with a "thick description" of political culture. In a manner similar to Burnham, McGerr focuses on the crucial mediating role of parties in rendering democratic politics meaningful and salient. In Burnham's formulation:

> The ultimate democratic purpose of issue formulation in a campaign is to give the people at large the power to choose their and their agents' options. Moreover, so far as is known the blunt alternative to party government is the concentration of political power . . . in the hands of those who already possess concentrated economic power . . . [N]o adequate substitute for party as a means of mobilizing non-elite influence on the governing process has yet been discovered.[40]

Unlike Burnham and all quasi-rational-choice theorists, McGerr does not depict parties as useful because they structure clear, alternative choices for the electorate, and thus enhance voter control. Instead, following the political culture approach, McGerr delineates the symbolic function of parties.[41] Parties and a pervasive partisan culture are the context for public, expressive rituals that construct and consolidate political identities in the nineteenth century. Elections are not a matter of private reflection as the voter decides between policy options. Rather, elections are elaborate ceremonies of publicly declared identification with parties. Election campaigns with their accompanying hoopla and histrionics were the first public institutions through which loyalty to party was repeatedly demonstrated and affirmed. Partisan newspapers with their emotional reports of party victories and defeats constituted the second. These public rituals helped to forge the popular affective political ties that were necessary to motivate high electoral turnout, thus strengthening the operations of mass democracy.[42]

For McGerr, politics and press have a positive role in the development of group identities, interests, and social ties.[43] McGerr does not reproduce the naturalized thin description typical of political science. In such accounts, politics consists of a voter, with an already given set of social interests, entering and exiting the voting booth.[44] Instead, politics for him is rich in symbols and meaning. In fact politics is better understood as a meaning-constituting activity than as a strategic arena. Politics is not (or not only) the allocation of scarce goods by authoritative decisions, but also the construction of collective identities through public rites.[45]

McGerr also points to the role of the press in constituting the public space for the display of political identities. He elaborates the concept of "political style" by which he means the different ways newspapers can represent politics, the rhetoric they employ, and the identities they make salient.[46] McGerr assigns the nineteenth century's press a central role in the propagation of a partisan political culture, and thus recognizes journalism's dynamic role in the public sphere.

Starting from 1870 however, McGerr says, newspapers dispensed with their typical theatrics of emotional partisanship. McGerr locates this reconstruction of political culture and the ideals of journalism in the political movement of elite, genteel reformers known as the Liberal Republicans and later the Mugwumps. Editors allied with these reformers recommended a journalism of principled independence. They banished the press's old, expressive advocacy and adopted a journalism of restrained, private reflection. For McGerr, this reformation of journalism and also political campaigns along more "rational," sober, and less ritualistic lines, accounts for the rapid collapse in voter turnout after 1896.

In sum, McGerr does not naturalize the present-day apolitical, objective, and differentiated press. He documents a possible alternative model, and he explains that the origin of our contemporary journalism was not a necessary development. On the contrary, it was a contingent, historical change depending upon power relations and the cultural views of a social elite. This new model of journalism emerged out of a class movement which imposed its own agenda on the political system for power and status reasons.

Notwithstanding its strengths, a number of problems plague McGerr's analysis. These problems stem, in part, from his conception of parties and press as vehicles for expressive rites. Of course, the democratic concerns underlying McGerr's study are evident right from the start, beginning with his book's title: *The Decline of Popular Politics.* Yet, McGerr's focus on rituals obscures questions of power in political parties, and neglects normative issues of democracy.[47] Typical of such a ritual mode of analysis, politics is considered an expressive drama of the community's values and experience, while the strategic and instrumental aspects of politics are screened from view. The conflicting goals, interests, and policies sought by groups and politicians, and the organizational forms used to pursue those goals, are invisible. McGerr recovers the crucial symbolic dimension of parties, but I claim this expressive dimension needs to be connected to strategic interests, style to content. Parties and their newspapers do not aggregate and report without distortion all the interests and views of civil society. Rather, parties are a mix of meaning, power, and interests. As organizations oriented to the strategic constraints of their environment, they jerry-build coalitions of supporters by making ideological and practical appeals. These appeals help to create public-political identities, but the elaborated identities are constrained, on one side, by the pragmatics of building viable political coalitions,[48] on the other, by the salience of pre-political identities and interests.[49] The political field is the ground for the elaboration of political identities, as McGerr suggests, and it has an autonomous logic depending upon the resources and constraints specific to it. But its logic does not exclude the strategic, and it also relies upon the array of interests and pre-political identities in civil society.

McGerr takes an important step forward in describing changes in this public-political arena and the variable role of the press within it. Never-theless, he inadequately describes the public sphere's institutional organization with its distribution of power and legitimacy among rival political actors. And, he insufficiently recognizes the influence of politics upon American journals. I argue instead that the press's public-political role depends upon its relative position within this public arena. As the structure of the public sphere changes, so will the press's particular public philosophy also evolve.

For instance, McGerr's history demonstrates that the preeminent speakers in the nineteenth-century public arena were parties. But the predominance of parties with their vast symbolic and material resources had consequences for newspapers, consequences ignored by McGerr. McGerr points to the elite political movement of Liberal Republicans that reformed the political ideals of newspaper editors and publishers.

But, in fact, this movement was too weak and too elitist to transform the views of the general populace. As long as parties could claim the mass allegiance of voters, journals were not free to travel their own road to independence and political neutrality.[50]

Transformations in journalism's avowed public mission depend upon alterations in the overarching public sphere. Against McGerr, this book contends that not until the "critical elections" of 1894–96 would the overwhelming power of parties diminish and provide an opportunity for journalistic revolt. After 1896, the Democrats and Republicans suffered a long-term decline in their legitimacy and control of political resources. In this context, and in conjunction with the Progressive movement's attack on "party machines," newspapers broke from parties and established their independence.

Freed from all allegiances to parties, newspapers were not removed from the contentious arena of public debate. Reporters still needed to justify their news selections in confrontation with other political perspectives. Therefore, the press elaborated a novel occupational ethic which drew upon cultural ideals articulated in the Progressive reform movements. Journalists defined themselves as impartial technical experts, providing factual and authoritative news accounts of the day's events. They saw themselves as serving the public interests, and above the contamination of politics. This new professional ideology helped to reconstruct the public sphere as it justified the press's new political role in public communication.

Chapter plan

This book proceeds in roughly chronological fashion, interspersing chapters that describe the political content of the press with those that analyze shifts in the daily papers' economic and political environment. Chapter 1 commences with the partisan press in the extremely politicized era of post-war Reconstruction, 1865–76. It offers a "thick" interpretive reading of the ideals and rites of this avidly political press. The newly liberated African-American appeared prominently in the editorials and narratives of Detroit's dailies. A close inspection of this reporting offers the opportunity for a critical assessment of the strengths and limitations of this era's politicized journalism. Chapter 2 turns to the economic machinery that sustained the post-bellum press. It explains the persistence of partisanship at a time when most historians have argued that party patronage and political payoffs to newspapers had ended.

Chapter 3 extends the cultural analysis of the partisan press into the late nineteenth century. In this "Gilded Age" the passions and issues of the Civil War had all but faded, yet partisanship continued to command the fervent loyalties of the average Detroiter. The chapter more fully documents the ritual nature of the fourth estate's symbolic practices. It comprehends the press not just as a bearer of information, but also as a crucial public stage upon which political identities were scripted and performed.

Chapter 4 details significant shifts in the business of journalism in the light of the economic upheaval embroiling American industry. The onslaught of mass production in the US and concomitant changes in distribution and marketing decisively affected the economics of Detroit's four dailies, and consequently their politics. Rising advertising revenue offered new profitable opportunities to entrepreneurial publishers, but also challenged their essential notions of what a newspaper should be. In the end, such economic permutations created necessary, but not sufficient, conditions for journalism to dispense with its public display of partisan bias.

Chapter 5 describes the political developments that finally culminated in the press's transformed public mission. Only after the "critical election" of 1896 and subsequent political reforms did papers disavow their past partisan identities. Through the public statements and private letters of Detroit publishers, the chapter documents a newly emergent professional ethic of objectivity. This chapter shows the novel public philosophy to be rooted in the dominant public rhetoric and political opportunities emerging in the early-twentieth-century Progressive Era.

The book concludes with a critical comparison of journalism's public philosophies in the nineteenth and twentieth centuries. How well did the ideals of public partisanship and the ethics of objectivity serve the purposes of a modern democratic society? How adequately did the two philosophies guide, protect, and sustain journalism as it pursued its distinctive tasks in the public sphere? Indeed, where could the press find the strength and wisdom to address democracy's paramount issues and ask the hard questions? Here, the conclusion recurs to this book's central theoretical premise – that the press is permanently entangled in the contentions of the public sphere, and journalism is secretly dependent upon the authority and truths generated in the citizenry's public deliberations. I suggest that only a proper reformulation of the press's relationship with democracy's unending public conversation will restore to journalism the prestige and perspective it needs to fulfill its democratic mission.

NOTES

1 Cf. Gienapp 1982.
2 Hallin and Mancini present a conception of the variable institutional structuring of the public sphere and the place of the press in their 1984 article.
3 Cf. Schudson 1986b: 44–5.
4 Schudson labels journalism an "uninsulated profession" (1978: 9).
5 This process occurs largely as the reporters draw upon tacit knowledge about the way the world works and what is important and true. As the "phenomenological" perspective suggests, these common-sense philosophies are constructed through day-to-day interactions among reporters and those higher up the corporate ladder. From this perspective, the press is a leaky boat. Claiming to float on the surface of politics, it is instead always taking on cultural waters from the surrounding political seas. The perspectives of "legitimate," powerful, and "important" speakers inevitably worm their way into media reports. Cf. Barsamian 1992: 26–7; Tuchman 1972.
    Without reference to journalism, Bourdieu discusses the unequal distribution of rights to name and speak in politics. See Bourdieu 1985. I discuss political rights of public speech further in chapter 4.
6 Schattschneider 1975: 2.
7 Lefort 1988.
8 Habermas 1974: 49; 1989. For a useful discussion of Habermas' ideas and the press see Hallin 1985.
9 On parliamentary publicity see Bobbio 1987: ch. 4; and Habermas 1989: 81–3. On political rights see Poggi 1978: 104–5; and Habermas 1989: 83.
10 Habermas 1974.
11 De Tocqueville 1945. V. II, 342–3, 119–22 and V. I, 188–95. Cf. Manca 1989.
12 On press and parliamentary secrecy Park 1960: 15; and for the American case Leonard 1986: ch. 3.
13 On the peculiar economic rights given to the press because of its political role see Pilgrim 1991.
14 Schudson makes an interesting attempt to reinvigorate this press ideal in his *The Power of News* 1995: ch. 10.
15 Habermas' later social theory provides at least the abstract categories for analyzing the variable historical forms of the public sphere and the political role of the press. He suggests that there are three rival principles that can govern the public sphere: money, power, and solidarity. We may further specify that these three principles are variably institutionalized depending on the class forces, cultural resources, and inherited political institutions of a given country. See Habermas 1986.
16 Cf. Nerone 1995. My notion of the "social" derives from Touraine 1981. Against all forms of reduction – whether to nature, efficiency, or strategic rationality – an adequate social theory must consider how the news is embedded in social relations traversed by culture and power. Schudson's consideration of the role played by technology and literacy in 1830s press changes is an important model of such a social conception.

17 Schudson 1978: 39–43. Also see McKern 1977 and Carey 1974.

18 E.g. Lippmann's argument in *Public Opinion* (1965 [1922]) against Upton Sinclair's *The Brass Check* with its attack on the press.

19 "These historians fell into the error of accepting the profession's own definitions of themselves and, in fact, were advocates of professionalization." So Terence Johnson writes without specifically referring to historians of journalism. See Johnson 1972.

20 Schudson 1978: ch. 1. On natural history see Tilly 1984: 97–102; and Johnson 1972.

21 See his timeline: Baldasty 1992: 5–6, 36–7. As a measure of partisanship, Baldasty offers qualitative judgments resting on his reading of papers and trade journals, e.g. pp. 128–9. A more quantitative measure covers only the beginning and end of his period – early 1830s and late 1890s – thus leaving unclear the precise points of transformation. Furthermore his measure of partisanship – relative amount of political coverage – is fairly crude. The content of the political coverage and if it is imbued with any bias or public partisanship is not studied. Regarding Baldasty's study, Schudson observes that while the relative amount of political coverage did decline during this period, the absolute amount did not: newspapers were expanding rapidly in size in the late 1800s (Schudson 1994: 269–70). Another measure of partisanship presented is the listing as partisan or independent from the annual advertiser directories, 128–33. I analyze this measure in my subsequent discussion of Michael McGerr.

22 He is more ambiguous about the meaning of commercialization on page 9. But the general thrust of the book is to denounce its destruction of the press's political mission.

23 Baldasty invokes shifting political culture along with visions guiding publishers. But, from his book title and chapter headings to his concise summaries, the dominant melody of his book resounds loudly: economics dictates the nature of the news. Baldasty does discuss a decline in partisanship during the 1850s and later (pp. 44–6). But he does not make any strong claims that this political transformation decisively affected journalism.

24 Baldasty 1992: 4–5 and cf. p. 8.

25 See Fiske 1989: ch. 2; Feher 1986: 39; Cohen 1996: 42–6. Also important is the idea that advertising exercises an "allocative function," distributing funds among publications. The shape of the market would differ if publications depended solely on readers for their revenues (see Leiss, Kline, and Jhally 1990: 121).

26 Schudson's account adopts a more sophisticated type of explanatory strategy than the one-way causality depicted here. The new press is part and parcel of this changing cultural and institutional constellation and not simply a derivative product. First Schudson shows that various autonomously developing factors are not by themselves sufficient conditions to explain the new penny press. For example, new printing techniques (that reduce newspaper costs and allow an expansion of the paper's circulation) are adopted and used only if they meet the interests and needs of social actors. But Schudson goes one step further in attacking this type of explanation. He deconstructs the idea even of necessary preconditions, in which causal

factors might seem to operate according to their own autonomous logic. Instead, such variables as literacy and independent technological developments are seen as being called into existence by a developing social demand (cf. Schudson 1978: ch. 1).

27 Schudson 1978: 18 and 25.

28 Alexander 1981: 29.

29 Cf. Hofstadter 1973, especially the introduction and chapter 3 and also the foreword by Lasch. In addition, see Wilentz 1982: 44–5.

30 Arendt's categories are evident in Schudson's analysis. He refers to her on page 30 and, in general; see Schudson 1978: ch. 1, especially 24–31, 58–60.

31 See Habermas 1989: 183–4, and in general ch. 20; also Habermas 1974: 53–5.

32 See the preface to his published dissertation: Schudson 1990; and Nerone 1987.

33 The earlier historical account of Frank Mott clearly notes the continued existence of an overwhelmingly partisan press until the late nineteenth century (Mott 1963).

34 Schudson 1978: 60, 58, 17, 121–2, 158.

35 Of course, Schudson never intended to reflect upon the role of power in the production of social consensus. I am using Consensus Theory as another name for pluralist political theory. Cf. Rogin 1987: ch. 2; McDonald 1989; Katznelson 1989; and Wilentz, 1982.

36 The government and press do not provide the opportunity for a participative political identity, but are a mere means for private accumulation.

37 McGerr 1986. McCormick traces out these paradigms in historical interpretation (1986: section one, "Trends in Historiography"). He analyzes four studies in the political culture of nineteenth-century party politics and notes "they are an unlikely historiographic school" (p. 126). He does not consider the rash of studies in political republicanism.

38 Blodgett 1976: 97. Blodgett more exemplifies the logic than transcends it.

39 The nineteenth century is favorably contrasted to the twentieth in Kleppner 1982, Jensen 1969, and Burnham 1982: ch. 1; Robert Westbrook points to this lost dimension of power in Westbrook 1983: 150–2. Burnham and McGerr do make some criticisms of the nineteenth-century party system: see Burnham 1982: 47; McGerr 1986: 7–9. More generally on parties as necessary to US democracy see Orren 1982.

40 Burnham 1982: 51 and 44. And see his essay, "The Turnout Problem" (1987).

41 In his notion of "political style," McGerr is indebted to the historian Jean Baker and in turn to cultural anthropologist Clifford Geertz (see Baker 1983). Carey in his classic work has shown the importance of the idea of ritual to understanding mass communications (Carey 1989: ch. 2).

42 McGerr 1986: 9, 14, 17–18.

43 Political identities are not just given but constructed in the public space of which the press is a central institution. Of course, the media are not the only organization involved in political identity construction. Others, such as various sub-cultures and interpretive communities, may well be more important. Falasca Zamponi presents a "creative," "dynamic" conception of

politics and its role in identity construction (1997). Also, see the discussion of the political construction of group identities and interests in the Introduction of Berger 1982.

44 Wilentz 1982.

45 Cf. the definitions of "politics" in chapter one of Poggi 1978. McGerr does not examine the role of social interests in the construction of political identities (cf. McCormick 1986: 118–19).

46 Ibid., pp. 9–11. This "political style" is in some sense comparable to Schudson's politics of journalistic narrative form.

47 Ritual is clearly (normatively speaking) a pre-modern form for the creation of social norms. Rituals represent a regression from the ideal of Habermas' public sphere where norms were subject to critical reflection and validation by open discussion (see Saretzki 1988: 56–7).

48 Cf. Przeworski 1985, Bridges 1984: 11–14.

49 Cf. Burawoy 1989; Offe 1984: ch. 9; and Oestereicher 1988.

50 Almost all the newspapers that bolted the Republican party in the Liberal Republican revolt of 1872 were back in the party fold within four years. Lost subscribers and declining advertising (not to mention lost political influence) all coerced the papers into returning to partisan correctness; see chapter 3.

1 Partisan news in the early Reconstruction Era: African-Americans in the vortex of political publicity

What was the essence of nineteenth-century press partisanship? Was it a political philosophy, or an especially opinionated and virulent form of journalism? Was it a particular relationship between writers and readers as members of a shared political community, or an economic strategy for increasing profits in a limited market? Was it a literary formula in which reporters could parade their biases as a matter of collective sentiment, or a public ritual designed to signal members' commitment to a political organization?

Partisanship certainly constituted a theory of journalism's proper public mission in American democracy. At times, Detroit's newspapers expounded upon their philosophy of partisanship and the duties appropriate to a daily paper. For instance, most journals published an annual prospectus publicizing their merits to potential subscribers. In 1872, as the election season opened, the Detroit *Post* issued a typical prospectus explaining its political mission. Hoping to capture all potential readers, the advertisement appeared in its columns every day throughout July and August:

For Grant and Wilson

To meet the demands of the Republicans of Michigan and to advance their cause, the WEEKLY POST will be sent to subscribers until after the election at the rates given below.

The Post has no sympathy with the sickly inanity that the Republican Party has accomplished its mission. No party has ceased to be useful while it retained the vitality which initiates all the practical reforms of its age and it is the crowning glory of the organization which has done so much for the country . . .

With these convictions . . . [etc.] the POST proposes to utter no uncertain sound during the canvass just now opening . . . and it depends upon those who are Republicans . . . to aid in extending its circulation.[1]

In this election-season publicity, the *Post* pledged to advocate the views of the Republican party, "to advance their cause," and to give the political community of Republicans a prominent public forum. It also argued that the ideal newspaper should be "a faithful organ" and "represent the [group's] sentiments during the campaign." In turn, the *Post*'s local rival, the *Detroit Free Press*, asserted that it would provide proper ideological guidance to all Democrats. If any Democrats were confused by the debates and news of the day, they could find clarification in its pages. In its prospectus for the 1868 campaign, Michigan's leading Democratic organ assured its readers:

The Free Press alone in this State is able to combine a Democratic point of view of our state politics and local issues with those of national importance . . . [It] will combine political news with a cool and dispassionate discussion of principles and men in such a manner as will afford to the people means of the best judgments as to the truth.[2]

As these public statements of principle suggest, newspaper partisanship was a public normative role. In professing allegiance to a party, the Detroit press assumed specific obligations, and in turn gained special privileges. The relationship between subscribers and journal did not consist in just an anonymous exchange of money for product in the market but, rather, a mutual vowing of commitments and duties as members of a political community. The individual journal was the organ of the political community, and commissioned with the task of expressing the group's ideas and its interests. Ties of solidarity and identification bound readers to their papers.

In return for the newspapers' service to the party, the readers–party members were obliged to support their party organ. Quoting again the *Post*'s 1872 overture to likely subscribers: "[The *Post*] depends upon those who are Republicans . . . to aid in extending its circulation." Similarly, the Democratic *Free Press* declared in its campaign prospectus of May 1868: "We urge the people of Michigan to continue to act and judge for themselves. Subscribe to your county papers. Sustain and maintain them first. They look out for your local interests, and they give a warm support to our national principles."[3]

At times a newspaper might betray the trust of the political community. In the summer of 1872, the Republican *Post* contended that the Democratic *Free Press* had violated the ethics proper to a political organ. The *Free Press* had tricked its subscribers when it abruptly shifted from opposing to supporting the candidacy of Horace Greeley as presidential nominee of the Democratic Party.

The Free Press' advocacy [of an anti-Greeley position] was designed to be a pledge and an inducement to all anti-Greeley Democrats to subscribe for that paper and rely upon it as a faithful organ to represent their sentiments during the campaign. Many of them did subscribe . . . in full faith that it would continue to be their organ and advocate their faith and policy. But the Free

Press has hoisted the [pro-Greeley] ticket and deceived and betrayed all those who trusted in its pledge.[4]

As the *Post* insisted, the daily paper was beholden to a community. The nineteenth-century newspaper properly functioned as an expressive organ of a pre-existing political community.

What accounts for the prominence of parties in public life and, in turn, the newspapers' unswerving political devotion? Throughout most of the nineteenth century, political parties strode triumphantly across the American political landscape. Historians describe the nineteenth-century polity as a government of "parties and courts." The United States peculiarly lacked any effective executive leader or disciplined bureaucratic administration. In the face of governmental fragmentation, these two political agencies – parties and courts – gave shape and coordination to federal policy-making and its implementation.[5] Several resources especially enhanced the power of parties to dictate the terms of American public debate. In addition to control over access to elected office, and conversion of governmental administrative positions into patronage jobs for loyal party workers, the party commanded the over-whelming support of the voting population. Parties demonstrated their ability to inspire citizen loyalty by record levels of voter turnout. In the late nineteenth century, electoral participation climbed to heights that the US has never again obtained – an average of 78.5 percent among the eligible male voters in presidential elections, 84 percent if one excludes the South.[6] Partisan identification was so pervasive that political inde-pendents were likened to some impossible third sex, a hermaphrodite species.[7] Because of their control over political resources and their legitimacy as the public representative of the people, the two parties spoke as the dominant, if not exclusive, voices on all issues of national importance.

In this context of the overweening power of parties, newspapers publicly pledged their allegiance to either the Democrats or their nine-teenth-century opponent, be it Whig or Republican. The nineteenth-century press openly paraded its partisanship.[8] This display of bias and partiality was taken as a proper and natural facet of American political life. As Michael Schudson and Michael McGerr have persuasively argued, this explicit avowal of sympathies was part and parcel of the ritual political culture of the nineteenth century. Because of the US's heritage of republican culture with its emphasis on citizenship as central to the individual's identity, and because of popular attachment to the visible local community, American politics entailed ceremonial displays of one's place in the local political order. It demanded a demonstration of commitment to a political party.[9]

Press, politics and the construction of the public domain

In our contemporary era, the mass media poses as impartial supplier of authoritative news accounts to readers for their private scrutiny and use. The press denies that it serves any specific group's interests, and rejects the idea that its rhetoric and interpretations influence the political opinions of its audience. Journalism stands above the disputes and interests of contending political groups. Furthermore, as an independent medium of information, the daily press works to insure that the news is not subject to the manipulations and demagogic efforts of groups striving to mold public opinion.[10] In general, the news is intended neither as a political stratagem nor as public dialogue, but as impartial document of the day's most important words and deeds.

Such a perspective, no matter how questionable for our era, distinctly hinders our comprehension of the workings of the nineteenth-century press. In the practices of the nineteenth century's partisanship, our contemporary journalism would only see a violation of its ideals of objectivity and independence: politically biased story selection and illicit editorializing by news reporters. Crucial dimensions of nineteenth-century journalism as an organ of a political community would be neglected. News as a ritual of group solidarity, as a tool for highlighting policy positions and their social consequences, and as an arena of public debate and dialogue – all central dimensions of nineteenth-century newspaper politics – would be obscured.

The Gilded Age's political notion of the news suggests that the distinctions that underpin journalism's modern ideals cannot be so easily maintained. Nineteenth-century news calls into question a series of separations sharply dividing an impartial journalism from the strategic conflicts of government and the impassioned deliberations of citizens. The press of today asserts that it is merely a neutral instrument in politics' dialogues and disputes. The nineteenth century's press, far from being merely an external observer, was centrally implicated in the construction of the parties' issue agendas and in the formation of the citizenry's political preferences. In fact, newspapers were esteemed on the basis of their "influence" – their persuasiveness and political authority.

Furthermore, a consideration of nineteenth-century newspapers in their close allegiance to formal political organizations reveals a special affinity between the press and polity. News and politics both rest upon an operation of publicity. In constructing their narratives, in elaborating their policy positions, media and government pierce the dusky shadows of everyday life. They function as a spotlight or "signal," to use the metaphor of news commentator Walter Lippmann.[11] Journalists and political leaders selectively illuminate social issues for public attention, extracting them from what society either accepts as consensual or simply ignores as natural. These glimmering facets of social life, refracted through the dramatizations of news crews and the pontifications of politicians, become recognized as problems of collective significance, potential matters of governmental action, and issues for social deliberation and dispute.[12]

Modern journalism pretends to register impartially social issues as if they were already given, natural topics of political dispute.[13] But the press, in fact, is crucial to the social construction and demarcation of this contentious public arena. Its coverage defines and sanctions or, in the phrase of Pierre Bourdieu, "performatively constructs" which issues and which views should properly enter into the public sphere.[14]

A closer examination of the functioning of the partisan press – their bitter polemics, their biased news, their proud public loyalties – will reveal the pervasively political dimensions of journalism. It will show the media's active hand in guiding the public's political deliberations; reveal their prominent participation in the construction of the parties' political agendas; and expose the press's role in the altogether more affective, public, and ritualistic political culture of the nineteenth century. In sum, it will demonstrate how the press expressed, reinforced, and defined the central institutional and cultural dimensions of democracy's public sphere.

In what follows, I detail the workings of the partisan press in the national Reconstruction Era that followed the war between the North and the South, 1865–76. The chapter melds a quantitative measure of political bias to a qualitative analysis of the underlying ideological themes of press advocacy. A particular issue that preoccupied the two parties and will occupy this chapter was the set of symbols, associations, and political discourses surrounding the African-American in the post-war period. Chapter 4 will then extend the content analysis into the final years of the century, and alter its focus by scrutinizing the political rites and aesthetic style of the partisan paper.

A measure of gilded age partisanship

The political biases of Detroit's newspapers can be tracked in both the news stories and opinion pieces across the span of the late nineteenth century.[15] In the early Reconstruction Era, 1865–76, the overwhelming preponderance of the editorials and a persistent share of the news filling up the columns of Detroit's dailies were slanted in favor of the preferred party.

Editorials are the genre in which newspapers most directly pronounce their views. In the nineteenth-century paper, they occupied a particularly prominent place. Their heavier weight in the total make-up of the journal was a matter of placement, space, and emphasis. Typically appearing on the inside page of a four- or eight-page paper, opinion columns filled approximately 20 percent of the journal's news space. In the 1880s and 1890s, as daily papers ballooned in size, editorials correspondingly fell as a proportion of the overall content. The post-bellum era was still an age of "personal journalism" when the public often identified papers with their proprietors. Newspapers amplified famous editorial voices onto the national stage, turning the likes of Greeley, Bowles, and Watterson into celebrities of the Victorian world. As chapter 2 argues, Detroit's journals too were most typically vehicles of political ambition and personal expression. Ownership of a paper was the *sine qua non* for speaking authoritatively within the councils of the state party. Even the placement of the editorials attests to the paper's openly avowed voice. Detroit's dailies typically printed their opinion pieces directly beneath the masthead's listing of owner and chief editor.

Throughout the nineteenth century's election seasons, the majority of the sampled editorials were partisan, evidently and explicitly. The newspaper posed forthrightly as the spokesperson for its party. Sometimes shrilly, sometimes sententiously, the press instructed the populace on the moral rightness of its party's policies and the corruptness, even criminality, of its foe. Outside of the campaign seasons, with election passions temporarily stilled, the percentage of editorials that were partisan fluctuated erratically. The numbers declined over the course of the late nineteenth century from 40 to 60 percent partisan in the 1860s and 1870s, to 18 to 34 percent in the 1880s and 1890s.

The Detroit press typically filled about one fourth of its news space with partisan stories during presidential election campaigns. In non-election seasons, biased stories occupied less than 10 percent of the news space. Editors introduced a political slant into their stories in two essential manners, which we might call "manifest" and "latent" partisanship, or "overt" and "covert."[16] In manifest bias, articles contained statements of evaluations and preference by the reporter–writer. In the second type of bias – latent partisanship – a story can support the interests and policies of the party even when a journalist makes no evident political evaluation. For example, without adding its own explicit judgments, the journal may devote a disproportionate attention to the favored politicians' words and deeds, while slighting the views of their opponents. Whereas such political preferences could be veiled, at a certain point the grossly unequal amount of space devoted to one party

Table 1.1. *Editorials in presidential election seasons*

	1868	1872	1876	1880	1884	1888	1892	1896
Partisanship as a percentage of editorials*	81	81	78	75	62	65	39	85

* In the sampled issues all editorials were coded for their political bias and their length was measured. The percentage is a percentage of the paper's space devoted to editorials.

Table 1.2. *Editorials in non-election seasons*

	1867	1871	1875	1879	1883	1887	1891	1895
Partisanship as a percentage of editorials	54	50	40	74	18	32	34	13

Table 1.3. *News in presidential election years*

	1868	1872	1876	1880	1884	1888	1892	1896
Manifest bias (%)	6	5	9	26	22	3	7	10
Latent bias (%)	9	18	12	14	17	23	9	30
Total Partisan News (%)	15	23	21	40	39	26	16	40

Table 1.4. *News in non-election years*

	1867	1871	1875	1879	1883	1887	1891	1895
Manifest bias (%)	2	0	0	2	0	1	0	8
Latent bias (%)	16	4	7	2	0	2	2	1
Total Partisan News (%)	18	4	7	4	0	3	2	9

over the other becomes evident. The bias, then, is no longer hidden but proclaimed and even required in an organ which is supposed to publicize the triumphs and philosophy of its party. This evident bias amounts to a proudly displayed badge of party loyalty by the newspaper.

What was the nature of the partisanship behind these numbers? What politics lay behind the press's overwhelming if not exhaustive partisan "bias"?[17]

The partisan news agenda: African-Americans in Reconstruction Era rhetoric

On April 9, 1865, General Robert E. Lee, commanding officer of the Southern army, signed a treaty of surrender for the Confederate forces.

With the war's conclusion, the combatants laid down their guns only to pick up their pens. Democrat and Republican, Rebel and Union sympathizer, Boys in Blue and Copperheads, carried on their battles in the pages of the press. Partisan journalism in the Reconstruction Era turned out to be merely the continuation of war by other means.

A consideration of the divisive issues of the Reconstruction Era will demonstrate the extent to which partisan interests permeated journalistic practices. Newspapers, in their robust alliances with political organizations, imported into the realm of print the issues and strategic calculations of the formal polity. By and large, partisan interests set the news agenda. The daily news did not simply reflect the existing balance of political forces, nor did it only reproduce society's prior principles of political (di)vision. Instead, partisan journalism played an essentially creative role in the depiction of political reality. Detroit's dailies labored shoulder to shoulder with the parties to construct those primordial cultural categories through which society perceived itself as split into friend and foe.[18]

In the years 1865–76, Civil War issues remained paramount in the press and the polity, but the two parties defined them differently. As political scientist E. E. Schattschneider explains, "[A]ntagonists can rarely agree on what the issues are . . . because the definition of the alternatives is the choice of conflicts, and the choice of conflicts allocates power."[19] For the Republicans the issues, of course, were the national union and the outrage of Southern treason. They persistently tried to depict the Democrats as the party of the Confederacy, Southern secession, and war for which the citizens of the North had paid dearly with the blood of their boys. In reply, the Democrats redefined the terms of the conflict, repainting the same issue cleavage in different colors, mostly black. Democrats insinuated that the war with its goal of union and abolition of slavery had a secret motive: the establishment of a despotic government by the Republicans, a centralized military state resting upon the support of "ignorant negro" voters. Tainted by their less than enthusiastic support for the Union in the Civil War, Democrats tried to mobilize a persistent popular racism against the Republican party's policies for reconstructing Southern society and government. Democrats, in part, appropriated their racist rhetoric from a commercial popular culture. In addition, the party of Jefferson and Jackson produced their own derogatory stereotypes of Black Americans. The Democratic press, embroiled in the bitter partisan battles, promulgated these harshly negative depictions in both their news stories and their fiction columns. As the Detroit *Free Press* editorialized,

The Radical [Republican] party, claiming to be the party of pure morality, religion, liberty and progress, has been in power only about seven years, and yet has crowded into that short period instances enough of oppression, violence, fraud, immorality, public robbery and corruption to utterly destroy any government but ours . . . Its next step may be to proclaim a dictator and openly set aside the constitutional government. In view of the character of the leaders of the party and the alarming outrages already committed by it, we have reason to fear they may resort to any measures no matter how desperate rather than relinquish power and plunder. . . . To secure power in the South they have disfranchised great numbers of white men and given the ballot to four millions of ignorant, incompetent negroes, led on by a few of the meanest white men . . . [etc., etc.][20]

These were the policy views repetitiously (and repulsively) advocated by Detroit's Democratic dailies. The excerpt parades some of the most prominent themes of Democratic editorials in the early Reconstruction Era, 1865–72. As the quantitative longitudinal measure indicated, the majority of newspaper editorials throughout the late nineteenth century pushed partisan themes (see tables 1.). While they repeatedly reiterated the central policy stands of the two parties, newspapers veered between bitter, vicious diatribes and beseeching pleas for reasoned discussion. Taking for example the *Free Press*'s editorials in the week surrounding the longitudinal sample date of February 15, 1867, one finds several issues consistently invoked.

Not just a melange of policy planks in a ramshackle political edifice, these Democratic issues formed a remarkably unified political ideology. And the editorial motifs most commonly dovetailed around one object of contempt and contention: the emancipated African-American. Indeed, Democrats and Republicans most often waged their political conflicts upon the terrain of the newly freed Black slave.[21] The rights and duties of the ex-slaves, their social situation and economic disabilities, even their physical nature and capacities, all formed grist for partisan polemics. Moreover, partisan news of the Reconstruction Era did not stop with the advocacy of national congressional policies for Southern Blacks, nor with criticism of the terrorism of the Ku Klux Klan. It encompassed more than views on the proper economic and political relations between the races in the South and on the role of federal troops in unreformed Southern state governments. In fact, journalists transformed the very physical body of the African-American into a charged symbolic nexus for the depiction of the nature, disorders, and promises of American society.[22]

Images of Blacks pervaded the Democratic newspapers and were not confined to any single journalistic genre, whether editorial, fiction, or telegraphic news dispatch. For example, the *Daily Union*, Detroit's

Table 1.5. *Major editorial themes**

	Total number of editorials in which theme occurs	Number of days theme appears	Average number of appearances of theme per day
Total of Editorials	103		14.7
Partisan Editorials	89		12.7
Republican policies are guided only by power interests, not principles	27	7	3.9
Republican party is			
• Despotic and anti-constitutional	15	7	2.1
• Immoral	14	6	2
Against Republican Southern Reconstruction policies	27	7	3.9
Against African-Americans	19	5	2.7
Against Black voting	7	3	1
On Blacks' social capacities	4	3	0.6
Vs. Republican tariff policy	7	5	1
Vs. Detroit's Republican city council as derelict in its duties	6	4	0.9

* *Detroit Free Press*, February 12–21, 1876. The themes are not exclusive; more than one theme may appear in an editorial.

junior Democratic daily, published the following array of articles in the sampled issue for October 15, 1868:

- a local crime story headlined "Brutal Murder by Negroes"
- a celebration of a local boy claiming affiliation with the Ku Klux Klan
- an editorial referring to the Republican goal of "the political supremacy of the negro"
- an editorial attacking Republican presidential nominee Grant for his views on negro suffrage
- an anecdote caricaturing a wedding of African-Americans replete with dialect speech
- a letter to the editor attacking Republican newspapers' distortion of the "temper, desires and views of southern Whites"
- a reprinted article from the South entitled "Beauties of Jacobinism" which impugns Southern Blacks and "Yankee carpetbaggers"
- a reprinted letter to the editor which discusses "indolent negroes" and the election

The issue of Blacks came up repeatedly in local political conflicts from the Civil War until the end of Reconstruction, and not only in relation to Southern policies. Michigan, like other Northern states, had to confront the possibility of enfranchising their local Black population. Such inhabitants, however minimal in size (1–2 percent), seemed to stimulate the active animus of a majority of Whites. Between the war's end and the ratification of the Fifteenth Amendment in April 1870, Northern states repeatedly rejected extending the franchise to their native Black populations. In the spring of 1868, Michigan, an over-whelmingly Republican state, defeated a state constitutional charter amendment that promised to remove racial restrictions from the electo-rate. The measure polled 39.3 percent in favor and 60.7 percent opposed. Such defeats, along with the resurgence of the Democrats in the 1867 elections, motivated "the Democracy" to play the race card again in 1868.[23] The Michigan Democratic platform for the fall 1868 campaign vowed "to keep this country as our fathers made it, a white man's government."[24] But national and state-wide Democratic losses in 1868 and the *de facto* establishment of Black suffrage through the Fifteenth Amendment convinced Michigan Democrats to acquiesce to the Black vote. In 1870, a state charter amendment to bring the state constitution in line with national law (as embodied in the Fifteenth Amendment) drew little partisan attention and fewer votes.[25]

Detroiters contested the status of African-Americans in a second local issue: the integration of Detroit's public schools. Between 1867 when the state legislature ruled segregation illegal and 1871 when the Detroit School board finally capitulated, school segregation simmered as an issue. Democratic newspapers repeatedly editorialized upon the topic, while Democratic city officials defied the legal enactments of Republican state authorities.[26]

Despite these local and the national conflicts, the Democratic odium directed towards Blacks did not derive from the actual threat of Black suffrage. True, congressional Republicans used the South's continuing failure to grant Blacks political rights as justification for excluding Southern states and their likely Democratic votes from national elec-tions. But in Michigan, the small Black population was not large enough to decide any state contest. Electoral power cannot explain the obsessive reference to African-Americans in Michigan politics.

Apparently, the Democrats believed that the Republicans and their Reconstruction policies were darkly stained by a too close proximity to the Black man. (The *San Francisco Examiner*, a Democrat journal, labeled its political adversaries, "the chocolate papers.") Indeed, since the origination of the Republican party, the expression "black Repub-lican" performed as standard Democratic invective. For example, Wilbur Storey, editor of the main Michigan Democratic organ, the *Detroit Free Press*, from 1853 to 1861 and later owner-editor of the important partisan and sensationalist journal the *Chicago Times*, "insisted that the Republican Party was always to be referred to as 'Black Republican' Party" in the columns of his paper.[27] The expression, because of its polemical edge, implied a measure of political orthodoxy whether pronounced by a Democrat or a Republican. Thus, *Free Press*'s managing editor William Quinby, upon hiring future Detroit mayor John Lodge in 1883, invoked this cliché of partisan rhetoric to communicate clearly to Lodge the political rules of the newspaper game.[28] "This is the Democratic state organ. Your father is one of the leading Republicans of the state, and of course you are a Republican also. I want you to see to it that you do not inject any of your Black Republican principles into what you write for the paper."[29]

References to Blacks pervaded the discourse of the Democratic party and its affiliated journals. As Jean Baker says: "[N]o matter where they began, Democratic set speeches invariably ended with blacks as the reason for higher taxes and tariff, the impeachment of Andrew Johnson, inflationary greenbacks, and Republican corruption. The Democrats looked at currency and saw the Negro, reviewed the impeachment and ended with the Negro, debated the purchase of Alaska and concluded with the Negro."[30] Blacks were thus central to a convoluted set of ideological representations elaborated by the Democratic party.

Let us untangle some of this imagery. According to Democrats, the project to free the Negro was illegitimate, and to grant him the right to vote an absurd endeavor. On the basis of his racial–biological nature the Negro was a foolish, superstitious child. He lacked the reason and the self-control necessary to participate in the White man's republican government. As the *Free Press* intoned, "this inferior race is [not] capable of managing affairs of state." African-Americans were "a degraded race of ignorant semi-savages."[31] Such partisan sentiments were reinforced by a hammering repetition. On subsequent days the *Free Press* editorialized:

"[the Republicans] have given the ballot to 4 million of ignorant, incompetent negroes" (May 10, 1868)

"an ignorant population" (May 12)

"ignorance and the most inferior of all races" (May 12, a reprinted editorial)

"ignorant negroes" (May 14)

"ignorance and vice are placed over intelligence and virtue – the inferior race is made the superior" (May 14)

"the white men of the South were deprived of all voice in public affairs while ignorant blacks, fresh from the field . . ." (May 20)

"It has placed the ballot in the hands of those negroes, ignorant and unfit as they are" (May 23) "the salvation of the blacks depends upon the infamy of putting the Southern whites under the rule of ignorant blacks . . ." (May 25)

And on the day from the longitudinal sample:

"the semi-barbarous African" (October 15, 1868)
"an inferior and uneducated people, who know nothing of their own, let alone the rights and wants of their fellow man." (October 15, p. 4)

To remove the Black from the natural hierarchy of races – to remove the slave from the master's control – was to permit license by those incapable of the self-restraint necessary for liberty. The natural outcome of such a lack of internal or external control was, in the jargon of the day, "outrages": Black attacks on Whites, specifically White women. Such outrages were repeatedly described in the Democratic press and were a politically motivated news selection, part of the partisan-driven news agenda. Thus, for example, our sampled issue of the *Detroit Union* of October 15, 1868 reports a local crime headed "Brutal Murder by Negroes." And, on January 1, 1868 the *Union* reprinted this story from the Democratic *New York Times*:

Outrage By A Negro In Maryland Upon A White Woman
Late on Sunday afternoon a most violent outrage was committed by a negro man on a most estimable married lady, in Hartford County, Maryland . . . This is the fourth or fifth affair of this kind which has happened in this county within the past year, in which negroes have been the actors and white women the sufferers.

Meanwhile, throughout May 1868, the *Free Press* publicized "depredations" occurring in the South, news of which was transmitted to them via the wire service and Southern Democratic newspapers.

THE SOUTH.
Official Report of the Florida Elections
. . . TERRIBLE TRAGEDY IN ARKANSAS
A MAN AND FOUR CHILDREN MURDERED BY A NEGRO . . .
At a small town called Lincoln . . . which was settled by freedmen, a negro named Cochrane was detected by another named Wm. Babcock in illicit intercourse with his wife and attacked him. Cochrane killed Babcock in the encounter and immediately took up with Babcock's wife who had four children. Next day all the children were found in the swamp with their throats cut . . . Ike Martin . . . informed the civil authorities who have laid the matter before the military. Cochrane is not yet arrested.

NEGRO SHOT AND ARRESTED . . . [etc.]
THE STORM . . . [etc.]
DEPREDATIONS COMMITTED BY NEGROES
Seven negroes attempted to enter [a] cotton shed on Washington street last night. They were fired upon by the watchmen . . . [etc.][32]

The editorial page spelled out in repetitious detail the not-so-veiled logic informing these news selections.[33]

In the month of May, the problem of "negro outrages" is invoked in editorials on the 9th and 10th but the fullest statement of the logic appears on the 31st in the following fantasy/editorial.[34]

THE TRUE CONDITION OF THE AFRICANIZED SOUTH

The effect of the policy pursued by the Congressional majority in the South can be seen by the condition of that section. In all the late [state constitutional] conventions negro delegations were admitted, and their action has brought disgrace and ridicule upon the nation. Propositions of the most indefensible and monstrous character have been submitted and argued by these men . . . Two ideas seemed to control the negroes. One was hatred of the white people among whom they reside; the other, to obtain a living without labor . . . [I]n the constitutions framed by them it is the vital element, in every day life they carry out this platform. Outrages upon white men, women and children are now common occurrences. Scarce a paper comes from that section without containing accounts of offenses committed by negroes at which the heart sickens and blood runs cold. Lesser crimes . . . are multiplied ten fold since the inauguration of negro equality. Bands of idle and worthless blacks pass through all the country plundering, destroying and burning . . . Behind these lawless blacks stand the Loyal Leagues [a governmental agency to insure for Blacks the right to vote], and then comes Congress and the Radical party . . . [etc.][35]

Such Democratic anti-Black rhetoric had a long history, dating back to the origins of the American abolition movement and later the emergence of the Republican party.[36] Much earlier, for example in 1863, the *Free Press* had publicized the accusations against a local Black man, on trial for "outraging" a young White woman. Years later all the major witnesses to the attack recanted their testimony, but at the time, the *Free Press* saw fit to headline its article "Horrible Outrage . . . A negro entraps a little girl into his room and commits fiendish crime upon her person . . . Full history of the shocking event."[37] Once the defendant was pronounced guilty, Detroit's White community rioted. The rampage was described in the pitiful 1863 account: "A Thrilling Narrative from the Lips of the Sufferers of the Late Detroit Riot, March 6, 1863." In the course of the riot several of Detroit's Blacks died, many were beaten, and hundreds were left homeless.[38] Commenting on the violence the *Free Press* remarked, "We regret the mob. If our voice could have controlled it, it never should have occurred; but what could Democrats do when the Abolition press were raising heaven and earth to claim the rights of white men to the experiment of nigger liberty."[39]

The Detroit riot was a pale echo of other Northern anti-draft riots of 1863, such as the New York City riot which claimed over one hundred lives. Such riots were triggered by popular resentment over the draft, high taxes to support the war, and the (largely mythical) threat of Black economic competition in hard financial times. As Jean Baker notes, Northern anti-draft riots quickly turned into mob attacks on Blacks. Rioters took African-Americans as the hidden hand operating behind governmental Civil War policies. Such popular mob action was fueled by the overheated rhetoric of Democrat newspapers and orators, which portrayed Blacks as malignant creatures – a threat to the social, political, and economic foundations of the social order.[40]

The political consequences of this selection of the news and its rhetorical treatment were hardly hidden for the Democratic editors and readers. As the *Union*'s weekly "Letter from New York" makes plain: "The constantly recurring intelligence of NEGRO OUTRAGES in the South does a great deal towards strengthening the Democracy in this section of the country."[41] Such stories, as the *Union* suggested, were important for deepening the political cleavages that defined the two parties, and for consolidating the partisan loyalties of Democrats and Republicans. Democrats publicized such news partly to emphasize Black Americans' incapacity for self-rule, and partly to counter the massive Republican production of news reports of Ku Klux Klan terror in the South.[42]

Democrats argued that, given the biological and cultural deficit that precluded Blacks from exercising self-control and autonomous reason, Black participation as equals in republican government would fail. Moreover, the Democratic papers suggested that this crippling of political democracy constituted the secret goal of the Radical Republicans in Congress. Blacks, as necessarily dependent, would require the perpetual help of the Republican party and the permanent tutelage of governmental agencies. Under the control and direction of the Republicans, they would surely vote for this despotic Radical government.

Blacks were part of a deliberate plan to despoil republican government and the natural rights of free-born Whites. Thus, the Detroit *Free Press* drew the invidious, but not coincidental, comparison between Republican policies in the South and North. "The party that demands that the elective franchise shall be extended to the ignorant negroes of the South, stands equally ready to disfranchise the intelligent voter of a city of the North."[43] Democratic newspapers asserted over and over again that the Republican goal was not negro equality but superiority in the South. As the *Union* explained, if General Grant won the presidential election in 1868, Republicans would be sure to take his victory as proof "that the people demand Reconstruction upon the basis of a military dictatorship under congress and the political supremacy of the Negro."[44] And, more generally, says Alexander Saxton, the moralistic claims of abolitionists had long been regarded with suspicion.[45] White workers feared that abolitionists and Republicans actually wished to deprive the White working-class of their "most scared rights," "the dearest privileges of freemen," as the *Free Press* repeatedly insisted.[46] They saw the granting of rights to Blacks as a loss of rights for White men. How can one explain this zero-sum equation? According to labor historian David Roediger, nineteenth-century White workers had been paid a "psychological, public wage" for accepting their dependent place in the American economy. These "wages" included political recognition and social prestige for all White males as free and equal political citizens endowed with inalienable rights. This status, central to White workers' identity, rested upon the deference and inequality of those who were not White and not male. From this perspective, Blacks could be made free only if White workers were made slaves.[47]

For Democrats, this violation of the two races' proper social roles could only have been accomplished by a force from outside civil society, by an excessive political power. Therefore, the *Free Press* equated the Congressional Republicans with French Jacobins and suggested: "Is it not strange that an influence so terribly destructive of sound morality as the rule of Radicalism has not broken up the foundation of civil society."[48] And the Detroit *Union* in publishing its annual proclamation of principles or "prospectus" linked governmental despotism to Black civil rights: "The Union opposes the centralization of governmental power; Opposes the supremacy of the military over the civic jurisdiction; Opposes the enfranchisement and social equality of the black race by Congressional activity."[49] Thus were linked what one historian of the *Free Press* calls editor Storey's central political tenets – "racism and states rights."[50]

Imagery of the childlike, permanent dependency of Blacks pervaded Democratic accounts, including their criticism of any governmental help to newly independent African-Americans starting out without land, tools, or capital. African-Americans were seen as seeking to "obtain a living without labor." In this context, the Democrats launched an attack on the Freedmen's Bureau, a government agency in charge of distributing aid to newly freed Southern Blacks and some Whites.[51] The *Free Press* editorialized on May 10, 1868: "They feel certain that with the help of the entire treasury . . . the army, the Freedman's Bureau and 4 million of negroes they can perpetuate their power indefinitely." On May 31 it opined: "Behind these lawless blacks stand the Loyal League and then comes Congress. Clothing and food are supplied them by the

Freedmen's Bureau and thus equipped [the Blacks] are prepared to act as the ready and willing tools of the conspirators at Washington." During the same time, the Democratic journal presented a front-page, verbatim account of the Michigan State Democratic Convention and detailed the indictments brought against the Republicans. "[The Republicans] declared white men disloyal until the contrary was proved, and declared all black men loyal without proof; it used federal power to control suffrage in the states; it established a Freedmen's Bureau to feed and clothe the blacks as pensioners on the national bounty."[52] Such rhetoric drew on the classical Jacksonian cultural repertoire that attacked both "corrupt" governmental institutions and indolent people of color using familial imagery.[53] Democrats wished to separate Negroes in the South from the too easy support of the maternal government and subject them again to the harsh discipline of their paternalistic master – the Southern White elite.

According to Democrats, Republicans desired to disrupt the natural laws governing the social order by placing Blacks in a position of superiority for which they were racially unfit. Blacks, as Jean Baker expounds, bore through the physical attribute of their skin color the visible sign of their inferiority. Black skin as a natural trait pointed to Blacks' natural, immutable social position as inferior to Whites.[54] Thus the epithet "Black Republican" and the continual recourse to the Negro in Democratic stump speeches emphasized the disorder being introduced into society's natural constitution by the Radical Republicans' political reign.

As mentioned previously, the *Free Press*'s owner Storey had ordered his editorial staff always to refer to the opposed party as the Black Republican party. About Storey, one historian writes, "His vitriol was unequaled . . . when he turned his attention to the Republicans and the abolitionist movement. He called the Republican party 'this monster of frightful mien – this party made up of white abolitionists, black abolitionists, and fugitives from slavery – this rabble of discord and destruction.'"[55] Storey's use of the expression "monster" in this context is doubtless not accidental. For monster refers to "any animal or plant that is out of the usual course of nature" and the word derives from the Latin for divine warning against the violation of God-given natural law.[56] Here we see the imagery of boundary mixing, a disordering of natural categories that consequently results in the creation of a monster, a Frankenstein.

This preoccupation with the violation of natural categories perhaps explains why Democrats and the Detroit *Free Press* obsessively returned again and again to the issue of Black–White "amalgamation," and why

Democrats equated the granting of political and civil rights to African-Americans with "an indiscriminate, unnatural, loathsome and hated sexual union of the races."[57] The fear of miscegenation in part revealed anxieties over the blurring of sharply defined, supposedly natural, racial differences. The hysteria pointed to the shakiness of the socially erected edifice of a Black–White racial dichotomy. This racial system smoothly classified individuals into categories, defined their place in the social hierarchy, and justified White power over Blacks, as well as securing the identity of White males in opposition to Blacks.[58]

The normally vitriolic rhetoric of the *Free Press* reached new extremes in this news story in which there is a double violation of the *Free Press*'s ideological premises: first, improper Black–White sex, and secondly a White woman freely consenting to wed an avaricious Black. Reporting on the elopement of a "white girl with a negro," the *Free Press* reporter added this observation: "[T]he girl is forever lost to decency and respect. Even should her separation from her negro paramou[r] be eternal, the finger of scorn would be pointed to her, to her dying day, as a white woman who disgraced her sex and common decency by consenting to become the wife of a black, ugly looking, disgusting negro."[59]

Republicans wave the "bloody shirt"

To this extended racist onslaught from the Democratic newspapers, the Republicans responded as best they could. On the one hand, the Republican journals, the Detroit *Post* and the Detroit *Advertiser and Tribune* stood forthrightly for human equality. The *Post*, the more orthodoxly Republican of the two journals, declared in its Prospectus for 1867 that, "[The *Post*'s] principles are based upon the immortal truths of the Declaration of Independence and the Divine Laws of the Universal Brotherhood of Man. Hence its motto is Equal Rights, Equal Justice for all Men."[60] The *Advertiser and Tribune*, too, repeatedly advocated political rights for the freed slaves.[61] Across the country, in San Francisco as in Detroit, Republican journals attempted to rebut the Democrats' racism, to denounce "the ineffable meanness which . . . [a Democratic journal] is capable [of] in its demagogical appeals to the despicable prejudice of castes and color."[62]

Beyond mere assertions of Black–White equality, the Republican papers mocked the Democrats' assumptions of the absolute superiority of all Whites by virtue of their blood. In the weekly letter from Washington, the correspondent for the Republican *Advertiser and Tribune* wrote:

Our Washington Letter
Saulsbury as a White Man of Intelligence . . .

From Our Own Correspondent   Washington, D.C., Jan. 8, 1867

Coming down from the Capitol last evening . . . I had a fine illustration of the character of some of the gentlemen . . . [defending President Andrew Johnson] I had just been listening to the solemn warnings of Cowan and Saulsbury against the frightful excesses of the [Republican] "Radicals," till I almost doubted the propriety of going forward quite so fast. Saulsbury . . . was positive on one point – the total unfitness of the colored race for elective franchise . . . When he was speaking I did not notice anything out of the way in his manner, but set him down, as I have one hundred times before, as one honest political bigot. I started home two or three hours afterwards, and to my disgust a drunken man was reeling to and fro on the sidewalk . . . To my horror as I came up with him I discovered the drunken man was the gentleman in the Senate who warned [Congress] of the unfitness of the negroes for the ballot![63]

Other news articles from the South helped to shore up Northern support for the civil rights of African-Americans. The papers reported the violence of Southern Whites against the freedmen, particularly in the context of a burgeoning Ku Klux Klan. Here, Republican papers worked hand-in-hand with Republican politicians in the production of partisan news as they published the results of Congressional investigations into Southern acts of intimidation and terror. For example, the *Post* devoted eight columns (or 24 percent of its news space) to the verbatim publication of the government's inquest into a Klan massacre in New Orleans.[64] From the Democratic point of view, Republican press accounts of Ku Klux Klan crimes were so much distorted party propaganda. The *Free Press* declared:

[Republican press] organs have undertaken once more to fire the Northern heart, and the consequence is that the columns of those sheets are again filled with police report editorials concerning the alleged lawlessness of the Southern States, especially as regards . . . the cruel treatment of negroes . . . Those who desire to test the truth of our remarks need only consult the Detroit *Post* of yesterday morning whose pages fairly reek with that kind of nauseous stuff.[65]

The wave of both Southern legislation and violence against Blacks and the resultant publicity helped to destroy any Northern support for President Andrew Johnson and his union party of moderate Republicans in 1866–67.[66] The *Advertiser and Tribune* itself turned from lukewarm to ardent supporter of Reconstruction measures.

Despite this strong response to Democratic racism, Republican defense of the besieged Southern Black was more often camouflaged in the rhetoric of Southern disloyalty than straight-forward support for equal rights. Republicans focused on the South's continued recalcitrance and the seditious support they received from "Copperhead"

Democrats. Republicans so often invoked the treason of the South that Democrats came to label this standard rhetorical move "waving the bloody shirt." The "bloody shirt" referred to the blood-soaked garments of the Northern soldier who had sacrificed his life to preserve the country. Simple strategic reasons guided the Republicans in their attempt to shift the definition of the Democrat–Republican conflict. The historian David Montgomery explains: "More Americans identified the cause of the Republican party with the cause of the Union than wanted Negroes to vote. It was for this latter reason that the Democrats were the party that talked incessantly of blacks."[67] Even Southern outrages were said to be aimed at Union soldiers and to demonstrate continued Southern rebellion against the Union. For example, the *Post*, in the sampled edition of 1867, editorialized against the "Rebel Democrats in Tennessee." The paper attacked Southerners who had entered into a "conspiracy to assassinate Union men and freedmen, particularly soldiers who had served in the United States Army."[68] And, in the edition sampled for 1868 the *Post* polemicized against belligerent Southerners. "North Carolina papers state that the rebels in that State are arming themselves with improved breach loading . . . rifles in expectation of a new rebellion in case [Democratic Presidential nominee and Vice President] Seymour and Blair are successful, for the purpose of trampling the reconstructed state governments into dust."[69]

As already noted, Detroit's two Republican dailies did not always see eye to eye on the proper Reconstruction policies. The *Advertiser and Tribune* was less inclined to support Black rights and punitive reconstruction measures against White Southerners, supporting the policies of President Andrew Johnson until late 1866. They also abandoned Reconstruction before the *Post*. In 1872 the *Advertiser and Tribune* flirted with the Liberal Republican party which announced as a plank in its party platform the speedy rehabilitation of the South and an abolition of Reconstruction measures. These policy differences reflected in part the natural competition of two newspapers aimed at the same market segment, but also party factional antagonisms. The *Post* stood with long-time state Republican leader, Senator Zachariah Chandler, while the *Advertiser and Tribune* was allied with Chandler's bitterest enemies.[70] Richard Slotkin, looking at the journals of New York City in 1874–77, has shown how each daily paper expressed the views of a party faction and, in turn, the interests of different elite economic groups.[71] Thus, competing party factions amplified, multiplied and muddied the two parties' debates in the public sphere.

To summarize, the Democratic party through the vehicle of its loyal press organs and speeches "on the stump" offered the voters a complex depiction of the problems of American society. With this portrait, it indicted the rule of the Republican party and its misguided policies. Republicans responded in defense of their Reconstruction policies and universal civil rights, but also, like a skilled matador, sidestepped the brunt of the Democrats' charge by waving the scarlet "bloody shirt." They stressed that the Democrats had defended the South's secession, which resulted in so much spilt blood, and that during the war Democrats possessed suspect loyalties. Republican and Democratic journals faithfully repeated these party lines, although they doubtless innovated in this editorial or improvised in that news story.[72] Their editorial pronouncements took up the unfolding events in Congress and in the South and encapsulated them in the political philosophy of the party in daily reiterated arguments. Political scientist Shanto Ingeyar has recently pointed to the overwhelming bias of contemporary news reporting towards the "episodic" over the "thematic."[73] The news of today, he claims, neglects to contextualize events in an overarching interpretation, a framework that can help explain the events' occurrence. Journalism of the nineteenth century surely suffered from the opposite malady – the rigorous explanation (as well as selection) of events according to a generalized political picture.

Unlike our contemporary papers, nineteenth-century newspapers stood under the protecting umbrella of a party's political legitimacy. Furthermore, as chapter 2 will show, the paper possessed a partisan readership that expected a strong display of partisanship by their journal. The partisan paper was thus authorized to explore systematically and repeatedly the various social implications of governmental policies in editorials and in feature articles. The news agenda was not dependent upon the occurrence of "news events" to justify the reporter's story selection. What would be forbidden to our contemporary independent and "objective" press as editorializing – as exposing the reporter's subjective point of view – could be thoroughly pursued by the nineteenth-century press.

Partisan newspapers had the merit of forcefully expressing alternative political views for the public. The *Post* acknowledged this political role in explaining the mission of partisan journals: "The secret of this influence [of papers on the community] is not so much that they furnish people with opinions ready made; but that they keep prominent and engrossing topics constantly before them, and throw all possible life upon these topics from every quarter . . . [Republican papers] are constantly stimulating this reflection and discussion [by the public]."[74]

On the other hand, the emphatic public dialogue of parties was contaminated by their strategic political calculations. Newspapers' partisan publicity aimed at consolidating the party's electoral coalition while splintering and weakening the opposed political alliance. This strategic definition of issue cleavages meant that papers directed their attacks not on the positions of the other party but on contrived images thereof. This, at least, was Lord James Bryce's perspective in the late 1800s:

[T]he aim of each party is to force on its antagonist certain issues which the antagonist rarely accepts, so that although there is a vast deal of discussion and declamation on political topics, there are few on which either party directly traverses the doctrines of the other. Each pummels, not his true enemy, but a stuffed figure set up to represent that enemy.[75]

Furthermore, newspapers, because they were aligned with the formal polity and its concern for the pursuit of power, did not report the broader range of views and voices in civil society. The public sphere, at least as represented by the press as the central medium of public dialogue and discussion, became absorbed in the extensively politicized and polarized debates between the two parties. Partisan interests set the news agenda. Information that did not conform to the party's agenda went unreported; issues that conflicted with the party's interests were suppressed.[76] The press's strategic reporting forced a departure from the democratic public sphere's highest ideals: open, rational deliberation among citizens over issues of the common good.[77]

Popular culture and the partisan agenda

But if press publicity followed the dictates of party interests, what explained the parties' particular choice of issue cleavages and cultural symbols with which to slice up the electoral pie? Why should Democrats obsessively return again and again to the issue of Blacks in America? From where did these electoral issues come, and what determined their attraction? After all, the mix of fear and fantasy animating the Democratic party's propaganda suggests something more than the calculating contrivance of political ideals. What were the sources of the Democratic press's racist rhetoric?[78]

Cultural historians Jean Baker and Alexander Saxton both point to the Democratic party's drawing upon, and reiterating, the racialist discourses of a prior commercial popular culture. Democratic orators and journals strategically utilized already-existing cultural resources in their efforts to split the available vote in ways detrimental to the Republicans. They deployed a repertoire of stereotypical representations of Blacks produced by popular commercial culture since the 1840s. For example, minstrel shows, "the preferred entertainment of the northern working-class from 1840 to 1880," manufactured comic caricatures of Blacks for the mass amusement of Whites. Whites, performing in blackface, created vivid and supposedly authentic portrayals of the lives, behavior, and character of Blacks. Along with such leisure-time commodities as lithographs, songs, and so on, minstrelsy rendered into concrete and comprehensible form the "abstract notions northerners held about blacks."[79] White audiences may have confused these contrived imitations – crude projective stereotypes – with real Black lives.[80]

In constructing their denunciations of Republicans, Democratic politicians and publicists made free use of this hoard of racist images and fantasies. In fact, Democratic journals mixed fact with fiction, topical events with popular humor's mimicry of Blacks, to report the news. Typically, journalistic claims of first-hand observation and factual descriptions of Black behavior conformed to popular cultural conventions and presented African-Americans as amusing, immature, foolish, and superstitious.[81] The *Free Press* in 1871 reported this incident from its regular news beat at the Detroit court house:

The case of Elijah Coombs, secretary of the Lincoln Hall Association, a political club composed of blacks . . . came up for trial before Judge Boynton yesterday. The want of harmony in the camp was occasioned by the alleged incompetence of the secretary, and his refusal to deliver his books in obedience to a vote of the association.
. . . According to a disinterested witness, "Uncle Josh took hole of Coombs and keerfully laid him down on de flor an' Mr. Sorrel, de President, took the books 'way from him." Mr. Coombs 'lowed as he was gwine to cut his livers out and Mr. Prater 'taliated by remarking something 'bout clubbin' Coombs' brains out."[82]

The use of caricatured dialect is designed to heighten the distance of the narrator (and his reading audience) from the Black speaker. The quoted Black appears as an unsophisticated primitive; he speaks only to mangle his syntax. His political club deliberates solely to confound all attempts at reasoned discussion. The narrator juxtaposes in an ironic manner his own formal, correct language to the informal, childish language of the quoted "disinterested witness." While the Blacks are depicted as a primitive other, they pose no threat but instead became material for comic entertainment.[83]

In another, later, example, the Detroit *Evening News*, an independent journal with occasional Democratic sympathies, titled one news story "Doctah Clawk." The headline, with its caricatured speech patterns, already prepares the reader for this genre of humorous, descriptive feature.[84] The sub-head "He Propounds His Views on State, National, and International Law" points to the pomposity of Doctor Clark. Clark, who is on his way to a political convention, is mocked as a self-absorbed and garrulous child, a parody of independent political reasoning. He is irredeemably tied to his "Ethiopian" physical nature.[85]

. . . The reporter explained that he was a NEWS man, en route to the convention. He made a wrong move in so doing, although the game came out all right in the end.

"Oh, well, you know me," said the colored gentleman. "My name is Clawk – Doctor Clawk – you know me for years."

"I should say so," said the reporter, with an aspect of reverential awe. "I have heard your name mentioned as a candidate for the legislature."

The doctor's body dilated visibly, and his face exhibited that genuine gratification which can only be expressed by the facial muscles of the Ethiopian.

"My name, sah, *has* been mentioned. But I don't care about it. I'm a man that is animated by principle. I go to all the meetings and lectures and political speeches, and I hear everything. I hear a republican speech, and I note it. I hear a democratic speech, and I note it. Then I balance 'em." The doctor swayed his body, and lifted his hands like a grocery scale. "I balance 'em, see."[86]

Baker suggests that Democrats mined the dark depths of popular culture to produce electoral gold. "Popular culture, a neglected expression of the historically voiceless, not only defined the nature of the Negro's inferiority but also provided a domain within which Democrats developed specific public policies. By using its language and symbols, party leaders linked popular sentiments to party agenda."[87]

The partisan agenda also penetrated into the fiction and humor columns of Detroit's journals. Newspapers most smoothly melded popular cultural conventions and party interests in their humorous, fictional stories. Alongside racist "news" and sketches, which mixed in unequal proportions the creative talents of the writer with the strategic agenda of the party and the popular prejudices of the citizenry, were regular humor columns that featured Black characters.

Until now this chapter has employed the terms "news agenda" and "selectivity" to indicate how partisan interests guided the political press's news choices. But such concepts incorporate a number of distinctions from our contemporary era, distinctions which do not illuminate, but definitely obscure, the workings of Gilded Age journalism. When we turn to fictional stories, the limits of the terms become doubly visible. Both "agenda" and "selectivity" take for granted a separation of the news-collecting organization from the events waiting to be harvested. They assume the existence of news facts prior to their journalistic representations and interpretation. Accordingly, reporters introduce their bias merely by choosing among already-existing facts and events. Yet, Detroit newspapers' publication of literary stories and comic features calls into question these differentiations. In their fiction columns, Democratic papers did not just select, "borrow from," or "draw upon" the facts and representations from an antecedent existing reality (or a previously existing popular culture, as Baker suggests).[88] Rather, they actively created reality's representation. Throughout its news and fiction, Detroit's Democratic press actively constructed Blacks as objects of disdain and derision.[89]

The Democratic *Free Press* became specifically renowned for the weekly comic column of Charles B. Lewis under the pseudonym M. Quad. M. Quad's most famous column "Brother Gardner's Lime Kiln Club" provided a broad comic burlesque of the antics of a Black social club debating such topics as the aesthetics of barber poles, the number of dogs owned by Detroit's colored population, and "de goneness of de past."[90] One contemporary of M. Quad remarks: "'The Lime Kiln Club' purported to be the discussion of a group of colored gentlemen with odd names like 'Give-a-damn-Jones,' etc. of various local types. Its dialect was not of the genuine southern negro but near enough to that of the northern to make it interesting and amusing."[91]

M. Quad's column along with that of fellow writer Barr's "Luke Sharp" achieved for the *Free Press* a national reputation as suggested by *Harper's* in an 1888 survey of "Western Journalism."

The Free Press may be said to have a dual character – to be sort of a Dr. Jekyll and Mr. Hyde in journalism. It is a strong Democratic newspaper . . . this for its local constituency; it is also a weekly literary and family paper, with a funny department that has given it a reputation and circulation in every part of the United States . . . The writer of the most popular humorous articles and sketches for the Free Press is Charles B. Lewis [whose nom-de-plume is M. Quad] . . . the expectation of finding something funny in the "Bijah" or "Lime Kiln Club" papers may cause one to buy it to read upon the cars or in a leisure hour.[92]

Charles B. Lewis' column rode the crest of a wave of humorists which emerged in the 1850s and swept over the pages of American journalism in the second half of the century.[93] While M. Quad was syndicated in Democratic newspapers across the country, equally partisan comics lambasted the Democratic party in the Republican press.[94] One such column was David Locke's "The Struggles of Petroleum V. Nasby" consisting of letters from an almost illiterate Democratic "copperhead" who resided at "Confederit X Roads," Kentucky. Nasby was "hypo-critical, cowardly, loafing, lying, dissolute."[95] Locke would wickedly lampoon Nasby's speech and writing as the crude dialect of a poor, Southern White Democrat, a sort of mirror image of the speech attributed by Democrat humorists to Blacks. Locke's Nasby paraded typical Democratic views such as negrophobia and a hatred for the

Union, opinions which, in Nasby's case as archetypical Democrat, were taken to be a product of ignorance, foolishness, and partisan venality. As popular tradition has it, Nasby kept up the spirits of President Lincoln during the war's most doubtful periods. The President would insist on reading various comic tidbits from the latest Nasby to his cabinet.[96]

While the Lime Kiln Club did not begin officially until 1878, M. Quad did humor parodies of Blacks starting from 1869 and his column was largely derivative of other humorists who scribed Democratic pieces such as Artemus Ward and Marcus M. ("Brick") Pomeroy.[97] Part and parcel of this vogue of newspaper comedy was a tradition of comic burlesque of Blacks. According to Kenneth O'Reilley, "During the postwar years the freedman often found himself and his speech patterns caricatured by Southern writers. Northern writers, spurred by a growth of 'Negrophobia,' soon followed suit and Lewis emerged as one of the first and most widely read writers to caricature Northern Negro speech."[98]

Conclusion

Throughout the period of Reconstruction, Democrats and Republicans fought over the right to lead the country. They battled for the attention and allegiance of American voters by presenting opposed policies for the post-bellum South and contrasting images of Black Americans. Journalism's close ties with the political system meant that the polarized rhetoric of the two parties was imported into its pages. One of the central propaganda ploys of the Democratic party was the continual, vicious portrayal of newly enfranchised African-American citizens. Detroit's Democratic journals followed suit by editorializing against civil rights for Blacks; selecting news that depicted the negative consequences of Republican Southern policies; and elaborating stereotyped images of the emancipated Blacks. To advance its strategic interests, the party extracted the unrefined racism of popular culture and processed and polished it in order to heighten racial antagonism and thereby gain votes. Since early Reconstruction, the Republican party had defended equal rights. However, by 1876 a variety of factors convinced the Republicans to abandon their Reconstruction policies. In effect they acceded to the racist depictions promulgated by the Democratic press. After 1876, Black Americans were no longer a political issue dividing Democratic newspaper from Republican. Black citizens retained their public journalistic presence only as the object of comic parody as the humor tradition developed by M. Quad and minstrelsy spread across the pages of the press without apparent regard for any journal's partisan preferences.[99]

As an extension of parties – their arm, their organ – American newspapers were the chief publicists and propagandists for the parties' policies. The entanglement of press and polity blurred the differentiations underpinning twentieth-century American journalism's highest ideals of independence and objectivity. Reconstruction-Era journalism was a political endeavor not just because of its partisan-motivated news choices, nor because it interjected evaluations into its news coverage. It was political because papers and parties linked their enterprises in constructing the parameters and contents of America's public sphere.

NOTES

1 *Post*, July 11, 1872. This prospectus at first led off the editorial page but later moved into the advertising columns. Other prospectuses noted:
   For the *Free Press*: 1867; on May 7, 1868 a prospectus/editorial "The Opening of the Fall Campaign,"; Jan. 1, 1871 New Year's Day Statement; 1872; July 11, 1876: 1; and August 8, 1880 ad for the *Free Press* "Campaign Weekly." In 1876 the *Free Press* ad says the subscriber will receive the paper for five months from the start to end of the campaign. Also an ad Sept. 23, 1876: 1.
   For the *Tribune*: 1872; 1875; 1883; 1884; Nov. 1, 1892: 3 Ad for the *Weekly Tribune* addressed to "REPUBLICAN COMMITTEES! . . . the most important issues of a political newspaper ever published in Michigan."
   For the *Union*: 1868 and 1872.
   For the *Post*: 1867; July 11, 1872.
   In 1880 and 1876 the election season prospectus started referring to the paper being advertised and offered at reduced group rates as a weekly campaign newspaper.
2 *Free Press*, May 7, 1868 "The Opening of the Fall Campaign."
3 *Free Press*, May 7, 1868. And see *Union*, May 22, 1872; *Detroit Post*, July 16, 1872: 2, col. 2.
4 *Detroit Post*, July 16, 1872: 2, col. 2.
5 Bright 1984, Skocpol 1992, Skowronek 1981.
6 Burnham 1982: 29–30.
7 Keller 1977.
8 Cf. Baldasty 1992, Dicken-Garcia 1989, Jensen 1971.
9 Schudson 1998: ch. 4; and McGerr 1986. More generally on the public, ritual nature of the political culture see Baker 1983; Skocpol and Ikenberry 1983: 6; Gienapp 1982. On public displays and republican political culture see Wilentz 1984: 87–97.
10 Schudson 1978: 134–44.
11 Lippmann 1965: 358. As Lippmann observes, the news is not, and cannot be, "the truth." A news report is not the full story, but only a partial one. Such considerations point to the reflexive, indexical concept of publicity

used here. Theories, deriving from phenomenological notions of the life-world, recognize that attention is a limited resource and always operates against the background of a series of taken-for-granted assumptions and cultural norms. Journalism should be conceived as a limited attention reflexively focused on delimited social aspects that are regarded as worthy of public consideration. In general, see the ethnomethodological interpretation of the news in Molotch and Lester 1974; Lester 1974.

Following Schattschneider, we can also recognize that publicity is a scarce, power-laden political resource. The prior exclusion of an issue from even being considered in political debate is seen by contemporary political science as an important operation of power. These "non-decisions" preclude diverse inequalities and social grievances from ever becoming recognized as an issue of contention. They are blocked from forming the basis for a social protest coalition. Cf. Schattschneider 1975; Lukes 1974; Honneth 1995: ch. 12.

It is only necessary to add to this picture of dynamic interaction within the public sphere that social actors are not oblivious to the stares of the media. Events are not innocent, spontaneous occurrences. Rather, social groups react to potential publicity and strategically construct how they will appear. Such writers as Boorstin and Molotch and Lester tell us that governments and corporations with their accumulated prestige and power are able to create, select, or repress the facts available to journalists, and their creations are always inflected by their particular interests. See Boorstin 1961: ch. 1; and Schudson 1978: chs. 4–5.

12 For Lippmann, publicity was socially produced and depended upon an institutional apparatus that could objectify and measure society. It requires a "machinery for reporting." Cf. Lippmann 1965: chs. 21, 23. As a Progressive reformer, Lippmann subscribed to technocratic dreams of an elite that could catalogue social reality and manipulate it for socially determined ends.

Both Hannah Arendt and Michel Foucault detail the historical expansion of arenas of publicity. For Foucault such publicity entailed a process of creation, objectification, and strategic control, while for Arendt it could also encompass a dialogical process of reaching mutual agreement over disputed norms and facts (Arendt 1959; Foucault 1979). Schudson applies Arendt's categories to the US press in the early 1800s (see Schudson 1978: ch. 1). Thomas Leonard analyzes changing reporting conventions as an expansion of journalistic attention to domains previously hidden (see Leonard 1986).

If we adopt Arendt's terms, the "political" domain in contrast to the "social," is defined by issues and divisions that are seen as "legitimately" contestable. The social domain and its publicity are instead characterized by norms and rules that have been naturalized. Contesting those norms becomes a matter of deviance, not legitimate disagreement. Deviance, in turn, is a problem for various social apparatuses – law, the professions – to rectify as they reestablish the normative order: (cf. Rogin 1987: 62–3). While both the twentieth- and nineteenth-century press filtered their stories through narratives of political society and of civil society – between articulated conflicts of contending powers and a normative consensual view of society's mores – the relative emphasis on contentions or integrative rituals shifted between the two periods.

13 For Molotch, journalism only gains a reflexive understanding of its political impact and the political construction of the news in exceptional circumstances, mainly when it serves the purposes of the ruling class (Molotch 1979).

14 Bourdieu 1991.

15 Some of the methodological issues raised here and elsewhere are addressed in my Methodological Appendix.

16 For more discussion see the Methodological Appendix.

17 In contrast to a contemporary perspective that sees news as information and entertainment for private individuals, partisan journalism can be viewed from three different analytical perspectives: news can be seen as a ritual of group solidarity, as democratic communication among party members, or as a strategic tool in the party's pursuit of electoral power. The historian McGerr forcefully analyzes the late-nineteenth-century press as an expressive ritual of partisanship (see McGerr 1986: 37–8, 40, 17, 21; also see Carey 1989).

18 Cf. Bourdieu 1991; and Falasca Zamponi 1992.

19 Schattschneider 1975: 66.

20 *Detroit Free Press*, May 10, 1868: 2. And see Mohr 1976: xiii–xiv.

21 Kenneth Burgess-Jackson argues instead that "constitutional issues" were the "most fundamental issue" of partisan dispute of this period (see Burgess-Jackson 1990: 306–11).

22 Baker, 1983: 257.

23 See Keller 1977: 71, 81 on the 1867 results.

24 Dilla 1912: 92–3.

25 Dunbar and Shade 1972: 53–5.

26 Katzman 1973: 84–90 and 22–25.

27 Angelo 1981: 65; and Scripps 1900: 14.

28 For example, in his 1946 autobiography William Allen White, the famous *Emporia, Kansas* editor, wrote: "and my mother, loyal to her dead husband and still a black abolitionist Republican who feared the rebels" to indicate the strength of his mother's political convictions. And to describe his boss's partisan loyalties: "He was a stalwart, wool dyed black radical Republican who was still fighting the battles of the Civil War" (White 1946: 163, 207).

29 Lodge 1949: 56.

30 Baker 1983: 256; Keller 1977: 51–2, 81–3. Or as the Republican San Francisco *Chronicle* wrote on June 17, 1869: "The Democratic Party just now seems to be based entirely upon shins, facial angles, elongated tibias and kinky hair. Without this capital, the party couldn't last a week."

31 *Free Press*, May 9 and 10, 1868. Also see Oct. 15, 1868: 2.

32 *Free Press*, May 30, 1868.

33 Cf. Slotkin 1985: 440.

34 I extensively scrutinized the pages of the *Free Press* of May 1868 to determine the repetition and continuity of news-editorial motifs.

35 *Free Press*, May 31, 1868: 2, col. 2.

36 Roediger 1991: 72–80, 140–4.

37 Angelo 1981: 86–7 cites the *Free Press* of Feb. 27, 1863. The court verdict

coincided with Congress's authorization of a draft to replenish the ranks of the Union army, March 3, 1863.

38 This account is presented in Holli 1976: 86–92; and see other accounts of the Detroit Riot in McPherson 1969: 1–24; McRae 1924: 4–5; and Katzman 1973:44–7.

39 Quoted in the preface of McPherson (1969: iv).

40 See the account of the New York riot in Montgomery 1981: 102–7:

> Military suppression of strikes, greenback inflation, the specter (for it was never more than that) of liberated Negroes flocking North, and the ubiquitous draft – what could have been better grist for the Coppery [i.e. Democratic] mill? . . . [At a Fourth of July rally against conscription] Copperhead orators pounded home the themes that the government's war effort was undermining the Constitution, that conscription claimed the lives of the poor in a rich man's war, and that emancipated Negroes were flooding the North.

Also, see Baker 1983: 245–9.

41 *Daily Union*, October 13, 1868.

42 See for example the *Union*'s commentary on the *Post*'s coverage of elections in the South, Nov. 6, 1868, 2; also, the *Free Press*, February 15–17, 1867, 4; Oct. 15, 1868, 4; Aug. 24, 1880, 4; Aug. 28, 1880; and Sept. 24, 1880, 4. And the *News*, Oct. 15, 1874, 2; Montgomery tells of the impact of such news reports on Northern Republicans in 1866 (1981: 69–70). Also see the *News*, Jan. 5, 1875, 2.

43 Feb. 15, 1867 and Oct. 15, 1868, 2; Oct. 9, 1868.

44 *Union*, Oct. 15, 1868.

45 Saxton 1971: 27, 132–6 Saxton analyzes Democratic party anti-Chinese propaganda in California and says indeed sometimes Chinese labor was used by capitalists in their battle with Caucasian workers. Also, Keller dicusses worker fears of Repblican "money-power." Keller 1977: 51–20.

46 *Free Press*, Feb. 13, 1867, 4; Feb. 20, 1867, 4.

47 Roediger 1991.

48 Quote from the *Free Press* of Feb. 15, 1867. References to the Republicans as "Jacobins" in the *Free Press* of Oct. 15, 1868 and May 7, 1868, 2.

49 *Union*, Dec. 15, 1868.

50 Angelo 1981: 72.

51 Quoted from the *Free Press*, May 31, 1868 . Other attacks on the Freedmen's Bureau in the *Free Press* in May 1868 besides those quoted below are May 4, 1868, 2, and May 28, 1868. Also see Dec. 18, 1868. Other payoffs to Blacks are mentioned on May 20, 1868, 2.

52 *Free Press*, May 31, 1868, 1.

53 This Democratic imagery of the freed Blacks paralleled historical depictions of Indians. In Rogin's psychological interpretation:

> The myth of the West establishes male independence through violence against [Indians] bad children of nature too closely, maternally bound. Imposing private property against communally living on the land, Indian policy makers hypostasized the bounded ego of the self-made man. Indian freedom by contrast, would have to succumb to self-restraint, hard work and emulation for these were, from the perspective of the dominant culture, the requisites of maturity. (Rogin 1991: 14)

Of course, Northern Republicans too were motivated by republican imagery to try and impose a model of disciplined liberal society on the bad social relations of the South. See Foner 1970: ch. 2; Burgess-Jackson 1990: 37–8.
54 Baker 1983: 256.
55 Angelo 1981: 72.
56 Thorndike 1958.
57 See, for example, the *Free Press* of Jan. 23, 4 and Jan. 29, 1867, 4 and Feb. 9, 1867, 4 as cited in Burgess-Jackson 1990.
   References to amalgamation were repetitiously invoked in the press, and indeed any Black participation in politics was labeled miscegenation. For example, the state governments of the South that permitted Black participation were called in the *Free Press* variously "miscegenation governments" May 14, 1868: 2 and May 4, 1868: 4; "mongrel constitution" May 9: 2, col. 2, May 10: 2; "miscegenation constitution" May 12: 2; "mongrel senators" May 20: 2. Also on May 9th the *Free Press* editorialized against "Hayti, Jamaica, Mexico or any other country which illustrates the evils of amalgamation."
58 Rogin 1987: 51–5 and 279; Gillman 1989: 81–6; Sundquist 1988. Furthermore, in Rogin's analysis, the sexualization and demonization of Black men as uncontrollable rapists and White women as helpless, virtuous victims fulfilled the purpose of policing the boundaries and depriving both women and Blacks of power.
59 Angelo 1981: 86.
60 The prospectus was repeatedly published in January through May 1867. See the *Post*, Jan. 5, 1867: 3 and May 7, 1867.
61 *Advertiser and Tribune*, Jan. 10, 1867: 2; Feb. 19, 1867: 2; Feb. 16, 1867: 2.
62 So wrote the San Francisco *Chronicle* (Republican) regarding the San Francisco *Call* (Democrat) Feb. 16, 1869; and see June 17, 1869.
63 *Post*, Jan. 10, 1867.
64 *Post*, Feb. 15, 1867: 2.
65 *Free Press*, Oct. 15, 1868: 4. American historians from 1890 through 1950 tended to adopt the Democrats' point of view. The news accounts of KKK terror, right or wrong, only had the purpose of strengthening Republican power and prolonging the mistaken experiment of Reconstruction; see, for example, Buck 1937. The revised point of view is strongly represented by Foner 1988.
66 Montgomery 1981: 66–72.
67 Montgomery 1981: 84.
68 *Post*, Feb. 15, 1867.
69 *Post*, Oct. 15, 1868.
70 I further discuss the history of these papers and their factional differences in chapter 2.
71 Slotkin 1985: 332–4. Montgomery describes the elite economic interests manifest in different party factions and policies. Montgomery 1981: ch. 2. These linkages of class and faction in Michigan can probably be traced out through the figure of James Joy who, as a leading Michigan Republican and a major owner of railroads, was a central player in the more conservative faction of the Republican party.

72 Speeches that were reported verbatim in the *Free Press* often tried to cast the Republicans as the party of the corrupt rich who were trying to exploit political power for private gain. The *Free Press*, however, rarely invoked such motifs in its editorials.

73 Iyengar 1991. Also see Carey 1986.

74 *Post*, Jan. 24, 1867: 4.

75 Bryce 1909: V. II, 214. For a more general discussion of the constraints on free expression posed by political and economic institutions see Goldfarb 1982.

76 For examples see Jensen 1971: 194–7; Goodwyn 1978, Folkerts 1985.

77 On the republican values of the press see Nerone 1993.

78 In part, party propaganda is governed by the strategic constraints of forging a viable electoral coalition. Parties appealed to inherited coalitions, which needed to be shored up, and to potential voters dissatisfied with their current political alliances. For example, Alexander Saxton explains that the Democrats' racist ideology fulfilled a number of functions, foremost of which was the need to defend slavery in order to retain the support of the party's southern wing. But here I sidestep most of these questions in order to address the popular cultural sources of the Democratic press's political appeals (Saxton 1975: 17; and, more generally, see Saxton 1990: 148–54, 105, 136–42).

79 Baker 1983: 214; and Saxton 1975: 4.

80 Ibid. 218, 220. "White southerners, who lived in closer contact with blacks had no need to visualize . . . but Northerners . . . What they saw . . . was their own imposition. With few exceptions blacks were not allowed on white stages" (p. 218).

81 Chapter 6 in Baker 1983 is an extensive catalogue of the conventions and logic of these stereotypes.

82 *Free Press*, Feb. 15, 1871.

83 An important discussion of the nineteenth-century use of dialect to portray African-Americans is Sundquist 1993: ch. 4; see also Howard 1985: 104–6. Interestingly enough, this brief news item probably constituted the original source for the comic column "the Lime Kiln Club," which was a featured attraction at the *Free Press* from 1881 until 1891.

84 As Frederic Jameson notes, "[A]mong the most important indices of generic expectations" are "the shifting in our distances from the characters, the transformation of the very categories through which we perceive characters" (quoted in Howard 1985: 105).

85 Minstrel players often called themselves and their comedic acts "Ethiopian."

86 *Evening News*, Oct. 12, 1874: 4. The *News* at this time was attacking Republican reconstruction policies.

87 Baker 1983: 213.

88 Quoted expressions from Baker 1983: 252, 253, and 257.

89 More generally, popular cultural conventions were influenced by the Democratic party. The founders of minstrelsy were disproportionately Democratic (Saxton 1975; 1990: 95, 102–5, 127).

90 One collection among others of Lime-Kiln comedy columns is M. Quad

(Charles B. Lewis 1882). Other columns of Charles Lewis are reprinted in *Quad's Odds* (Detroit: Tyler, 1875).
91 Holden 1927: 424.
92 White 1888: 690. And on the *Free Press*'s reputation see O'Reilly 1979: 130; Holden 1927: 424, 428.
93 Catlin 1945: 355 and 350; O'Reilly 1979: 114.
94 O'Reilly 1979: 126–7. O'Reilly tells us that Charles B. Lewis' column "the Lime Kiln Club" lasted from 1877 to 1891 whereupon he departed from the *Free Press* for Pulitzer's Democratic *New York World*. In New York Lewis initiated a new feature parodying Blacks which was titled "Cotton Blossoms." The *New York World* induced Lewis to leave Detroit with a salary reputed to be at least $8,000.
95 Keller 1977: 47. On the Democrat "Brick" Pomeroy see pp. 49–50.
96 Ibid., 47–9; Buck 1937: 20–1.
97 Keller 1977; cf. M. Quad's *Free Press* column for Dec. 7, 1878.
98 O'Reilly 1979: 117; Saxton 1975: 26.
99 The main reasons for the Republican party's abandonment of Reconstruction were: the *de facto* seizure of control of most Southern state governments by Whites; the displacement of "Radicals" from positions of power in Northern Republican parties; a lack of popular support for continued federal military intervention in the South; and lastly a new political philosophy articulated by the Northern, genteel intelligentsia that melded a racist Social Darwinism with economic liberalism. See Foner 1988: 483–4, 488–99; Keller 1977: ch. 7; on the case of California see Saxton 1971: chs. 4–6. On this new political philosophy also see: Bender 1987: ch. 5; Montgomery 1981: ch. 9; Fredrickson 1965: 192–4.

2   Economic engines of partisanship

Why did a partisan press persist throughout the late nineteenth century? The answer to this question lies in the structure of the press's economic and political environment. By scrutinizing a series of political crises afflicting Detroit newspapers from 1866 to 1900, this chapter investigates the pressures buffeting journals as they sailed the sea of partisan political opinion and attempted to maintain their profitability. My conclusion: a curious combination of politics and markets reinforced the public biases of journals. Urban markets across the nation were inundated by a plurality of daily papers, from Detroit's handful up to Chicago's dozen and New York City's fifty journals.[1] In the face of such rigorous competition, newspapers were forced to segment the market. They refined their sales appeal in order to capture a select share of the available readers. Differences in class, ethnicity, and especially party allegiances defined these slices of the market. Competition and the consequent division of the market along the lines of popular political preferences ensured a lively partisan press.

Thus this chapter argues that the operations of the market itself reinforced the press's political allegiances. But, in addition, this market dynamic possessed political underpinnings. Economics alone determined neither the basis, nor the extent, of market segmentation. Politicians, desiring favorable publicity and the prestige that accompanied the ownership of an influential sheet, invested heavily in the journalistic market. This "political capital" guaranteed that a multitude of dailies would be engaged in the struggle for survival and profitability. Political investors, thus, reinforced the tendency of papers to divide, instead of aggregate, their audiences. In the end, politics decisively influenced the structure of the market.[2]

Historians still today debate the mechanisms that sustained the American press in its political advocacy, and why in the end this machinery broke down and partisanship was abolished. Typically, media scholars exclusively stress the role of the market or the polity, while interconnections between the two are ignored. Michael McGerr, for example, situates the beginning of the end of our partisan press in the 1870s–1890s, an era of rapid economic transformation encompassing profound shifts in the nation's systems of sales and marketing. McGerr, however, dismisses purely economic explanations and, instead, provides a political account for journalism's changes. He tells us that the ending of party subsidies and government patronage to newspapers along with expanding market opportunities after the Civil War meant a newspaper *could* pursue a sales- and profit-maximizing strategy of political neutrality. But, he asserts, "By themselves, the material changes in the newspaper business did not destroy partisan journalism . . . [E]ditors had been willing partners, not slaves, of party. Freed by their profits, they did not necessarily want to run away."[3] The cultural beliefs of editors sustained their practices of partisanship. For McGerr, an alteration in editors' and publishers' attitudes towards politics helps explain the rise of a non-partisan press. He discovers this alteration in the elite, reform movement of Liberal Republicans. The new political culture of the Liberal Republicans freed editors from obedience to parties, and allowed them to follow the imperatives of the market.

McGerr's emphasis on the political culture of journalism forms an important corrective to much of journalism history. But, despite his seeming heterodoxy, he adopts many of the assumptions of mainstream historical analysis. McGerr joins numerous other scholars in presuming that the market inevitably promotes journalistic neutrality or even objectivity.[4] Without the political restraints and cultural obstacles to a newspaper's pure pursuit of profit, such as government subsidies, party patronage, or the strong political views of editors, papers would adopt a posture of political neutrality. Journals would select the least divisive political content in order to offend as few readers as possible, and thus maximize their sales.

Against McGerr's internal focus on the attitudes of owners and editors and his overly simple economic analysis, this chapter returns to the press's economic environment. It wishes to complicate McGerr's depiction. It is necessary to consider the total economic environment, the "ecological context," and more specifically the set of newspapers that constitute rivals for available market resources.[5] This "organization-set" analysis suggests that, in a competitive newspaper environment, the rational economic strategy for maximizing a journal's audience and profits cannot be a mass appeal to an undifferentiated audience. As Glenn Carroll remarks, unspecialized mass newspapers "aim for the center of the market but are forced to differentiate themselves from their competitors by developing some unique or special appeal."[6] An undifferentiated sales appeal will lose readers to journals that more precisely tailor their editorial content to an audience segment's particular desires. Just as with the competitive market of US radio stations that find it necessary to appeal to specialized musical tastes, American publishers in the 1800s could and did appeal to a reading audience stratified along class, ethnic, and especially partisan lines.

Researchers studying other countries have documented national presses that are fractured by party affiliations and political preferences. These authors, however, explain the political specialization of newspapers exclusively by the partisan segmentation of the subscribing audiences, not by reference to competitive newspaper strategies: "[N]ewspapers consistently shift to a strategy of audience-maximization through the adoption of generalized content materials. [But,] the extent to which this shift can take place is a function of the degree of polarization and segmentation in the reading audience." Most particularly, it is party preferences and political cleavages that "prevented a shift towards a non-controversial content. Attempts to maintain a neutral attitude were not well received by the readership."[7] My analysis of the partisanship of Detroit newspapers subscribes to this focus on audiences divided by party loyalty, but joins it to Carroll's emphasis on the role of a competitive market in enforcing such specialized appeals.[8]

While "ecological theories" of the competitive market's impact on the editorial strategies of individual newspaper organizations may be a construct of twentieth-century social science, such ideas were not totally foreign to the nineteenth century. Indeed, Gilded Age newspaper entrepreneurs developed remarkably similar ideas to guide their investments in profitable press enterprises. For example, James E. Scripps, founder of the innovative, cheap, and sometimes independent *Detroit News*, outlined a similar notion of audience segmentation, market niches, or in his words market "fields." His 1879 speech – "Some Elements of Success in Journalism" – to a gathering of Michigan newspaper publishers argued against too many papers competing for the limited resources of a city's market. "Newspapers are planted by scores in places and under circumstances in which they cannot by any possibility succeed and this in great measure accounts for the great number of newspaper failures." "The remedy for supernumerary papers is consolidation . . ."

Beyond arguing for reduction in the number of papers in order to benefit from economies of scale, Scripps urged papers to specialize in order to possess "a sufficient field," that is, an adequate sales market.

As a rule, there is never a field for a second paper of precisely the same characteristics as one already in existence. A Democratic paper may be established where there is already a Republican; or vice versa; an afternoon paper where there is only a morning; a cheap paper where there is only a high-priced one; but I think I can safely affirm that an attempt to supplant an existing newspaper . . . of exactly the same character has never succeeded . . .

So strongly am I impressed with the disadvantages under which papers other than the leading ones labor that I would even abandon the profession rather than waste my energies upon a newspaper that was not in some important respects at the head of the list . . . All other positions involve only years of toilsome labor and no reward.[9]

Scripps claimed that any new journal must distinguish its audience. The successful periodical would appeal to a market segment not previously addressed by established journals. Otherwise the publisher would be permanently handicapped in the race for sales and advertising dollars. An undifferentiated paper would fail. Furthermore, he suggested, the major market appeals are predicated on price, partisan editorial content, and whether the paper is published in the morning or evening.[10]

In the second half of the nineteenth century, despite the decline of government and party subsidies to newspapers,[11] and notwithstanding increases in capital investments and the rising influence of advertisers,[12] the press remained political.[13] Partisanship – imposed by strenuous market competition, a readership with set political loyalties, and politicians as investors seeking laudatory publicity – was an effective, profitable economic tactic. An examination of Detroit's daily papers from 1865 to 1900 will demonstrate the market opportunities and constraints confronting journalism and how publishers managed to negotiate the balance of party, audience, and advertiser.

Trials and Tribulations at the *Detroit Free Press* in 1872

In 1872 a crisis enveloped the governing board of the *Detroit Free Press.* Unfolding over the summer and early fall, these events illuminate the economic pressures on a newspaper, pressures that arose from readers when a paper deviated from expectations of its proper partisanship. As the national election campaign of 1872 approached, the Democratic party desperately sought an effective strategy to reverse its persistent losses to the Republicans. That year upper-class reformers, disgusted with the corrupt administration of President Grant, had bolted from the Republicans. They launched the independent party of "Liberal Republicans," and chose as their presidential candidate newspaperman Horace Greeley. The Democrats, hoping to capitalize on the Republican disaffection, also nominated Greeley for President.

The endorsement of Greeley, however, entailed the reversal of numerous long-standing Democratic policy positions. In the 1850s and

1860s, Greeley had gained a national reputation as a leading, early crusader for the abolition of slavery. In his outspoken editorials for the *New York Tribune* he had always supported Black civil rights and Republican reconstruction policies, while viciously attacking the Democrats. The Democrats' act of political expediency was a "hard worm to swallow," and many faithful party members rebelled.[14]

The *Detroit Free Press* was a veteran Democratic newspaper, indeed the leading one in Michigan. Its service to the party had gained it the typical rewards of state printing contracts, postmaster positions for its publishers, and a body of loyal readers.[15] But, in 1872 two of its owners, Colonel Freeman Norvell and Henry Walker, were old-time Democrats who refused to endorse Greeley. They rebelled at "swallowing" their Democratic pride and principles. According to the reminiscences of reporter Edward Holden, the *Free Press*'s remaining proprietor, Editor William Quinby, took alarm at Norvell and Walker's daily, strident repudiation of Greeley in the pages of their journal: "[Quinby] believed the *Free Press* would lose prestige among the steadfast loyal and intelligent followers and leaders of the Democratic party should it prove disloyal to the party's official actions . . . In his opinion the party could better afford to support the absurd nomination of Mr. Greeley than go to pieces over such an issue."[16] Indeed, Quinby only needed to consult the pages of his competitors to observe this threat mobilizing. Certainly, the cheap Democratic workers' daily, the *Union*, was glad to publicize the *Free Press*'s difficulties. Similarly, the Republican journals, the *Advertiser and Tribune* and the *Post*, were quick to highlight the divisions within the Democrats. The *Union* publicized one report:

The FREE PRESS Censured By A Democratic Convention

The Clinton County Democratic Convention . . . passed a resolution censuring the FREE PRESS for its actions in not publishing the speeches of leading Democrats at the late Greeley ratification meeting at the Young Men's Hall.

It is due to the FREE PRESS to say that the reason the speeches were not published is because no pay was offered that paper for doing so. The call for the meeting was published by the FREE PRESS and paid for by the Democrats of this city. It was supported by the committee who had the matter in charge that the FREE PRESS would publish the proceedings as a matter of news. Democrats through out the state will take notice, however the Free Press is no longer a news paper, at least as far as the publishing of the proceedings of Democrats meetings is concerned – unless it is paid for it.[17]

The Republican *Post* gloated at the disarray in Detroit's Democratic ranks shortly after the Democrats' Baltimore convention nominated Greeley. They published this letter-to-the-editor:

A Democratic Paper Wanted

To the Editor of the Detroit Post:

Help is wanted. The Democracy are without a paper. Anxious squads of Democrats were about the news room and post office today awaiting the arrival of the FREE PRESS, and hopeful that its [editorial] leader would be for Greeley and Brown – but oh! the disappointment! The FREE PRESS can't see it, and consequently the subscribers can't see the FREE PRESS and nearly all are ordering the FREE PRESS stopped. Torn and mutilated FREE PRESSES are upon the street . . . What shall be done?[18]

Editor Quinby, recognizing the mounting threat to the fortune and future of Michigan's "leading organ of the Democratic Party," opposed the political stand of his partners. A stalemate developed. One side or the other must capitulate. Other papers predicted the abrupt surrender of the *Free Press* to political and economic exigencies:

Swallowing A Candidate

[T]omorrow or the next day we shall see the DETROIT FREE PRESS going through the same process [as the NEW YORK WORLD] in a small way. Like an ancient hen struggling with a piece of garbage whose dimensions were not accurately estimated beforehand, the [FREE PRESS] will be seen choking away at the subject for a while . . . But it will worry Greeley down and . . . advocate the ticket.[19]

Finally, after days of "painful suspense," Quinby succeeded in raising the requisite capital to buy out Norvell's interests, and the *Free Press* was able to swallow "the garbage" of Greeley's nomination.[20] From 1872 until the political upheaval in 1896 Quinby ran the *Free Press* as the state's major Democratic organ. For such loyal service he received an ambassadorship in 1891 as well as a healthy accumulation of newspaper profits.[21]

What can this political tempest tell us about the economic workings of press partisanship? First, we should note that the *Free Press* directly appealed to a political community, and this audience expected the paper to perform in a clear partisan manner. The organ should endorse and firmly support the party's candidates and policies, and not just in editorials, but also in the news. Secondly, when the paper strayed too far from these partisan standards, party leaders and loyal party members responded with criticism and warnings. Such admonitions might be ineffectual if not backed up by the threat from rival papers. Indeed, new competitive threats are an essential part of the market logic described here. It is the danger from an alternative journal, one which more closely mirrors the interests and views of the audience segment, that compels the politically wayward newspaper to retreat to a posture of political loyalty.

And, in fact, both real and potential Democratic rivals haunted Quinby and the *Free Press* in the summer of 1872. On the one hand, breathing down the neck of the *Free Press* and attempting to make the best of the tensions between the party and its official organ, was the *Detroit Daily Union*. The *Union* had vigorously endorsed Greeley as the Democrats' candidate immediately following his Liberal Republican nomination in May. As the *Free Press* resisted the party's ticket and as protests rolled in, the *Union* added as much wood to the fire as possible – deriding the *Free Press*'s stance and publicizing Democrat dissatisfaction. To the heated protest of the *Free Press*, the *Union* proclaimed itself the state's premiere Democratic party organ.[22] On the other hand, Quinby learned "that influential Democrats were talking of establishing a loyal rival to the *Free Press* in case of its faithlessness to the party."[23] A new political organ would threaten the *Free Press*'s monopolization of the Democratic market segment and endanger its economic viability.

Punishing the *Advertiser and Tribune* in 1866

Quinby knew better than to believe such threats were idle. As a long-time Detroit newspaperman, he certainly was mindful of past events at the *Advertiser and Tribune*. In the mid-1860s, this Republican organ had bucked the state party's control and refused to endorse the party's complete slate of candidates. In response to this political disloyalty, a "joint stock company" of prominent party members founded a rival Republican sheet, the *Detroit Post*, in 1866. The new organ, wrote journalist Edward Holden, was intended to "offset the lukewarm if not hostile influence of the *Tribune* and at the same time [to] properly chastize it."[24] The publishers appointed Carl Schurz, the prestigious political statesman, as editor. Schurz would keep the new paper properly partisan, and ensure its vigorous support for orthodox Republican policies.

This leads to our third observation on the financial mechanics of the partisan press. Much of the capital invested in the nineteenth-century newspaper (at least in Detroit) came from politicians in hot pursuit of elected office.[25] Indeed, as Chapter 3 argues in more detail, ownership of a party organ – possession of a journalistic mouthpiece – crucially enhanced a politician's prestige and power. In the end, not only did a given partisan market segment and the competitive menace from newspaper rivals induce papers to express clear partisan loyalties, but such partisan correctness was also enforced by a party elite threatening to establish an alternative organ.

Complicating any straight-forward portrait of party power over party journals, however, were the factional feuds that fractured both the Democrats and Republicans.[26] Indeed, the conflict between the Republican party and its Detroit organ can more properly be understood as a battle between factions. Typically at stake in these intra-party squabbles were such mundane concerns as the distribution of election spoils, for example: governmental positions as postmasters and custom house clerks; or alternatively there were significant issues to be wrangled over, for instance: civil service reform and Southern reconstruction. In the flurry of bitter words and festering rivalries, no journal could remain loyal to all factions, (although some tried by a stance of even-handed neutrality.)[27]

Early on, the Michigan Republican party had fissured into warring camps, a war which also embroiled Detroit's Republican press. The party split between Michigan's senior senator, Zachariah Chandler, and up-state Republicans.[28] Depending on whose account one reads, the factional antagonisms revolved around Chandler's aggressive Radical Reconstruction policies, his iron-fisted control of the state party, his failure to distribute fairly political spoils, or his vulgar personality. In the immediate post-bellum period, the *Advertiser and Tribune* began to slide into the anti-Chandler camp. In response, the Senator and his "political machine" established the *Post* to speak for their faction. Regardless of the reasons for this party-paper fight – whether reflecting a schism in the Republican political church or an individual act of heresy by the *Advertiser and Tribune* – the introduction of the *Post* sparked an immediate decline in the circulation and profits of the *Advertiser and Tribune*.[29] The *Post* only survived eleven years, but until its dying day the two Republican journals doggedly waged a war of insults and political arguments.[30]

The example of the *Detroit Post* shows that politicians invested in the urban newspaper market in order to gain supportive publicity for their electoral campaigns and policy positions. A systematic examination of "political capital" in Detroit's dailies will further illustrate this trend.[31] Let us first look at the *Detroit Post*. The *Post*, as we know, was founded with Senator Chandler's money. Other stockholders included senatorial candidate William Howard, Governor Henry Crapo, and future senator Thomas Ferry.[32] In 1877 the *Post* and the *Advertiser and Tribune* merged to form the *Post and Tribune*. In 1880 this decrepit party sheet received a capital transfusion. Future senator and Republican boss, James McMillan, "who was beginning to entertain political ambitions and the hope of securing a party leadership in Michigan, bought a considerable part of Hiram Walker's interests. He found the load rather heavy so on March 3, 1881, he induced several staunch Republicans to combine with him." These investors included Republican power-broker and 1883 senate candidate James Joy and the future governor Russell Alger.[33] In 1891 the paper was sold to independent publisher James Scripps. At the time of its sale, among the owners was Senator Francis Stockbridge.[34]

Before Quinby acquired control in 1872, Detroit's second major daily, the Democratic *Free Press*, was not so much owned by politicians, as directly run and edited by party hacks. Publishers Wilbur Storey and Henry Walker did not seek elected office, but lived off the party and its largesse in the form of governmental appointments and printing contracts.[35] In 1905 Quinby's son sold controlling interest to Republican leader and Congressman Colonel Frank Hecker, and Charles Freer and William McMillan. McMillan, son of Senator James McMillan, was contemplating a run for the Senate.[36]

Detroit's second Republican organ, the *Detroit Journal*, did not appear until 1883. According to newsman and archivist George B. Catlin: "The new investors made their venture because one of the liveliest and most bitter modern presidential campaigns was coming on and they hoped to profit politically if not financially and to be able to unload the Journal on other venturers."[37] By 1884 the *Journal* was floundering and in desperate need of new funds. In 1886 and again in 1892 Senator Thomas Palmer invested large sums of money in the two-cent afternoon sheet.[38] Later, in 1908, the *Journal* reviewed this early history and derided its former owners: "The *Journal* as an old-fashioned Republican party paper made no progress and no financial success. The Republican office holders and office seekers looked upon the *Journal* then as a sort of ladder by which to climb up to the plums, and when the plums were reached, the ladder was kicked over to paddle its own canoe."[39]

The fourth newspaper, the Democratic *Daily Union*, was formed in a printers' strike and styled itself a "radical Democratic" newspaper. One of its owners, Thomas Hawley, served as Democratic city alderman in the 1870s.[40] The *Union* paper was sold to Scripps' *Evening News* in 1874.

Lastly, the independent and sometimes Democratic *Evening News* relied on the capital of James Scripps and whatever funds he could scrounge from his assorted brothers and sisters. Although Scripps became a state representative late in his life, in his days as a publisher he evinced no desire for governmental office.

To summarize, political capital played a substantial role in Detroit's newspapers, especially in the organs of Michigan's dominant party: the Republicans. This capital sustained the newspapers' role as political media – as partisan journals designed to propagate a partisan public opinion – instead of merely commercial vehicles. Of course, the resulting political journalism was narrowly defined. It worked to consolidate the interests of the party and its candidates, not to enhance broad public debate. Political capital promoted a partisan content directly, through the control of newspapers by political party interests, and indirectly, by the threat of potential competitors for a market segment, as seen in the 1866 launching of the *Post* and in the example of the *Free Press* in 1872. Furthermore, these politically motivated investments stimulated partisanship by the founding and financing of new or struggling journals, thus ensuring tight newspaper competition and the necessity of (partisan) market specialization.

To be sure, this exaggerated competition entailed economic consequences, in addition to political pressures, for Detroit's dailies. Even politically motivated investors could not entirely neglect profit, and too many newspapers were battling for the same market share for all to profit. In fact, this was one of James E. Scripps' arguments in his 1879 address to the state convention of publishers. He polemicized against the entry of a second newspaper into any given market segment. Furthermore, he explicitly took the bitter competition for the Republican market as one of his examples of economically disadvantageous competition. But by 1878 Scripps noted that "unhealthy competition" in Detroit had been "done away with by the daily press resolving itself into two good dailies of the opposite politics" (the *Free Press* and the *Post and Tribune*), along with Scripps' own cheap, afternoon journal, the *Evening News*.[41] In 1875 Chandler had been defeated for reelection to the US Senate. The two Republican papers, representing pro- and anti-Chandler factions, lost all reason for prolonging their economically harmful contention. They merged in 1877.[42]

"Political Schizophrenia" at the *Detroit Tribune* in 1891

There exists an obvious counter-argument to the claim that competition for delimited market segments fortifies press partisanship: the ownership and control of newspapers by party officials and candidates. Such politicians cultiviated their own well-honed political interests and needed no guidance from partisan readers to ensure a proper editorial policy. Both the case of Quinby's *Free Press* and (as will be shown) that of the *Tribune* in 1891, however, demonstrate that an exclusive reliance on political ownership alone fails to fully explain newspaper politics. The publishers of these two journals possessed no clear political interests of their own, yet they still marketed their papers to a particular, partisan audience segment.

Consider the case of the Republican *Tribune* in the 1890s. By 1877, Senator Chandler had passed on. The *Post* and the *Advertiser and Tribune* consequently resolved their political differences and merged, eventually assuming the name the *Tribune*. For some commentators, Michigan's premiere Republican publication never overcame the damage to its finances incurred in the earlier rivalry between the two party factions and their respective organs.[43] In 1891 the economically troubled *Tribune* was sold to James Scripps. Scripps always believed in buying competing press properties and consolidating them into his afternoon paper. But this sale was contingent upon the agreement of Scripps and his managing editor, Michael Dee, to maintain the *Tribune* as an advocate of Republican policies and candidates.[44] Under their direction, the *Tribune* should not adopt the policies of their other journal, the *Evening News*, with its vague support for the Democrats and its advocacy of public ownership of the municipal streetcar system and the elimination of all import tariffs. Editor Dee telegraphed the head of the state Republican party in Washington:

To Senator James McMillan
Capt W H Stevens has Tribune matter in his control. Would you be kind enough to wire him early in morning . . . that you would be satisfied with me as director of Republican organ. He is a little fearful that I would be fool enough to sacrifice my business to my opinions. If you assure him on this point he would be satisfied I intend to make first class Republican paper and have abundant means to do it.
        M. J. Dee[45]

Dee, perhaps for the sake of gaining control of the newspaper, explained that he was not about to sacrifice his economic well-being to maintain his "political integrity." He implied there was a business logic in keeping the *Tribune* faithful to the Grand Old Party. This logic was due neither to Republican ownership, nor Republican payoffs. It derived from the political preferences of *Tribune* subscribers. And, in fact, after their purchase of the *Tribune*, Dee and Scripps diligently advocated Republican candidates and positions. Dee and Scripps lacked "political consistency" as they promoted Republican policies in the morning *Tribune*, while supporting the Democrats in their *Evening News*. Detroit papers gleefully mocked their "split political personalities," their political schizophrenia. For example, the *Free Press* pontificated:

Mr. Scripps Entangled
Mr. Scripps' morning conundrum [the *Tribune*] bore false witness [against Democratic candidates] . . . It continues the charge of corruption. Meantime, the afternoon vent of Mr. Scripps' eccentricities [the *News*] seems to think very well of the Democratic city ticket . . . This is Mr. Scripps' way. If he kicks a

man in the morning, he will pat that same individual on the head before sunset. If he smites a citizen hip and thigh in the afternoon, he will apply balm to his wounds at the earliest opportunity in the day following. If he preaches [the Republican policy of] high protection in the [*Tribune*] organette, he can be relied upon to give tariff reform a boost [in the *News*] . . . He roars honest money in the still watches of the night and howls free silver in the daytime. This is an infirmity with Mr. Scripps. He cannot help it. Consistency was omitted in his make-up. It is a misfortune because it leaves his utterances without the force of sincerity.[46]

While the shift in *Tribune* ownership appeared to the Democratic *Free Press* as an opportunity for political propaganda, to the Republican *Journal* it was an economic boon. The cheap evening *Journal* matches my model on three key points. First, it represented the invested political capital of an individual or group pursuing elected office. Second, it often expressed the views of a political faction of the Republicans – in the 1890s the views of Governor Hazel Pingree's reform wing against those of party chief Senator McMillan and his corporate allies. Lastly, the *Journal* competed with the *Tribune* for the same partisan market share, thus pressuring the *Tribune* to retain its circulation by heightening its appeal to Republican readers. For example, early in 1891, with the *Tribune* now of doubtful Republican loyalty after its sale to Scripps, the *Journal* spied its chance to become the leading Republican periodical in the state. In a public announcement the *Journal* editor Brearley reasserted the partisan loyalties of the paper. Henceforth the *Journal* would not hide its explicit affiliation with the Republicans.[47] And, in the early 1890s, it regularly proclaimed on its editorial page: "Larger Circulation than any other Republican Paper in Michigan."[48]

In any case, Scripps' *Tribune* trudged along the partisan path till 1896, a year of momentous political upheaval for the two parties. That summer, William Jennings Bryan captured the Democrats' presidential nomination and endorsed a program of radical populism against the wishes of the party elite: "the Gold Democrats." In Detroit, as in the rest of the nation, party leaders, voters and newspapers deserted the party in droves.[49] The Democrats dwindled to a minority. While the *Free Press* and its publisher Quinby quit the Democrats for McKinley and the Republicans,[50] Scripps took the *News* and the *Tribune* into the Populist–Democratic camp. The subsequent turmoil at the *Tribune* provides one last example of the market pressures on a newspaper – incentives to report news with a partisan bias in order to retain the approval and subscriptions of Republican readers.

The *Tribune*'s abrupt turn to the Democrats in 1896 restored "political integrity" to Scripps. For years he had attacked monopolies, the tariff, and political corruption in his *Evening News*. Now he could speak also with his "true" voice in signed editorials in the *Tribune*.[51] Of course, this change did not go unnoticed and leading Republicans quickly protested against the *Tribune*'s political deviation. Ex-Governor Russell Alger, a venerable power in the state party, wrote to Scripps, pleading for a return to the Republican ranks:

The *Tribune* has long been the leading Republican organ of the state and while you own its title and are paying its bills, still in a sense it is the property of the organization that has made the country great. It seems to me, it is your duty to permit it to heartily support both the ticket and platform. Can you not assure the Republicans of the state that, no matter what your views may be, the *Tribune* shall support the party heartily?[52]

Scripps for his part tried to move the Republican party in his direction and to conceal the break. He published news reports implying that Michigan Republicans did not endorse the party's national platform of a "gold standard" for the currency. Across the front page headlines read: "STIRRED UP!" "Republicans in Michigan Don't Like Gold," "GIVE THEIR OPINION," "Majority of Them Favor the Platform of 1892," "WAS A GOOD THING," "The Tribune's Stand is Endorsed By Many Republicans."[53] Similarly, the *Tribune* printed readers' letters to demonstrate wide-spread Republican support for the paper's pro-silver, anti-gold position.[54] The *Journal* and other Republican papers around the state would have none of the *Tribune*'s tricks and angrily drummed Scripps and his morning organ out of the party.[55]

Conclusion

This chapter examined the market interaction of the English-language dailies in the Detroit metropolitan area from 1865 to 1900. It suggested that focusing on the ecological context – the competitive pressures confronting the press – would explain the individual newspaper's marketing strategy, its political stance, and its editorial content. From this perspective the chapter detailed how Detroit's journals split the available newspaper readers into market segments based upon political preferences. As journals distinguished themselves politically, mass audiences and party elites developed expectations about the appropriate level of partisan bias in their papers' news and editorials. These expectations were enforced, on the one hand, by the threat of boycott by readers and politicians and, on the other hand, by the risk that a rival partisan newspaper would capture one's market share of subscribers. Furthermore, "political capital" – funds invested into journals for the sake of politically advantageous publicity – helped perpetuate the competitive market environment. As a consequence, newspapers were persuaded not to adopt a "generalist" marketing strategy of an undifferentiated, politically neutral market appeal, but instead to pursue a specialized, partisan one. Thus, a complicated economic machinery, underpinned by political resource and identities, generated a vigorously partisan press.

NOTES

1 Fifty-five dailies in New York City in 1890 according to census data cited by Lee (1947: 731). Chicago's dozen English-language dailies in 1890 were led by the *News* with 200,000-plus circulation. The next five papers distributed between 36,000 and 60,000 copies. The last six journals possessed much smaller distributions. There were also nine foreign-language dailies. See *N. W. Ayer & Son's Newspaper Annual* (1890): 120–31.

2 If we were to propose a theoretical explanation for this market–polity interaction, we might say that markets always assume a particular construction. This form is based on political intervention and political definitions of the "rules of the game." It is part of the logic of markets to appear innocent of all social intervention, all the while state and society subsidize certain forms of property and market transactions over others. No market is free of political influence, starting with what Marx called "primitive accumulation" up to today's crucial state support of housing markets and transportation infrastructures. Cf. Fischer 1996.

3 McGerr 1986: 110 and 112.

4 An example is Baldasty and Rutenbeck 1988. But on p. 68 they provide an important alternative view to their straightforward opposition of market versus politics, profits versus press partisanship. This alternative more closely corresponds to the view of this chapter. Other examples are Hallin 1985: 128–9, but see his qualification on 144; and the general tenor of Rubin 1981: 3, 7–8, 37–40, 56–65.

5 Hirsch writes that culture-producing organizations can be studied from three angles: the first angle is occupational roles, professional culture and attitudes; the second focuses on the organizational structure – its division of labor and its coordination; and the third focuses on the organization's political and (mainly) economic environment. This chapter concentrates on the last level. See Hirsch 1977.

6 Carroll 1984: 17.

7 Amburgey, Lehtisalo, and Kelly discuss the case of Norway (1988: 155, 157).

8 Carroll operates with a "population ecology" theory of organizations. Such a framework naturalizes the boundaries and types of interchanges between organizations and their environment, usually assuming an economic relation. Sociology's "new institutionalist" approach to organizations and their environments is better able to analyze the way politics influences newspaper organizations. As my comments on political capital should make clear, this economic interchange in fact possessed political presuppositions that influ-

enced the terms of the exchange. Other chapters discuss the way politics helped define the nature of the news and journalism's proclaimed public mission. For a theoretical discussion of new institutionalism and journalism see Kaplan 1998.

9 Scripps 1879. Also see the summary of Scripps' paper in the *Free Press*, Jan. 8, 1879: 7.

10 Scripps' recommendations were generally followed by publishers in the late nineteenth century. Knight, in a summary of census data, found that the second and third daily newspaper entrants into a city's market tended to differentiate themselves from earlier established papers on the basis of time of publication and party affiliation. See Knight 1968.

11 An important monograph on the workings of patronage from state and local governments to partisan newspapers is Dyer 1989. Because Dyer confines her analysis to her selected time period, she does not speculate on when and why such patronage ended, nor how the abrogation of such financial subsidies affected the partisan news content of papers (See her p. 4 and footnote 121).

   On the national level, the definitive account of governmental patronage is Smith 1977. Smith reports that governmental political payoffs were ended in the years 1860–75. However, the consequences that this poses for press partisanship are unclear. On p. 231 Smith writes that although federal subsidies to papers were abolished, "now plenty of party newspapers existed, distributed over the country with advertising incomes and large subscription lists, and not dependent upon party subsidies." But on p. 246 he suggests the opposite view: that the ending of governmental subsidies meant the end of formal press partisanship (and in general see also xi–xii, 3, 12–13, 58–60, 231, 241, 246–7).

   This vagueness has not stopped other historians from using Smith to say that the abolition of governmental patronage was the crucial factor in the ending of press partisanship. Schiller, for example, writes, "In his major interpretation of patronage and party journalism at the national level, Smith details the development of the party press up to its final eclipse in 1875" (Schiller 1981: 12; and see Schudson 1978: 65).

12 Cf. Baldasty 1992; and 1991.

13 My emphasis here is on public identities. Such public newspaper identities as "formally partisan" can entail a wide range of practices in fulfillment of their partisan duties, as chapters 1 and 3 detail. Furthermore, even formally "non-partisan" independent journals may possess a latent, unacknowledged bias towards the two major parties. And, of course, since objectivity is an illusory ideal, papers necessarily have a perspective or bias in reporting social reality.

14 Baehr 1972: chs. 5–6.

15 Catlin 1926b.

16 Holden 1927: 427.

17 *Detroit Daily Union*, July 1, 1872: 2; and see July 7, 1872: 2 and May 5, 1872 among other articles.

18 *Detroit Post*, July 13, 1872: 1; also see July 16: 2 and July 17: 3, and the *Detroit Advertiser and Tribune*, July 3, July 8, and July 10, 1872: 2.

Similarly, the *Cincinnati Commercial* lost readers and advertising when it bolted from the Republicans to the Liberals in the same 1872 election; see the account in Curl 1983: 72–3. Milton McRae describes similar dynamics for Chicago papers around 1895 (1924: 130–1).

19 *Advertiser and Tribune*, July 10,1872: 2.
20 Holden 1927: 427.
21 Campbell and Guest 1948.
22 See the *Union*'s "prospectus" May 22, 1872 and its articles on May 14 and June 1, 1872.
23 Holden 1927: 427. In 1880 a series of feature articles, entitled "Our Journalists," appeared in the weekly *Every Saturday* and described the newspapermen of Detroit. In the sketch of Editor Quinby this same claim is repeated: "Mr. Quinby, with rare sagacity, saw that the refusal of the *Free Press* to support the regular [1872] nominee of the party of which it was the acknowledged state organ would result in the establishment of a rival paper" (Joseph Greusel Papers, Scrapbook Vol. 13, Burton Historical Archives).
24 Holden 1918: 69. Also see the account by Stocking 1915, and *Union*, Nov. 12, 1868; and *Advertiser and Tribune*, Jan. 7, 1871.
25 Cf. Dyer 1989: 2–5, 26–7.
26 In the 1870s the major Republican factions were the Stalwarts and the Half-breeds; cf. Keller 1977: ch. 7. Senator Chandler was a Stalwart. My chapter 1 mentions some of the policy issues separating the *Post* from the *Advertiser and Tribune*.
27 Baehr describes the scramble to invest in and gain control over the *New York Tribune* by different New York Republican factions after Horace Greeley's death November 29, 1872 (Baehr 1972: ch. 7).
28 The senior senator for each state typically controlled patronage within the state from the national government. He usually ran the state party organization and was at the center of all factional disputes. See Rothman 1974: 833–7.
29 Changes in the circulation and income of the *Advertiser and Tribune* are described in the article "Interesting Inside History," *The Libel News* April 9, 1894 (Burton Historical Archives, Detroit Public Library (anon.)).
30 Cf. the *Union*, November 12, 1868: 2. For examples of the *Advertiser and Tribune*'s anti-Chandler and anti-*Post* editorials and news examine November 28, 1868: 2; January 7, 1871: 2; July 11, 1872; January 1–7, 1875. At one point it calls the *Post* "the Daily Chandler Suckling."
31 In looking at the political capital invested in Detroit's dailies I neglect the German papers and the various short-lived newspapers such as the *Telegram* and the *Times*.
32 Applegate 1907: 66.
33 George B. Catlin, "Detroit Journalism" (Ms. in George B. Catlin Papers, Burton Historical Archives).
34 *Detroit Free Press*, January 19, 1891: 5.
35 Angelo 1981: chs. 3–4. This probably represents an earlier form of partisan newspaper economics. It rests on the patronage payments typically pointed out by newspaper historians.
36 Ibid., 115–16.

37 George B. Catlin, "Story of the *Detroit Journal*, 1883–92" (Ms. in George B. Catlin Papers, Burton Historical Archives).

38 Ibid.

39 Actually an article from the *Kalamazoo Telegraph* reprinted in the *Journal*, Oct. 16, 1908: 12.

40 *Detroit Journal*, Jan. 31, 1894: 4.

41 Scripps, op. cit. This thinking typically guided Scripps and his brother Edward of the Scripps-McRae (later the Scripps-Howard) newspaper chain. For more on Scripps and his *Detroit Evening News* see chapter 4.

42 Cf. the announcement of the merging of the *Advertiser and Tribune* and the *Post* into the *Detroit Post and Tribune: Advertiser and Tribune*, October 13, 1877: 2; *Detroit Post and Tribune*, October 14, 1877: 4.

43 See Holden 1918: 69.

44 On Dee see Catlin 1926a.

45 Telegram, January 15, 1891 from Michael Dee to Senator James McMillan (Senator James McMillan Business Papers, Burton Historical Archives). And cf. the *Free Press* Jan. 19, 1891: 5.

46 *Free Press*, October 15, 1892. And see similar attacks in the *Journal*, January 26, 1892.

47 *Journal*, October 14, 1908: 8–9: "Birth and Early Years of the Detroit Journal."

48 See the *Journal*, February 21, 1894.

49 This turmoil suggests why press partisanship weakened after 1896. The massive shifts in voter allegiance in 1894–96 and the subsequent fall in electoral turnout 1896–1924 disrupted readers' long-term, strongly felt partisan loyalties. As popular partisanship collapsed, so did the utility of partisan journalism as a marketing tool. But this takes us beyond the boundaries of this chapter's topic into that of chapter 5.

50 See the *Free Press*'s "Declaration of Independence" from the Democratic party, July 12, 1896: 12.

51 Signed editorials–e.g. the *Tribune*, June 12, 1896: 2.

52 Published June 22, 1896 in the *Tribune*, p. 2, with a reply by Scripps.

53 *Tribune*, June 22, 1896: 1 and June 23: 1.

54 Cf. *Tribune*, June 23, 1896: 1–2, and June 25: 1.

55 The *Journal* reprints the comments of condemnation by various state newspapers on "The Tribune's Bolt" July 1, 1896: 4. And it refutes the *Tribune's* claims that Michigan's Republicans have pro-silver currency views, July 3: 1.
    Pound says that the "*Tribune* never quite recovered from its advocacy of 'free silver' . . . [T]here clung to it the fatal odor of radicalism in a state turning from agrarian economics towards policies more in tune with its high future in manufacturing" (Pound 1964: 146).

3 Rituals of partisanship: American journalism in the Gilded Age

On October 13, 1876, as the early election returns from Indiana and Maine began arriving in Detroit newspaper offices, the editors of the *Free Press* prepared to celebrate the grand Democratic triumphs. The October elections were considered as a bellwether sign. They promised certain victory in the national vote in November. To proclaim the good news to all Democratic readers, the editors crowded page 1 with woodblock prints of proud, strutting, crowing roosters, the very symbol of the Democracy. Thus the *Free Press* prominently and publicly displayed its identification with the Democratic cause.[1]

American newspapers in the last quarter of the century continually demonstrated their commitment to the Democrats or the Republicans as part of a more general public culture of partisanship.[2] Despite the repeated claims by such historians as Michael McGerr, Daniel Schiller, and Gerald Baldasty, Gilded Age newspapers by and large did not depart from the ranks of loyal party papers.[3] The nature of this partisanship did, however, change. The dailies of Detroit emphasized less rigorous discussions of the issues that divided the party from its foe, and more the symbolic invocation of traditional party loyalties. Newspapers reinforced the established party ties of voters in order to rouse them to the polls at election time. This change in press politics reflected the broader transformations of the two Civil War parties. In President Grant's second term of office, 1872–76, the Democratic and the Republican parties underwent a metamorphosis from "parties of principle" to pragmatic "organizational parties"; they shed the ideals and inflamed passions of the Civil War battles. Nevertheless, both parties continued to sustain their prominence in the public sphere by invoking traditions of party loyalty, distributing patronage and election spoils to party workers, and effectively monopolizing electoral power.

These late nineteenth-century changes in press politics and, more generally, in political parties afford the opportunity to critically re-examine the supposedly democratic nature of nineteenth-century US parties. While newspapers' pervasive displays of political allegiance elevated politics into an all-engrossing activity for the populace, such rites also helped to remove specific policy issues from the critical scrutiny of public opinion. Into this gap between party and public, corporate interests were able to enter and exercise their influence over governmental decision-making.

Transformations in the Third Party System, 1856–96

The historian Alexander Saxton once observed that "In human affairs . . . there seems to be a law of dissipation of principle according to which the daily life of any established organization tends to erode its declaring faith." Social theorists have variously glossed this as "the routinization of charisma" (Weber); "the iron law of oligarchy" (Michels); or "the priority of dead labor over living" (Marx).[4] In virtually all cases the organizational forms imposed by the strategic pursuit of goals take on a life of their own and come into conflict with the group's original purposes.

Saxton's law of ideological decay as the unintended consequence of organizational forms perfectly describes American political parties. During the Reconstruction Era (1865–76) both parties cast off their much bloodied principles for the pragmatic pursuit of elected office. Eric Foner encapsulates this change as the movement from "the ideological politics of the Civil War to professionally managed politics of the Gilded Age." Such a transition commenced early in President Grant's first administration (1868–72), but was not completed until the end of Reconstruction.[5]

As previously mentioned, several factors explain the diminution of Civil War controversies over equal rights for African-Americans. With the passage of constitutional Amendments Thirteen, Fourteen, and Fifteen, the Northern electorate believed that issues of Southern reformation had been resolved. In addition, divisive new issues confronted the managers of state parties. These policy questions threatened to fracture the coalition that formed the basis of the Republican party. To meet this political danger, Republican party managers dumped their Reconstruction policies, although they continued to rely upon traditional party rhetoric. They repeatedly denounced the Democrats as the party of the traitorous and recalcitrant South. The Democrats sarcastically labeled this Republican tactic "the waving of the bloody shirt," and replied with calls for reform against the manifest corruption of President Grant's administration.[6]

Both parties united around the issue of the tariff as the site of political battle for the years 1880 to 1896. As an issue, the tariff possessed multiple utilities. It articulated the interests of the two parties' regional bases of the industrial North versus the agricultural South. It also allowed the two parties to divide up the financial support of commercial and manufacturing capital in the North. Lastly, the economic issue of industrial protection from overseas competition quickly took on symbolic overtones. Democrats could claim that protection was part and parcel of the general Republican attack on individual freedom and on the cultural traditions of ethnic groups by an overly active state. The Republicans, in turn, argued that import tariffs protected American jobs and working-men's wages.[7]

Ideological decay also occurred through a shift in political personnel directing the parties. The elections of 1872–76 rewarded those politicians less inclined to uphold the issues of the Radical Republicans, especially when these issues might prove an electoral liability. The Republicans who first rose up with the new party in the late 1850s and avowed the radical abolitionist program, were displaced by a younger generation of politicians. These new leaders proved themselves more adept at moving the levers of party power – patronage, symbols, and behind-the-scenes organizational maneuvering.[8]

Party and democracy in critical election cycles

This transfiguration of the American political system can be characterized in terms of both normative democratic philosophy and the critical election theory of political historians. In democratic philosophy, the triumph of pragmatic parties is seen as a retreat by parties from their democratic role in political socialization and public-opinion formation. Parties as fundamental bearers of public discussion are superseded by parties as strategic vehicles for the capturing of political power. The presentation of principled, opposed positions and the stimulation of debate inside and outside the party organization is replaced by the strategic stylizing of policies to optimize voter support while internal dialogue is suppressed as potentially harmful to election chances. In this manner, party organizations migrate from the public sphere's vigorous popular debates to formal, elite, organized politics.[9]

From the viewpoint of historians of US voting, American party systems typically undergo periodic cycles of realignment at "critical elections." Parties oscillate between a politics of principle and a politics of organization according to their stage in the cycle. Realignment first begins as the dominant parties and their electoral coalitions enter into crisis. New contentious social problems – such as slavery in the 1850s and economic justice in the 1890s – force their way into the political arena. The interjection of these issues may require a popular mobilization. In any case, fresh controversies capture the attention and involvement of disaffected parts of the population, and are often accompanied by a surge in polarizing ideology. Infused by these ideologically charged questions, social interests and party politics come into close alignment, and the differences between parties appear clear and substantial. No matter which side emerges victorious in the critical election, there typically occurs a reshuffling of electoral coalitions and office holders, and consequently a change in governmental policy. Such elections, says Walter Burnham, constitute one of the few times in America that policy decisions are made by the public and enforced by parties.[10]

After the "critical election" and its realignment of voters has transpired, the new party system solidifies. The policy cleavage that divides the Republicans from the Democrats creates social alliances and establishes a distribution of power. The expression of any new issues might disrupt the existing political alliances. Therefore, new, potentially complicating issues are suppressed for the sake of the already-established organization of power. Further, the American polity with its two party, winner-takes-all election races can articulate relatively fewer issue-cleavages than European multi-party systems. The attempt to maintain the existing power base results in a rigidification of policy stances. Political leaders seek to eliminate the threat posed to their electoral base by principled conflict over interests and values. Instead, they buttress their positions of power through the distribution of non-divisive governmental benefits and symbols that are vague enough to reinforce the coalition without antagonizing any coalition members. To replace the articulation of significant policy options, and yet sustain party member loyalty, Gilded Age parties also developed immense organizations.[11]

Changes in partisan journalism in the late Reconstruction Era

The decomposition of principled politics in the late nineteenth century inevitably affected journalism. For example, the drama that unfolded in the 1872 election season at the *Free Press* (see chapter 3) was triggered precisely by the Democratic party's pragmatic "New Direction." In seeking a much desired, but elusive, electoral victory, the Party gambled on the unlikely candidacy of Horace Greeley who had lambasted the Democratic Party's policies for years.[12] Similarly, the Republican establishment's funding of the *Detroit Post* in 1866 reflected, albeit in confused form, the conflict between traditional party principles and the calculating pursuit of electoral power. Between 1872 and 1896, partisan newspapers, like parties, became less the proponents of particular views and policies and more the supporters of the party as a power-aggrandizing organization.

At times, papers explicitly justified their commitment to party victory, their strategic orientation. The *Post*, for instance, in its 1872 prospectus claimed to be convinced of the rightness of the Republican party's principles and, furthermore, that the party contained the majority of the country's moral people. The Republican party retained "the vitality which initiates all the practical reforms of its age." Therefore, the newspaper believed it was necessary that Republicans win power and implement their policies. "With these convictions . . . the POST proposes to utter no uncertain sound during the [election] canvass just now opening." The Republican organ would do its utmost for party victory. For its part, the Democratic *Free Press* vowed, "uncompromising advocacy" and to "aid the cause to the extent of its ability."[13] In this journalistic bellicosity, the strategic requirements for party victory quickly triumphed over the public sphere's traditional ideals of free, open, and critical discussion. Partisan sheets promised to support the party without quibbling or wavering; without significant debate over the merits of party policies; and without exception in endorsing the party's diverse nominees.

In general, journalists and intellectuals bemoaned the loss of principled debate from the columns of the American press. In 1883 Chicago publisher Melville Stone took the occasion of an address to the Michigan association of publishers to quote the *North American Review*'s summary derogation of current press politics.

Journalism has become, very generally, the voice and the echo of a party . . . There is no longer a patient, lucid discussion of underlying principles, as in the days of the old Federalist. Party organizations have come to find their focal points no longer in principle and measures, but in men and spoils. Patriotism seems to have utterly gone out of politics, and left ravenous lust for office, plunder, and power as the sole centripetal organizing forces. Journalism cannot rise higher than [this] foundation spring of sustenance . . . [etc.][14]

The pragmatic turn in Gilded Age politics entailed two major consequences for journalism; even as papers remained partisan, the extent and very nature of their political commitment evolved. First, while editorials remained solidly partisan, the amount of partisan news dwindled, at least in non-election periods. This pacification of Civil War passions was already apparent by 1871. During the off-election year of 1867 18 percent of the daily news was partisan, but by 1871 and then thereafter, papers filled 7 percent or less of their columns with politically biased news. Only during election campaigns would newspapers return to their former full-blooded political advocacy.

The drop off in partisanship between elections and non-election periods suggests that the reading public had become relevant only as the voting electorate, and not as a participant in political opinion formation. The party focused on mobilizing voters to the polls, not on year-round indoctrination in the party positions. A journal's formal partisan affiliation could, it seems, entail a flexible amount of political advocacy. Such partisanship varied over time depending upon pressures from the press's political and economic environment.[15] As the century wore on, and as no new political actors effectively seized the public's attention, newspapers increasingly juggled stories of a political character with those that were social or "human interest." They complemented their partisan news and views with stories of no clear political import. Of course, no society is ever so polarized and politicized that the news consist only in reports of political contention and conflict. Nor is any society so much governed by habit and consensus that the press merely expresses and reinforces society's taken-for-granted norms in tales of crime, scandal, and deviance. But, in the 1880s and 1890s, as the policy divisions between the Democrats and Republicans seemed to lose their urgency and saliency (and as newspapers expanded), political news diminished.[16]

Furthermore, beyond the straightforward decline in partisan content, the very style of the press's political advocacy shifted. Partisan reporting stressed more the "horse race" aspects of election races than substantive issues. In contrast to twentieth-century election news, this fixation on winning and losing was not a matter of cynical detachment from the rhetorical assertions of politicians. Rather it was the occasion for cheering on the favored party. Late-nineteenth-century partisan journalism incessantly celebrated the party's political triumphs and insistently promoted its policies. Papers were not neutral media promoting private reflection and sober debate; they were rabid partisans which boldly paraded their biases, their allegiances, and their political faith. Let us examine this late-nineteenth-century journalism – with its flamboyant political style and its alternative public philosophy – in more detail.

Demonstrative partisanship

The partisanship of the papers was an emotional, public display of support, allegiance, and commitment. The *Post* swore in 1884, "Lukewarm or non-committal it will never be" in supporting the Grand Old Party.[17] Newspapers as vehicles of communication and persuasion for a party could, of course, attempt to hide their biases, their partisanship, their political preferences. In essence they could replace an overt display of preference with a covert, hidden one. In fact, journals often selected for coverage news events, speeches, and quotes that favored their party, all the while presenting their selections as neutral, technical choices. Indeed, since the early years of the century a rhetoric of naturalistic observation and non-partisanship was available to journalists to camouflage their partisanship.[18] This tactic of covert partisanship, remarked William Stocking, editor of the *Detroit Post and Tribune*, was continued well into the twentieth century (as a manipulative tactic of newspaper managers).[19] Indeed, these covert journalistic evaluations still occur today, albeit in a less conscious and less conspicuous manner. Still, in scrutinizing nineteenth-century journals, it would be a difficult enterprise to sort and separate the instances of covert bias from the newspaper's more explicit, active support for the party. At a certain point the ruses of covert partisanship – the immensely unequal distribution of news space between parties and the vastly disproportionate number of quoted remarks in favor of one's party – become obvious. They turn into one more deliberate exhibition of partisan fealty.

The partisan press complemented its surreptitious forms of political advocacy with much more evident, overt displays of preference. In its headlines, its illustrations, and its stories, the press explicitly and hence formally sided with one party. Newspapers typically printed:

- Explicit evaluations for or against a party in both the news and headlines;
- Candidate endorsements that were published continually from the party's nominating convention up until the election;
- Notices of party meetings and calls for rallies, effectively turning the paper into a party bulletin board;[20]
- Woodcuts celebrating the performance of the party in the latest elections, and front-page editorial cartoons;[21]
- Quips and jibes jeering the other party's policies and personnel;
- Grossly unequal amounts of news coverage devoted to the activities and speeches of the two parties' notables;
- Diverse articles predicting imminent electoral success and accounts of election rallies exaggerating the numbers in attendance, the quality of the speeches, and the enthusiasm of the audience;
- And, of course, an editorial page devoted to defending the party's principles and policies.

Such diverse narrative devices exposed the press's political commitments. The open advocacy of Gilded Age journalism implied that no independent, neutral standpoint could exist outside of the contentions and conflicts of politics. Instead, a periodical was necessarily the proud, public spokesperson for "the Democracy" or the "Grand Old Party." For newspapers, the public realm was exhausted in the disseminations and dissimulations of the two parties.

Michael McGerr classifies this press politics as a central component of last century's "political style."[22] In the Gilded Age, newspapers participated in a pervasive partisan culture where the citizen enthusiastically and publicly displayed his political ties and commitments.[23] McGerr effectively analyzes these political performances as public rituals. Such rites, according to his Durkheimian cultural analysis, have the role of expressing society's core values and instituting society's central classificatory schema.[24] The continual, collective dramatic portrayal of partisan commitments consolidated popular political identities. It also transformed political parties into concrete, meaningful entities for the Americans. In campaign rites as well as in press narratives, parties were conjured into all-encompassing, living, breathing animate political beings. In this public theater, the whole of the political world was translated into simplified us-against-them narratives. Such political stories permitted easy comprehension and strong emotional identification.

According to such historians as McGerr and Jensen, this public demonstration of partisanship bound citizens to parties and oriented voters in their electoral choices. For McGerr, the political identities thus enacted effectively motivated nineteenth-century voters to year after year of high electoral participation.[25] In contrast to today's low election turnout, public apathy, and fluctuating political loyalties, nineteenth-century parties and their papers forcibly galvanized political participation. Elections became less a matter of instrumentally choosing between different policy options and more a matter of publicly expressing identity and affirming solidarity.[26]

The stress on public participation and political identity drew on nineteenth-century cultural codes of republicanism which emphasized political citizenship as central to the individual, White male's identity. Party rallies were one more occasion for the staging of public dramas of citizenship, with Fourth of July parades another. In these rituals the participants affirmed their status as equal, participating members in the political community.[27] Both themes – the public dramaturgy of partisanship and affirmations of political citizenship – are evident in the following news story. (In this instance, the *Free Press*, in the fashion typical to Detroit's dailies, relied on a temporary correspondent, a stringer, to write up the local party rallies and to add partisan flavor.[28]) I quote at length this early account of an upstate Democratic rally not only to demonstrate the ritualistic reporting of a political rite, but also because it invokes several other important cultural motifs: the exaggerated accounts of party performance to stimulate party morale; the rhetorical preponderance of military metaphors; the celebration of popular sovereignty; and, finally, melodramatic depictions of a Manichean struggle between good and evil.

FROM GRAND RAPIDS
Enthusiastic Outpouring of the Democracy
A MAGNIFICENT TORCHLIGHT PROCESSION
Stirring addresses by Hon. John Moore, S. C. Coffinberry, Wm. P. Wells and Others . . .

From Our Own Correspondent
From this beautiful and interesting "Valley City" of Western Michigan, I have good news to send you. There has been to-day the largest outpouring of people, and the most enthusiastic political gathering ever seen . . . [This is conceded on all hands.] It is proudly proclaimed by the friends of the people – the supporters of Seymour and Blair, and the point is fairly yielded by the dyspeptic [Republican] Radical print of this afternoon, notwithstanding the manifest mortification and chagrin shown publicly by its editors and proprietors on the streets as the long procession passed by.

Not less than ten thousand men at the lowest calculation have been in attendance here to-day, to unite in the renewal of their fealty to the cause of truth and justice – to declare again their faith in the principles of Democracy, and to add their voice to an appeal to the people to rescue the country from the straits insane Radicalism, ambitious to perpetuate its power, has plunged it . . .

[The rally parade started,] moving like an army with banners across Canal Street, through the long covered bridge spanning the noble Grand River, threading the streets, on the "west side," returning to the city proper and passing in a triumphal procession through the town.

The grand procession was headed by a squadron of Rangers about one hundred strong, following which was drawn the Valley City band wagon by six splendid horses upon each of which rode a lad neatly attired in red, white and blue . . . Next came a large open wagon bearing above a score and a half of young ladies – one for each State in the Union – with "the Union forever" as their motto . . . Forty-one workmen from Berkey Bros' chair factory and cabinet shop, wearing uniforms, caps and capes were borne in a wagon drawn by six horses. Upon one side was the following: "The workingmen of Berkey's shop support the people's candidates, Seymour and Blair," and on the other

"We workingmen – without persuasion or force – will vote for our Mason [Candidate Seymour] as a matter of course."

Following this was a team drawing a number of craftsmen of Wood's wagon shop, with the tools of their trade . . . [etc.] A hundred and sixty wagons or more followed in the procession, many of them from the surrounding towns, and bearing mottoes of various devices, but all blazing with patriotism and alive with enthusiasm . . . [etc.]

Many private residences and places of business were adorned with flags and tri-colors during the day, and hundreds waved on the procession from doors and windows on the crowded corners of the streets.

. . . At half-past two o'clock the ranche was filled to listen to addresses by the standard-bearers of the Democracy and other eminent speakers, but upon being called to order it was found that not one-half of those desiring to hear could gain admittance. Col. A. T. McReynolds called the assemblage to order and introduced the Hon. William P. Wells of your city, who proceeded to speak for two hours in masterly argumentative address, mainly upon the Radical reconstruction measures, which was listened to with marked attention. A full report of the address will be printed hereafter.

The jam at the doors was so great . . . that Hon. S. C. Coffinberry, our candidate for Lieutenant Governor, proceeded to Road's House, where he entertained for an hour and a half an audience packed to the last inch of standing room . . . the assemblage at the hall adjourned to make preparations for the evening's programme . . .

The exercises of the evening comprised a splendid torchlight procession of two miles in length, with banners, transparencies and bands of music, fireworks and illuminations and a blaze of glory generally, followed by speaking at the ranche till past eleven o'clock at night by Messrs. McReynolds, Moore, Wells and Church.

In the closing of one of the speeches it was said: Be discouraged by no defeat; not even if the news to-night [from early October elections] should not bring the hope which we desire; still the Democratic party is mighty and will prevail. Our principles are as eternal as the hills. Renew the vows under the constitution and the Union. Determine that you will stand by it . . . Do this, fellow citizens, and the blessings of your children after you shall rise up and shall rest upon your memorial from generation to generation and from age to age (Long continued applause.) . . .

Vox Populi

McGerr praises the nineteenth-century rituals which made public identities salient for the American citizenry. In the tradition of Durkheim and Geertz, he takes the ritual as a consensual expression of the community's views. Valuing the ability of late-nineteenth-century parties to mobilize voters, however, he fails to recognize how power influences the construction of partisan-group identities. Furthermore, he universalizes the Gilded Age's ritual production of political identity as the only means to involve the citizenry in the ongoing issues of government.[29]

In contrast, as Pierre Bourdieu observes, political rituals have an instrumental function hidden behind their expressive role. They not only produce group identities and express supposedly shared belief systems, they also create unequal political capacities to name and represent social reality. From this view, McGerr's political rituals can be best understood as procedures for the delegation of political power.[30] Indeed, if we examine historian Jean Baker's short list of nineteenth-century electoral rites, we see that the unifying feature of these political rituals is the delegation or transfer of legitimate power away from citizens into the hands of political officials. "American presidential elections were such rituals . . . [T]hey were composed of a series of episodes – party [nominating] conventions, ratification meetings, seren-ades [of the candidate] and mass rallies, culminating in the ultimate expression of public life, voting."[31]

Such rites specifically invoke the power of popular sovereignty. But their genuflection before the people's will is only a step in a process that ends with the conferral of political power upon society's anointed representatives. These celebrations of the workings of democracy occur precisely at the moment when the citizen's capacity for public speech and action is entrusted to the party or the representative. Political rites, which mark the beginning and end of popular involvement in politics, make parties (and in turn party officials and partisan papers) the sole legitimate representative of group members' interests.

Gilded Age political parties, in this context, became "political fetishes."[32] Having been delegated the right to speak for their members, they were taken as substantive entities worthy of popular loyalty and public devotion. Indeed parties and their allied papers were a continu-ally manufactured "fictitious social entity" (Bourdieu) that monopolized the nineteenth-century public sphere to the exclusion of other political organizations and identities. Given the automatic identification of party members with their party, the question of whose interests the Democrats and Republicans actually represented was never raised.

This political fetishism is clear in a speech given to the Michigan Publishers Association. In 1884, Editor A. J. Aldrich addressed the "Relation of the Newspaper to Politics":

The love of party is probably stronger than admiration for any journal . . . As a rule . . . aggregated wisdom is nearer correct than the opinion of "the remnant" or at least the best policy for party action; and the newspaper must be identified with some existing party. No journalist can secede and set up for himself. A paper without a party is a rudderless ship; and I have always seen that about election time the so-called independent paper manages to swing far around enough to support the opposition candidates . . .

. . . [The journalist] should be independent, not so much of his party which is quite apt to follow right convictions, but he should be ready and prompt to censure the follies of party leaders and criticize intelligently the errors which they occasionally attempt to incorporate into the party creed. As a member of the party whose principles he must advocate and whose candidates he must support he has a legitimate right to do this [criticism], and the rank and file of the party will generally endorse his course especially if he keeps close enough to the people to feel the beatings of their great heart.[33]

Aldrich wished to defend some measure of journalistic autonomy. But, by taking as natural the dominance of parties in the public arena, he was forced to accept the press's subordination to party. Editor Aldrich papered over the contradiction between journalism's historical ideals of independent, critical reporting and commentary, and the pressures on journals to support without question their party and its policies.

Bourdieu's theory of political representation highlights the inequalities in defining social reality – disparities that result from the procedures of political delegation. Rites of delegation detach political representation from processes of public-opinion formation. The party representative, as authorized spokesperson for the group, is not subject to the group members' control on any specific policy issues. She or he is not obliged to justify particular decisions to the public. However, once freed from popular scrutiny, the representative becomes vulnerable to other forms of power. This diffuse loyalty of the party members allows other social powers – organized economic interests – to exercise their influence over particular political decisions. As I discuss later, delegation supports the privileged representation of select social interests.[34]

Battle cries

Parties and allied papers consciously tried to reinforce their dominance over legitimate political discussion. Indeed, many of the traits of the partisan press can be comprehended as part of a general aggrandizing strategy to claim for parties all rights of public speaking and to police all potential dissident voices. To accomplish this goal, newspapers emphasized the strategic dimensions of politics, not the communicative. Politics was conceived as a war, not a reasoned dialogue. Such imagery, then as now, splits the political field into two mobilized groups who must defeat their opponents at all costs. The overriding imperative of winning requires the suppression of internal dissent and the denigration of third parties as only aiding the victory of the foe.[35]

This emphasis on the strategic aspects of politics explains, in part, the profligate use of metaphors of war to describe the "election battlefield." Jean Baker and Richard Jensen both note the continual recourse to military terms in the political rhetoric of the era. For Jensen, the main electioneering style of the nineteenth century was "based on the explicit metaphor that the two parties constituted organized armies that fought it out on election day."[36] Military imagery permeated both campaign events and their literary renderings in the pages of the press. For example, in the above-quoted account of a Grand Rapids rally, the grand procession "was headed by a squadron of Rangers" and when the parade began, it moved "like an army with banners . . . threading the streets." In newspaper prose, the opposed party became "the enemy camp." Rallies were conceived as shows of force, while elections held in the months prior to the big national elections constituted "preliminary skirmishes" where "small detachments" were deployed to test "the enemy" for "weak points." Dissent and conflict within the party "demoralized and scattered" the party's supporters, or opened a "breach in the Democratic party wide enough for its complete disruption." Dissident papers and politicians "stirred up discord in the Democratic ranks" and were "giving aid and ammunition to the enemy." Columns of print, thus, were akin to columns of soldiers as papers traded accusations of betrayal and sabotage. The *Saginaw Courier*, for instance, denounced the *Free Press* as a traitor that was "endeavoring to create in the interests of the common enemy a 'fire in the rear.'"[37]

Newspapers employed this strategic notion of politics to assert the two parties' natural monopoly over popular representation, and to deride all new-born, alternative parties. Invoking the zero-sum logic of the political field, journals argued that a vote for a third party could only contribute to the victory of one's despised political opponent, whether the Democrats or the Republicans. Thus, the Liberal Republican Party, the Greenbackers, the Prohibition Party, and the Populists were each, in their turn, denounced.[38] In 1872, the Republican *Post* denied that there was any difference in principle or practice between the Liberal Republicans and the "party of secession," i.e. the Democrats:

By the action of the Baltimore Convention, yesterday, HORACE GREELEY was baptised and rechristened into the Democratic fold . . . He now stands before the Republic no longer as a "Liberal Republican" candidate or an independent candidate but as the Democratic party candidate . . .
    We thus have the old battle between the two old parties once again . . . On the GREELEY side are all the bad old elements, the Ku Klux, the secessionists, the rebel chiefs . . . the ignorant and vicious and criminal classes . . . [39]

And twenty years later the *Journal* assailed the Populists:

A Cemetery Party
Freedom and slavery, protection and free trade, honest and dishonest elections are principles. On them the people of this country are divided into two great parties.

The only effect the third party [i.e. Populist] can produce in this election will
be to elect [Democratic candidate] Cleveland . . .[40]

Voice of the party

The two parties, Detroit's journals argued, were the only relevant public
speakers, the only true representatives of democracy's will. In turn,
newspapers aspired to be the substantive embodiment of the party, the
authorized voice of the people. In this context, the press's public
preeminence did not derive from its role as external observer of the
American political drama. The press did not just provide an authoritative account of the day's most important words and deeds. Rather, a
share of a paper's prestige and power derived from its ability to present
its own words as the party's official decrees. In some sense, the press's
pronouncements defined social reality. The merging of newspaper with
party organization and party members is implicit in the *Free Press*'s
prospectus of 1868:

We urge the people of Michigan to continue to act and judge for themselves.
Subscribe for your county papers. Sustain and maintain them first. They look
out for your local interests, and they give a warm support to our national
principles. If you can afford more than one regular paper, take the Democratic
organ of your State. The Free Press alone in this State is able to combine a
Democratic point of view of our state politics and local issues with those of
national importance . . . While [other states' papers'] Democracy may be
unquestionable, and as such most valuable, they are not as valuable or important
as are our own newspapers, which discuss our State affairs and throw light on
our own interests. Those who can should subscribe for them, after they have
subscribed to the local and State organs. In this way alone can the immediate
interests of the people of this State be best understood . . . [41]

This aspect of speaking for the party is most evident in the exchanges
between newspapers, which took the form of diatribes rather than
dialogues.[42] The party organs, by taking each other as the appropriate
interlocutor, implied that the two parties exhausted the relevant spectrum of political viewpoints. At the same time, they confirmed the
debating papers in their role as legitimate surrogate for the parties. For
example, in its editorial response to Republican journals' attacks, the *Free
Press* assumed the mantle of official party defender: "There is not only no
possibility that the Democratic party will sanction or permit the revival of
a 'wild-cat' currency. . ."[43] The *Free Press* elided the difference between
paper and party by making authoritative pronouncements on the party's
future actions and policies. Earlier, in 1871, the Democratic journal had
condemned similarly preemptive speech by a Republican paper.

[Among its pronouncements, the *Tribune*] . . . editorially proclaims in its most dictatorial and offensive manner that the "Tribune has had occasion heretofore to allude to and condemn these and similar transactions [of the leaders of the Michigan party]. It is high time there was an end to them . . . The Republicans of this State will no longer put up with such outrageous tyranny and injustice from men who forget they are servants and arrogate to themselves the prerogatives of masters . . ."[44]

As organ of the group, as their advocate and public defender, the newspaper had to represent them in public, to speak for them. Nevertheless, the definition of the group and the determination of its goals and who should engage in "the right naming," in the *Free Press*'s felicitous phrase, were necessarily conflictual activities.[45] In its imperialist aspirations to be the sole definer of party philosophy and policies, the newspaper of course had numerous rivals and critics. "[T]he Free Press claims to speak for the Democratic Party. Pshaw! The Democracy of Michigan pays no attention to, and cares nothing for her utterances . . . The leading Democratic paper is evidently not the Free Press."[46] Dissension was inescapable in a public sphere riven by bickering party factions, competing party papers, and conflicting social interests.

Various nineteenth-century categories – such as "influence" and "preeminence" – judged a paper's capacity to speak for the group, to have its word accepted as a convincing representation. For example, in an 1884 interview, the new manager of the *Post and Tribune* professed: "I am a republican and shall try to make the Post an influential party organ."[47] And, in 1876 the *News* commented:

What a good thing it was for the [Republican *New York*] Times, as a newspaper and as a property, that the [*New York*] Tribune helped the Democrats four years ago . . . When [the *Tribune*] left the Republican party [the *Times*] quickly and quietly stepped into its place and has held its position ever since, increasing in influence and in money value daily at the expense of its neighbor across the way.[48]

Other factors bolstered the press's prominence in the public arena: a journal, if not the indisputable voice of the unified party, was at least the semi-official organ of a faction or leading politician. Its pronouncements were thus important, even newsworthy. Furthermore, in an era when polls were non-existent, newspapers themselves were taken as a major gauge of public opinion. Therefore, Detroit's papers regularly (albeit selectively) quoted other Michigan sheets.[49]

Spirit of Michigan Press

For Lieutenant Governor, the Honorable H. H. Holt of Muskegon, is prominently mentioned and he seems to have the support of the Republican journals of the State . . .[50]

And, the *Detroit News* in its first three years of publication 1873–75 printed abstracts of the other Detroit newspapers' editorials.[51] The *Free Press*, for its part, surveyed the response of the important New York dailies to the nominations of a national ticket by the Republican party:

NEW YORK

The City Press on the Radical Nominees . . .

Of the nominations made yesterday the *Herald* says Grant is stronger than the party and Colfax is the most popular man of the party, and the Republican ticket is a strong one.

The *Times* says: The people have faith in Grant, and the selection of Colfax is eminently judicious.

The *World* says the ticket would have been a strong one five months ago. It is completely Western and wholly Radical. Grant is without popular qualities, but a successful military career heals a multitude of defects. Colfax is, perhaps, the most popular man in his party, but on the whole the ticket is not a strong one . . .[52]

Rallying the party faithful

The relatively fixed political affiliation of voters explains numerous traits of the partisan press. It accounts for a journalism that often "preached to the converted." Instead of persuasive arguments, the press engaged in ridicule and verbal jousting which could be appreciated only by established partisans. Newspapers, for example, regularly followed their more extensive editorials with short jokes and witticisms aimed at the opposed party's supposed foibles.[53] These sarcastic jibes took for granted that the readers were united with the paper and party in desiring a good laugh at the enemy's expense. In its abbreviated and cryptic form, the jibe assumed that the reader knew who was friend and foe and what was the nature of the conflict. The *Free Press* in 1891 illustrates this practice:

NOTES AND COMMENTARY

It is not so easy to see high tariff blessings through glass upon which the price has been raised–[Louisville Courier-Journal.]

Senator Hoar still believes that he has the country at his back. That is true but it's going the other way–[Springfield Republican.]

A child without a mouth was recently born in Mississippi. Nature evidently designed him for a model politician of the Quay type.–[Buffalo Express (Rep.)] . . .

The Philadelphia Press charges Senator Don Cameron of the heinous offense of smoking fragrant Havanas in the Democratic cloak room of the Senate with ex-confederate Brig. Gen. Butler of South Carolina. What would the Press have them smoke? Connecticut short sixes or clay pipes?–[Boston Herald.] . . .[54]

Already in 1876 the *Evening News* contended there was an excess of these mindless witticisms at the expense of substantive arguments:

Such weak, thin childish campaigning as the Free Press carries on must be a source of contempt and ridicule down at the national headquarters. It has hardly a dozen columns of serious, candid, truthful statement or argument during all this campaign – nothing but flippant, shallow puerilities all through. No one Democrat or Republican, who has habitually read the Free Press can fail to have been struck by this fact. The Post on the other side is no more candid and truthful, but certainly displays more force. To think our centennial campaign should sink so low![55]

To find comparable political phenomena in our own era it is necessary to leave the US for other countries where parties still dominate the public sphere, for example, Italy. There the populace retains a strong affiliation with the dozen or so parties. The citizenry does not relate to parties instrumentally – as offering a series of policy alternatives for critical scrutiny. Instead, the electorate cast "their vote as a statement of subjective identification with a political force they believe to be integrally . . . identified with their own social group. This affiliation is expressed not only during elections; it continually characterizes relationships between most Italian citizens and the parties, and consequently deter-mines the symbolical context within which political communication is developed."[56]

Media scholar Paolo Mancini explains the consequences for jour-nalism. Given enduring popular attachments to parties, political com-munication dispenses with educating or persuading the electorate. Rather, it is aimed at other elite political actors for the purpose of negotiating policies and alliances. The mass audience, for its part, is a passive spectator that only looks for messages confirming its political beliefs. Furthermore, this public is familiar with the technical language of politics; citizens watch the news and elite political communications with the hope that their favorite will win a clear victory over rivals. The partisan audience roots for the success of their faction.[57] A century earlier the *Detroit Union* condemned just this type of partisan public:

The vast majority of men only attend one class of political and religious meetings, read the papers of only one side, slur over the hard arguments, seek to be amused, and at any rate determine if possible to remain in a contented state. Faith is a good thing – but blind faith which has avoided honest controversy, has produced all the persecutions and all the wars of history . . .[58]

As elucidated by Jensen, fixed popular affiliations profoundly affected the practices of American parties and, in turn, news reporting. The task for parties and their allied papers in an era of tight electoral competition became mobilizing their electoral troops and getting them *en masse* to

Table 3.1. *Average space devoted to morale-building news and editorials (in columns)*[59]

1868	1.90
1872	1.63
1876	1.70
1880	6.40
1884	9.07
1888	1.74
1892	2.21
1896	17.08
1900	1.34
1904	2.12
1908	2.02

the polls. Political actors generated publicity for a number of reasons, but convincing voters through substantive debate was not one. Their goal, says Jensen, was not to persuade an independent electorate but to energize already-convinced party members. The public spectacles of partisanship, which were staged in election rallies and magnified in newspaper accounts, were aimed at mobilizing the party faithful and intimidating opponents. Campaigns comprised a series of morale-raising events that built to a crescendo election day.[60]

Between 1865 and 1908 Detroit's partisan journals during campaign seasons devoted about two columns of news and editorials each day to morale-building articles. An article can be classified as morale-building if it suggests that the favored party's chances of winning are good or improving and, more specifically, that the party is united, strong, and expanding, while the opposed party is in disarray. The *Detroit Tribune* of October 15, 1888 illustrates the variety of morale-building narratives typical to the partisan paper. Within its four pages one finds: a news report deriding a Democrat rally; three commentaries and analyses predicting a likely Republican election victory; a story of a Detroit Democratic family converting *en masse* to the Republicans; an editorial jibe over factions in the Democratic Party and two accounts of conflicts internal to the Democrats; and, lastly, news of local election bets where no Democrats were willing to place money on the Democrats' chances of winning.

The press certainly recognized its role in mobilizing voters. The *Tribune* lectured its readers in preparation for the forthcoming electoral campaign:

But before the convention assembles the Republicans of the state should begin to reorganize for the spring campaign. They suffered defeat last fall because too many Republican voters remained at home on election day . . . The Republicans

of Michigan can elect their ticket in April if they will go to work as they should
and get out a full vote on election day . . .[61]

This practice of rallying the troops through exaggerated news reports
was well known. The *Tribune* exposed its logic in their publication of an
internal communiqué of the Democrats.

DEMOCRATIC BLUSTER

The Democratic leaders have evidently issued orders to their agents all over the
country to indulge largely in brag and bluster during the closing days of the
campaign. It can not hurt them, unless they are foolish enough to back up their
assertions with bets, and it may help to capture some timid and doubtful voters
whose chief anxiety is to be on the winning side. Accordingly we find Democrats
all over the State claiming the election of Tilden with a great pretense of
confidence. How this "Dutch courage" has been manufactured is amusingly
illustrated by the following circular from the Democratic State Central
Committee of Ohio . . .

Editor Democrat, Bowling Green, O.:

Dear Sir – National success is assured. There is no event in the future more
probable than the election of Tilden and Hendricks. The feeling in the state is
intensifying, and if our friends will do their duty we will wheel Ohio into line.
We are claiming the state for November. In your paper, from this to the seventh
[of November], *claim the national contest and this state also.* BE EARNEST IN
THIS MATTER. DO IT EXULTINGLY AND WITH THE UTMOST
CONFIDENCE. Do not be lukewarm in this, but fervent. The Republicans are
greatly alarmed. They feel that the fight is gone. They are drooping. Keep them
there. Press the advantage which the situation assures. There is much to be
gained from this course. Demand the polling of every vote, that our victory may
be overwhelming and last through the years. Claim the state with confidence
. . . Hold meetings, everywhere in your county. Exult at your meetings and press
each one to go forward with assurance of victory.

> Very truly yours,
> John G. Thompson, Chairman[62]

The *Evening News*, for its part, denounced such standard partisan
tactics:

The party papers instruct their correspondents to whoop it up for the party
candidates, and the consequence is that these young gentlemen are compelled
to make predictions during the campaign which are recalled only with shame
when the [election] returns are in . . . [The *News*] sympathizes with the
conductors of party organs who are compelled to do so much lying for their
parties, because they are in many cases gentlemen who would not do it for
themselves . . .

The practice of the organs claiming a sweeping victory every time in advance
for the whole ticket may possibly have its influence sometimes upon the weak
and vacillating who wish to go with the crowd and be on the winning side . . .[63]

Newspaper articles that specifically focused on campaign events – on magnifying the spectacle of party rallies – were still common, if less extended, at the century's end and continued into the early twentieth century. Generally, each election issue devoted a minimum of a half a column of print to the reporting of (from two to thirteen) rallies around the state. If the party gathering occurred in Detroit, the space devoted to the rally swelled to one to three pages of minutely printed text.[64] The *Free Press* regularly published its rally stories in columns entitled "The Campaign," for example:

YARPLE AT DOWAGAIC
The Opera House Packed and Hundreds Unable to Reach the Doors.

Dowagaic, October 14.–(Special.)–The meeting addressed by Hon. George L. Yarple at the opera house to-night was a grand success. Mr. Yarple always draws a full house here, but was never greeted by a finer audience than he was to-night, the large opera house being packed to its fullest capacity while hundreds were unable to get inside the building. A special train brought a large delegation from Niles and the street parade of hundreds of torches and several brass bands made an imposing appearance.

Mr. Yarple's address . . . On the tariff question the speaker was particularly forcible and eloquent. He showed how, under the present system of tariff taxation, the farmer is compelled to buy in a protected and sell in a free market . . . etc., etc. He held the close attention of the audience till 11 o'clock, and many were loath to leave the hall at that late hour, so great was the desire to listen to his eloquent words.[65]

This article was chased by:

Hon. Free Estee at Gallen

Gallen, October 14.–A large and enthusiastic Democratic rally was held here last evening at the town hall. The Hon. Free Estee, of Mount Pleasant, was the orator and he held the crowd spellbound with his eloquence and facts. He is the right man in the right place and succeeded in setting a good many of the old hard-headed Republicans in and around Gallen to thinking that the wool maybe is being drawn from their eyes . . . .[66]

In the world of the partisan press, it was difficult to determine the truth. Each side exaggerated the size and grandeur of its own rallies, denigrated the parades and speeches of its opponents, and attacked the veracity of the rival newspapers. The exaggerations led the *News* to chastise the partisan rags: "Most of the partisan newspapers in these odd days before the election are fine specimens of printed frenzy. Alcoholic products are not the only means by which intoxication is produced. A general election every two years in Michigan would necessitate the erection of a few more lunatic asylums in the state."[67] In 1876, the *Free Press*, for example, traded charges of misrepresentation with the *Post*: "If the Post lies about the procession last night as it lied concerning the Reform [i.e. Democrat] parade of Wednesday night the public will have one more confirmation of the fact that the Detroit Post is one of the most offensively abject and servile partisan organs that ever disgraced journalism."[68] While in 1892, the *Tribune* felt compelled to rebut one Democratic report: "James Slocum of Holly, the hustling editor of the Oakland City Advertiser and a staunch Republican, was in the city yesterday. Mr. Slocum states that the account in the Free Press of the Republican meeting in Holly the other evening was a tissue of lies and the meeting was an enthusiastic and large one."[69]

Even ostensibly neutral news agencies like the Associated Press were irresistibly drawn into the vertiginous world of politicized accounting. In the elections of 1876 and 1884, both Democratic and Republican journals accused the Associated Press of providing unequal coverage of their campaign events.[70] The wire service could not stand aloof from the polarized divisions defining the polity.

How did readers react to the epistemological uncertainty of multiple, conflicting, and distorted news reports? The *Union* suggested that party members blindly followed the claims of their favored journals. But, the English observer, Lord James Bryce, asserted that readers responded with cynicism to the partisan publicity: "In America . . . a leading article carries less weight of itself, being discounted by the shrewd reader as the sort of thing which the paper must of course be expected to say."[71] "[The] average public is shrewder, more independent, less readily impressed by the mysterious 'we.'"[72]

Political melodrama

Jensen asserts that spectacles of partisanship had a strategic task.[73] They increased the enthusiasm of the party members and thus propelled them to the polls. The *News* (above) disputed the strategic values of these mass party rallies and the subsequent newspaper reports. In contrast, the Scripps paper suggested that such partisan tales in their fantastic form convinced no one. It is my contention that both Jensen and the editorial staff of the *News* misinterpret the cultural logic involved in such campaign-reporting and rallies. The news was not meant to be a straightforward representation of the facts that would therefore convince readers of the likely outcome of the ensuing election. Rather, the news invoked the subterranean logic of the melodramatic plot to endow such seemingly mundane political trivia with portentous meaning.

While the *News* bristled at the exaggerated claims of parties en-tangled in political conflict, such rhetoric may have suited an electorate habituated to the narrative conventions of melodrama. As Peter Brooks writes, the conventions of melodrama were particularly relevant for the nineteenth century and, we may add, for the battles of American political parties. Emerging from the Civil War with their violently opposed views of right and wrong, Democrat and Republican parties were rival claimants to be restorers of a morality that was no longer self-evident in the nineteenth-century world. One would have to be convinced of the fundamental import of the victory of one party over the other to see the working of this melodramatic theater.

Melodrama was one more instance (along with minstrelsy) of political leaders using the repertoire of popular culture to effectively convey their message to the electorate. As Lawrence Levine states, melodrama was strikingly present in nineteenth-century popular culture and a mainstay of American theater. But, beyond its evident utility as a shared medium for communication, melodrama had several generic features that made it particularly advantageous for party leaders. Indeed, melodrama helped imbue the battles of the two parties with a readily comprehensible and transcendent significance.[74] Melodrama took as its ground the nineteenth century's loss of any evident transcendent moral code; morality has retreated from public life, but still dwells hidden beneath the surface of the mundane world. In melodrama, the interaction of the central characters actually turns out to be the metaphorical depiction of the ceaseless conflict between good and evil. The play commences with the hero/heroine's goodness unrecognized by society, indeed denied. Absolute villainy triumphs temporarily and heartlessly torments the guileless virtuous hero. But, gradually, in moments of revelation and astonishment, the true natures of the protagonists are exposed. The conflict is resolved by society's acknowledgment of real virtue and the expulsion of evil from the social body. In its equation of the public's recognition of virtue and villainy with the resolution of the story, melodrama was a democratic art.[75]

Parties, eager to attribute exclusive significance to their continued battles, appropriated the codes of melodrama. Melodrama's simplified binary logic, with its exclusion of any middle ground between polarized protagonists, replicated the desired dualism of the political field. In the Manicheanism of melodrama, the two protagonists were embroiled in an absolute ethical struggle. Even if the differences between the two parties were minimal, melodrama could help to depict the Democrats and Republicans as polar opposites entangled in a dramatic conflict of the utmost importance. The victory of one party over the other would determine whether good or evil ruled the world. No wonder charges of treason and treachery were attached to those who turned from their traditional party. Such plots suggested a dramatic coherence to election rites. During the campaign the populace might be confused by the lies and duplicity of the evil party. But the contest would be inevitably resolved by the vote – a final moment in which one party was revealed to be virtue triumphant, while the loser was driven from power.[76]

In all these theatrical devices, political melodrama reflects what Jean Baker has described as the nineteenth century's endowing the political sphere with a transcendental religious significance. This religious–melodramatic logic was evident in the various journalistic narratives of "conversions." The very term "conversion" suggests a personal transformation to a new church or religious doctrine. As the *Post* exclaimed, "Let every Republican go to work on his own hook, converting as many of his neighbors as possible to the true political faith." Conversion relates to the typical melodramatic device of moments of dramatic astonishment, of public revelation of the hidden virtue or immorality of the characters. Tales of recognition of the party's virtue and hence conversion were typical in the partisan press.[77] For example:

[The Democratic official] Mr. Magone remarked, "In this campaign the democratic party will poll its full vote. I do not know the name of any democrat, of any influence whatever who is not supporting Tilden heartily, while at the same time there is not a report from a single town or county which does not contain a good list of converts from the enemy."[78]

The *News* scoffed at the literal significance of an unknown voter in upstate Michigan switching sides to the Democrats.

In startling headlines the Michigan Democratic bible [i.e. the *Free Press*] sets forth before the gaze of an astonished world the fact that one William Ricksby, of St. Joseph, has been converted from the error of his ways, and hoisted the name of [Democrat presidential candidate] Tilden at the head of columns of the St. Joseph Republican. That fixes Berrien county.[79]

What the *News* considers as an insignificant gesture, the Democratic *Free Press*, using the conventions of melodrama, imbues with a greater significance. The voter's conversion was part of a more general movement towards the virtuous party. Virtue, previously misprized, was now becoming recognized, and would soon be redeemed. The individual conversion was a first sign of a broader public revelation. For example, the *Free Press* on October 15, 1888 reports:

HE GIVES STRONG REASONS

Why H. J. Waterbery, of Lansing, Will Vote for Cleveland

ALWAYS HERETOFORE A REPUBLICAN, BUT NOW THROUGH
WITH THE PARTY . . .

Lansing, October 14.–Mr. H. J. Waterbery of this city, a gentleman of prominence and of large personal influence, . . . has always, heretofore voted the Republican ticket, but will this year vote for Cleveland and Thurman, Burt and the whole Democratic ticket . . . As [his reasons] are such as have had great weight with many others and have caused like action on their part and as they will be of wide interest they are given somewhat at length . . .

The spectacle of party rallies with their crowds of fervent partisans and their parades, uniforms, torches, and banners could not be used to factually predict likely election turnout. Rather, the mass gathering reveals the citizenry's always increasing, fateful recognition of the virtue possessed by the party. "Not even a silver man would debate that last night's sound money meeting was the biggest event of the campaign in Detroit up to date . . . Many a supper was gulped down last evening in the haste of citizens to get down to the Auditorium and enthuse with the ever growing sound money majority."[80] The public's display of belief in the party may ignite a similar revelation in other voters. Or, it may provoke a quaking terror in the enemy. Parallel to the growing confidence of the righteous party was the paralysis through doubt and dismay that strikes the foe. Indeed, since the enemy's strength was founded not on truth or morality but deception and duplicity, it was destined to crumble and fall. The Democratic official thus advised his colleagues: "Claim the state with confidence. Do it with such confidence as to carry conviction to our friends and terror to our enemies."[81]

Given this melodramatic cultural logic, we can understand some of the typical symbolism of election rallies. As Jean Baker tells us, election rituals made repeated use of light and fire. "Immense bon-fires," torchlight parades, illuminated lanterns, and so on, signified the coming light of public revelation carried by the party.[82] In the end, the exaggerated theatrics of partisan belief, like the hyperbole of melodrama, perhaps reflected the difficulties of importing a cosmic significance into the basically pragmatic strategies of political organizations.

The symbiotic ties of corporations and organizational parties

The rites of parties and their papers sustained popular political loyalties. But, as Mark Twain and Charles Dudley Warner's metaphor of the "Gilded Age" suggests, the era's gaudy political veneer concealed more mundane, more corrupt, forms of politics. Journalism's histrionic narratives of popular sovereignty and partisanship were designed to stimulate continued party allegiances. But this diffuse loyalty to parties, unconnected to any specific policies, permitted more specialized economic interests to exert their control over political officials.

Starting in 1872, parties resorted to new organizational and symbolic politics to meet the threats posed by novel issues to the party's electoral coalition. These new pragmatic politics, though, made parties dependent upon outside funds. To organize rallies, pay for stump speakers, distribute political pamphlets, and support the myriad of party workers, Democrats and Republicans needed increased flows of money.[83] The wealthy and corporations, most specifically railroads and utilities, supplied these contributions to which parties became increasingly addicted.[84] In turn, corporations (especially those needing public franchises and governmental grants) could not escape the fees levied by parties, not if they wished to survive and remain competitive.[85] In fact, Morton Keller suggests that it was not as much the economic elite's control of politics as capital's inescapable dependence on the corrupt, party-controlled government that forced large companies to cough up money for party activities.[86]

However, this picture of two rival institutions – parties and corporations – coerced into rough cooperation might be too strong for Michigan. In the Wolverine state, political power and economic wealth tended to flow into each other until they were indistinguishable and finally merged in one person: Senator James McMillan, head of the State Republican party (mid-1880s to 1902).[87] McMillan was both the state's most powerful politician and a central figure in Michigan's corporate ownership. His financial interests trailed through several of the largest companies in the state, including Michigan's network of transportation – from the Michigan Central Railroad Company, to train car manufacturing, steamship lines, and Detroit's local streetcar system.[88] In addition, as Marie Heyda notes, "he had a voice in almost every great industrial enterprise in Detroit."[89] The rest of the Republican leadership were similarly involved in the major industrial and commercial interests of the state. McMillan was merely a typical figure of this elite political class.[90]

As senior Senator and head of the Republican state party he was in charge of distributing federal patronage and also handing out funds and favors to state legislators.[91] The party head was expected to act with a degree of largesse, and the funds for election campaigns and party events frequently came from his own pocket. (And, of course, he needed to own, or be allied with, a daily journal which would function as his personal mouthpiece.) In exchange for his dispensations, the boss effectively influenced the state legislature in all important enactments, including his own reelection to national office.[92]

After battling McMillan and his control over the Republican party for four years, the reform mayor of Detroit, Hazen Pingree, angrily condemned the mix of money and power governing the US: "Trusts and combines rule the Congress, and the corporations are represented in the administration. The Canadian Pacific [Railroad] is the real government of Canada, just as the Pennsylvania Railroad is the government in the State of Pennsylvania. In Michigan, the Michigan Central rules the legislature."[93]

Parties and corporate interests formed a united front in the pursuit of a common goal – private enrichment without any obligation to the public good. Or, perhaps, it is more accurate to say that they did not recognize the distinction between the policies which benefited parties and corporations and those laws which helped society as a whole.[94] In the end, parties, pursuing increased autonomy from voters and from well-defined policies, subordinated themselves to elite economic interests. As a source of power, the number of voters was replaced by the quantity of dollars. Newspapers with their rites of partisanship constituted an important instrument of this elite control of politics.

Conclusion

In the Gilded Age, papers married their fortunes to parties in order to maximize both their power and profits. Journals accepted parties as the sole legitimate representatives in the public sphere. Thus when the strategic electoral calculus of Democrats and Republicans shifted from the issues of the Civil War to an emphasis on inherited partisan identities and symbols, newspapers followed suit. Editors and publishers turned to the ritual production of popular political identities. They repeatedly publicized, indeed magnified, the achievements of the parties, and celebrated partisan commitment. To sustain their efforts at party propaganda, papers drew upon the diverse cultural codes of popular melodrama, political republicanism, and bellicose military metaphors. These exuberant partisan expressions certainly stimulated citizen engagement with the affairs of government. However, they did not serve an expanded public dialogue. Rather, into the public sphere's potentially broader and more variegated exchange of opinions, newspapers imported the strategic interests of organized politics. Public debate, as delineated and publicized by the nation's press, was systematically marred by strategic exclusions and distortions. Journals dismissed issues which potentially undermined their party's coalitional base and they denigrated all potential rivals to the two major parties.

Of course, these policing efforts achieved only limited success, especially as the century wore on. Outside the mainstream political and journalistic institutions, wave after wave of insurgents rose up. Excluded social interests organized their own means of public discussion and political representation. Farmers initiated a broad social movement first with the Grange, then the Alliance, and finally the Populist Party.

Women occasionally took to the streets but more often to their own network of clubs for discussions and the elaboration of an alternative social sensibility. Organized workers created political parties, union representation, and a vigorous labor press throughout America's major cities.[95] But not until the press officially broke from its allegiance, indeed its subservience, to parties would these social groups gain greater access to the wider reading public.

NOTES

1 Also see the Roosters on Oct. 12, 1876 and Sept. 14, 1880, *Detroit Free Press*. Reporter John Fitzgibbon reminisces about the Roosters in the *Detroit Evening News*, Dec. 30, 1927: 17.
2 McGerr 1986; Melder 1992.
3 Ibid. But see McGerr's qualifications on p. 120; Schiller 1981; Schudson 1978; Baldasty 1992.
4 Saxton 1971: 23; and see Pizzorno 1981; Horkheimer 1973.
5 Foner 1988: 485; Baum 1984: 4–6; Keller 1977: ch. 7; Montgomery 1981: 359–60.
6 Mohr 1976: Introduction; Foner 1988: 487–8; Keller 1977: 251–5.
    See *News*, Oct. 15, 1874: 2 col. 1. Democrats reply to the bloody shirt: *News*, Oct. 19, 1876 "The Local Campaign." And see the *Free Press* editorials Aug. 24, 1880: 4, col. 2 and Sept. 24, 1880: 4; also *Free Press*, Sept. 17, 1876. See *News*, Oct. 23, 1876: 1 for the Republican invocation of the "sanguine garment."
7 Shefter 1983: 465, 467; Keller 1977: 376–80, 553–4, 556, 559–61; Melder 1992: 114–15.
8 Ibid., 253–6, 556; Shefter 1983: 463–4; Foner 1988: 485.
9 Kircheimer 1969; Offe 1984: ch. 9; Cohen and Arato 1992: 51–8; Habermas 1986: 8–9, 13–15.
    Some of the terms of this analysis have been worked out by political scientists who argue that the US needs "responsible parties." See Orren's concise summary (1982).
10 Rogin and Shover 1970: xvi, 3–5; Burnham 1970: ch. 1 and 26–9; Burnham 1982: ch. 3; Jensen's typology of nineteenth-century political styles – organizational-"rally" styles and mobilizing "crusade" and "missionary" styles – partly parallels this two term oscillation; see Jensen 1969.
11 Schattschneider 1975: chs. 4–5; Jensen 1969: 38, 43; Skocpol and Ikenberry 1983: 93–4. Important in this context is the Civil War pension system and the Grand Army of the Republic. For Michigan see Heyda 1970.
12 Keller 1977: 262. I thank John Pauly for his suggestion that this transformation in American politics was also important for journalism.
13 *Free Press*, July 11, 1876: 1.
14 Stone 1883: 9. Stone was publisher of the *Chicago Daily News* and later director of the Associated Press. His criticisms of parties and papers were typical to Liberal Republicans and later the "Mugwumps." Complaints about unprincipled politics were common among the genteel intelligentsia.

They longed for the principled exchange of ideas that appeared to matter during the Civil War and its aftermath. Keller 1977: 277, and in general 268–79.

15 McGerr 1986: 120; Jensen, McGerr, and the *Evening News* note that the early 1890s represented a nadir in popular excitement. *Evening News*, August 1, 1891. 1896, instead, with its infusion of new political issues into public debate, marked a return to an extensively politicized, partisan journalism.

16 Politics fell to 20 percent as a share of the leading stories. Rubin 1981: 58, 82. In Baldasty's content analysis, politics figured as about half of a sample of ante-bellum papers, but only 19 percent of metropolitan papers in 1897; see Baldasty 1992: 153–7. These percentages do not measure whether the political news had a partisan bias. Schudson points out that Baldasty presents a relative measurement. Metropolitan journals at this time were rapidly expanding in size. The absolute amount of political news was not declining. Schudson dates human interest news (or "news" *per se*) back to the 1830s; Schudson 1994.

17 The *Post*'s statement "Under New Management," Aug. 1, 1884 and Nov. 7, 1884.

18 See Schiller 1981; and Leonard 1986: ch. 1.

19 Stocking 1915.

20 Virtually all the Detroit dailies that I sampled (except for the *Evening News*) carried notices of their party's meetings. The newspaper issue from the fall Presidential election season published notices of the gatherings for rallies, speeches, and organization meetings. These were published day after day. But also the issue sampled for spring of the preceding year printed each day a call to convene the party's late spring state-wide and county nominating conventions. The spring state convention would select candidates to run for the university regents and for the state supreme court.

21 For example, *Detroit Journal*, July 2–7, 1892.

22 McGerr 1986: 9, 14, 17–18. Jensen also presents a typology of five different political "styles" in his "Armies, Admen and Crusaders"; Leonard discusses the origin of a democratic "vernacular," that is, the development of cultural forms that could dramatize and make politics salient to the general populace. See Leonard 1986: chs. 4–5.

23 On a pervasive publicly displayed partisanship see also Gienapp 1982; Baker 1983; and Melder 1992: 30–1.

24 McGerr 1986: 37–8, 40, 17, 21. See also Geertz 1973: ch. 4; Carey 1989: ch. 1; and Wuthnow 1987. An important source for McGerr is Baker 1983; also cf. Skocpol and Ikenberry 1983: 93. On parades and processions as a dramaturgical self-representation of society see Darnton 1984: 109, 116, 120–5, 140.

25 McGerr 1986: 23; Leonard 1986: ch. 7; Keller 1977: 242. Exuberant, demonstrative partisanship, says McGerr, led to high levels of voter participation. These affective politics and parties were attacked by the genteel intelligentsia in the form of the political–cultural movement of Liberal Republicans. For McGerr, the Liberal Republicans never win any political power but do effectively reform American political style, replacing this

demonstrative partisanship with a more restrained, private, reflective politics. This change in political styles leads to a fall in voter participation after
1896 (*Evening News*, Aug. 1, 1892). The *News* models this anti-demonstra-
tive view, while commenting on the relative indifference of voters in the
1892 election campaign, e.g. Oct. 15, 1892: 4.

26 Jensen 1969: 38, 45, 50; McGerr 1986; and see the contrast of Progressive
Era and Gilded Age conceptions of citizenship and politics in Schudson
1998: ch. 4.

27 See the account of the Fourth of July parade in the *Free Press*, July 6, 1876.
Also Wilentz 1984: 87–97. Roediger identified such citizen rights as part of
the "wages of whiteness." White male workers might have to suffer the
indignities and dependence of wage-labor but at least, unlike Black slaves
and women, they were free, independent citizens in a community of equals.
Since such public rituals as the Fourth of July were a celebration of "white,
male" citizen rights, Blacks were often violently excluded (Roediger 1991:
57, 141).

28 *Free Press*, Oct. 15, 1868. The 1872 campaign prospectus "The Tribune as a
Newspaper" boasts of complete coverage of "every political meeting held in
Michigan of any special magnitude" (*Tribune*, July 30, 1872: 2).

29 It is by now a standard theoretical move when confronted by such Durkheimian accounts of social ritual and cultural values to turn to Marx. What are
supposedly consensual expressions of shared social values turn out to be the
unequal expression of views that in turn enhance the power of one group
over another; cf. Lee 1988. For an alternative picture of the nineteenth
century, one which is strongly critical of the lack of participation in the
mainstream parties, see Goodwyn 1978.

30 Bourdieu 1991, 1985; Rogin 1987: xvii–xviii, 293–300, and chs. 3–4.

31 Baker 1983: 264.

32 Cf. Marx 1972; Bourdieu 1991; Rogin 1987: ch. 4.

33 Aldrich 1884. See similar claims about the impossibility of independence in
the *Post*, October 5, 1884: 4. The Republican sheet asserts that a lack of
declared partisanship will necessarily result in a concealed bias.

34 Cf. Habermas 1977: 8–9; Rogin 1987: xvii–xviii, ch. 4. Bourdieu, following
Hobbes' model of representation, dogmatically asserts that all representation
means the elimination of the popular influence upon the representative. For
an alternative model see Plotke 1997.

35 Examples are as diverse as Orwell's *1984*; Carl Schmitt's *The Concept of the
Political* which attempted to suppress the heterogeneity of civil society
through its invocation of politics as decisions the sovereign must take when
confronting a foe; and the suppression of alternative voices in Croatia and
Serbia in their civil war, e.g. "Croatia Clamps Down on Opposition," *San
Francisco Chronicle*, May 13, 1993: A8.

36 Jensen 1969; Baker 1983: 288–91, 300, 302.

37 Quotes passages from: Headline *Tribune*, Oct. 15, 1892: 3; *Free Press*, March
16, 1872; *Free Press*, Feb. 16, 1891; *Tribune*, Feb. 13, 1891; *Free Press*, Jan.
14, 1891: 19; *Tribune*, Jan. 12, 1891: 4; *Evening News*, Sept. 26, 1876: 2,
col. 2; *Post*, July 13, 1872.

38 For examples of attacks on Prohibitionists by the Republican *Post*, Oct. 15,

1872 and Oct. 5, 1884: 2 as enhancing the electoral chances of the Democrats. In turn, the Democrat *Free Press* criticized the Prohibitionists Oct. 15, 1892. And for an attack on Greenbackers see Aug. 28, 1880 and Oct. 15, 1880 "The Greenbackers and Republicans."

39 *Post*, July 11, 1872.

40 *Journal* July 1, 1892 and other attacks Oct. 15, 1892: 2.

41 *Free Press*, May 7, 1868.

42 Cf. Bryce 1909: V. 2, 274.

43 Etc. *Free Press*, Sept. 7, 1892.

44 *Free Press*, Jan. 5, 1871.

45 *Free Press*, May 7, 1868.

46 *Union*, May 15, 1872.

47 *News*, Aug. 1, 1884; also e.g. Nov. 3, 1886.

48 *News*, Sept. 26, 1876.

49 Cf. Baehr 1972: 199. William Stocking, an editor of the Detroit *Post* described his paper's public preeminence in its early years: "Editorially [Morley] wrote very little but he was in touch with the leading Republican politicians of the day and in full accord with the ideas represented by the dominant branch of the party. The combination on the whole was a strong one and the Post was a decided power in Michigan politics until it consolidated with the Advertiser and Tribune . . . in 1877" Stocking 1915: 891.

50 *Post*, July 11, 1872: 2. Other examples: the *Free Press*'s selection of quotes on the senate contest labeled "Spirit of the State Press," Jan. 14, 1883, or the *Union* on Dec. 8, 1869 "Spirit of the State Democratic Press."

51 E.g. the *News*, Jan. 2, 1875: 2 "To-day's Opinions."

52 *Free Press*, May 23, 1868: 1.

53 Partisan "jibes" appeared in about 80 percent of my sampled papers from 1872 through 1900, including both election and non-election years. They took as their target the other party's policies, personnel, or election chances. The quantity of these partisan witticisms fluctuated between two and twenty-four, with a usual number of five or six. Before 1872 there were less jibes.

54 *Free Press*, Jan. 3, 1891: 4.

55 *Evening News*, Oct. 24, 1876: 2.

56 Mancini 1991: 142. Mancini speaks of pre-1989 conditions.

57 Ibid., 149. The US too has such elite negotiatory communications, but as Mancini notes, they often occur in more specialized, elite media such as the *New York Times* or the *Washington Post*.

58 *Union*, Feb. 14, 1871: 2.

59 The amount of news coverage drastically increased when the party rally took place in Detroit, as in 1880, 1884, and 1896.

60 Jensen 1969: 34–8. Jensen does not see their role as rituals creating partisan bonds of commitment. Also see Baum 1984: 8–9; Keller 1977: 545; Burnham 1970: 72–3, 95–7. For another view see Baker 1983: 301–2. And compare Stephen Skowronek's explication of "the strategic calculation of government officials as they pursued political power" and how this affected the possibilities for civil service reform (1981: 166–70).

61 *Tribune*, Jan. 10, 1892. Another example is a report of a Democratic rally: "In the closing of one of the speeches it was said: Be discouraged by no

defeat; not even if the news to-night [from early October elections] should not bring the hope which we desire; still the Democratic party is mighty and will prevail" (*Free Press*, Oct. 13, 1868: 2).

62 *Advertiser and Tribune*, Oct. 31, 1876. A similar account is in the *Post*, Aug. 15, 1876: 2.

63 *Evening News*, Oct. 11, 1890. Such criticisms were already made in 1844. See Jensen 1969: 38.

64 In my sampled issues two such Detroit Republican rallies occurred; in 1884 a chronological description of the events and a verbatim report of the speech filled a full page of text in a four-page paper. In 1896, two and a half pages were devoted to the Gold Democrat–Republican rally by the *Journal* and the *Free Press*.

65 *Free Press*, Oct. 15, 1892: 2.

66 Ibid. And see the *Free Press* four years later (Oct. 15, 1896) in another sampled issue for its rallying articles. The *Evening News* in its passion for Bryan for president presented similar articles enthusing over popular turnout for the Great Man.

67 *Evening News*, Nov. 6, 1892: 4.

68 *Free Press*, Oct. 14, 1876.

69 *Tribune*, Oct. 15, 1892.

70 For charges of Associated Press bias see: *Evening News*, Sept. 24, 1876: 2; *Post*, Jan. 13, 1875 and Oct. 16, 1884: 1; *Free Press*, Sept. 26, 1876: 2; Sept. 27, 1876: 2; Oct. 4, 1876: 2; and Oct. 10, 1876: 2. Schwarzlose refers to these controversies as occurring across the nation in 1876 and 1884 (1990: 124–30).

71 Bryce 1909: 272. And see McGerr 1986: 22.

72 Ibid., 275. And cf. *Free Press*, Aug. 29, 1880: 4, col. 3. on pure party organs:

> Representing the ambitions or purposes of a politician and his clique, its ablest and most disinterested utterances get little credit for their ability or boldness, and the public attaches no more weight to its views than it would to those of the man or men behind it. People just as soon think of the salesman in the store delivering disinterested and weighty opinions upon the quality of his employer's goods.

73 Jensen 1969: 36–7.

74 Levine 1984: 51. And on the use of melodrama as a political code see Falasca Zamponi 1992: 85–90; Clark 1990. More generally, see Baker 1983: 213, where she writes, "By using [popular culture's] language and symbols, party leaders linked popular sentiment with party agenda."

75 Brooks 1985: 31–2, 43–4, 49. Melodrama placed society in the position of final judge; the play's resolution depended upon the populace's recognition and acclaim of the hero's previously hidden virtue. But melodrama is also democratic in the strong (and imaginary) sense of a society made transparent to itself. Evil furthers its ambitions through hidden conspiratorial machinations. Virtue rules, in the end, through publicity.

The underlying parable of "occluded morality" typically gives the melodramatic plot its dramatic charge, along with its elements of psychological pathos, and gothic horror.

76 Brooks 1985: 17.

77 Baker 1983: 269–78; *Post*, Oct. 15, 1872; Brooks 1985: 27, 15, and ch. 2.

78 *Evening News*, Oct. 25, 1876. Other examples of "conversion" are: the *Post*, Oct. 16, 1876; Oct. 15, 1884: 1 and 12; a bolt from the Democrats in *Journal*, Oct. 15, 1892; *Free Press*, Aug. 8, 1880; *Tribune*, Oct. 14, 1888.
79 *Evening News*, Oct. 16, 1876.
80 *Free Press*, Oct. 15, 1896.
81 Cf. *Free Press*, Sept. 24, 1876: 1; *Advertiser and Tribune*, Oct. 31, 1876.
82 Baker 1983: 295–7. The *Evening News* (Oct. 19, 1876) reports an immense bonfire at a Detroit Democratic rally; a defense of torchlight parades is printed in the *Evening News* Oct. 26, 1876 by a writer who signs him/herself Kerosenist; the *News* provides an account of a Detroit Republican rally in 1876 replete with torchlight parade. Comparing the two parties' rallies the *News* writes, "in this kerosene contest, the Republicans are certainly ahead." *Evening News* Sept. 25, 1876. Other local torchlight processions are referred to in the *Post* Oct. 17, 1868; *Advertiser and Tribune*, Oct. 15, 1868: 1; *Free Press*, Oct. 15, 1868; *Union* 1872; and *Post* Oct. 15, 1884: 1 "Detroit Ablaze." In 1892 the *News* claims torches were disappearing. Cf. Melder 1992: 32.
83 Keller 1977: 243, 245, 536, 542, 562.
84 Montgomery 1981: 60–1; Rothman 1974: 833–7; Keller 1977: 536–7, 542–3, 562; Shefter 1983: 464, 467–71, 481, 483.
   McCormick says this reliance on corporation funds increased in the 1890s, once civil service started proscribing levied fees on party appointed governmental workers. McCormick 1981.
   On railroad influence on state government see Utley 1906: 150–1; Catlin 1926a: 637–9; Foner 1988: 466–7; Shefter 1983: 469–71.
85 Rothman 1974: 836–7; Sarasohn and Sarasohn 1957: 11.
86 Rothman 1974: 828, 833, 835–6; Foner 1988: 468, 486–7; Keller 1977: 531, 536, 543, 562.
87 McCormick characterizes this convergence for New York State: "Sharing similar values as well as interests, the two elites mutually thrived through the interchangeability of economic and political power" (1981: 141). Cf. Foner 1988: 465–6.
88 On McMillan see Rothman 1974: 819–20, 838; Heyda 1970; Sarasohn and Sarasohn 1957: 10–12. On the Democratic counterpart of McMillan see Bolt 1970; Pound 1948.
89 Heyda 1970: 191.
90 On Michigan and Detroit's elite see Zunz 1982: ch. 8.
91 Rothman 1974; Sarasohn and Sarasohn 1957: 9–12; Bolt 1970: 27, 60; Heyda 1970: 194; George 1969: 199.
92 Rothman 1974: 820, 827–30; Sarasohn and Sarasohn 1957: 10; Heyda 1970: 194. On the earlier Michigan Republican boss Zachariah Chandler see George 1969: 98–9. Also see various letters to Senator McMillan, September through November 1893 requesting funds and donations. Senator James McMillan Papers (Burton Historical Archive). On these processes in New York State see McCormick 1981: 141–50, 155, 162.
93 Pingree 1895: 15.
94 Heyda 1970: 196, 200.
95 Fine 1956: ch. 9; Clemens 1993; Oestereicher 1986; Goodwyn 1978; Wiebe 1967: chs. 3–4.

4 The two revolutions in urban newspaper economics, 1873 and 1888

In the early and mid-nineteenth century, the strong competition among journals and the enduring political loyalties of readers produced and reproduced a vigorously partisan press; publishers enlarged their power and profits by selling their paper to an audience composed of faithful party members. In the late nineteenth century, however, a radical transformation in newspaper economics undermined this political equilibrium. Beginning in the 1870s, new cheap dailies invaded the urban newspaper markets and rapidly captured an expanding readership. Indeed, these one- and two-cents papers created the first mass, nearly universal, audience for American journalism. From being an elite leisure activity, "taking a paper" became a standard rite and daily routine for the American family. Journalism finally realized its long-cherished dream of delivering the news to every American, of incorporating all citizens into the "republic of letters."

Soaring advertising revenues further transformed newspaper economics in the 1880s and 1890s. The ensuing economic upsurge created new millionaire publishers. At the same time, the boom initiated what Svennik Hoyer has called the "consolidation phase" of urban newspaper markets, and by the early 1900s the transformed conditions of manufacturing and vending newspapers intensified the competition among journals. The press joined the US business community in a mania of mergers, buyouts, and closures. Ultimately, this consolidation wave led to a concentration in metropolitan markets across the country.

In 1919, George G. Booth, publisher of the Detroit *Evening News*, cast a retrospective eye over this history and labeled these tumultuous changes the "first" and "second revolutions" in Gilded Age journalism. This chapter details these two economic revolutions through the particular case of one innovative publisher and his newspaper – James E. Scripps and the Detroit *Evening News*. Scripps, in fact, blazed the trail for cheap, popular newspapers in industrializing cities across the Midwest. As *Harper's Magazine* claimed in 1888:

One of the most notable features of Western Journalism during the past few years has been the rise and success of the penny and two cents newspapers. The first journalist of the West to discover the demand for journals of this class and to act upon his discovery was Mr. James E. Scripps, the principal owner of the *Detroit Evening News* . . . This was the pioneer of the cheap newspaper in the West . . . [1]

In important ways the press of Detroit foreshadowed the rise of Joseph Pulitzer's and William Randolph Hearst's "new journalism."

This chapter discusses the economic innovations in popular journalism, and then turns to their implications for the political role of the press. It shows that the new profit orientation of newspapers created a complex dynamic weakening journalism's embrace of partisanship, although the final rupture did not come until later. Throughout the late 1800s, Detroit's dailies maintained their formal public partisan identity; with each election campaign, fresh waves of partisan enthusiasm broke over the press. Indeed, not until the political turmoil of 1896 and the political reforms of the Progressive Era, were such obligatory ties of formal partisanship disrupted and then renounced by the print media, as chapter 5 describes.[2] In the Gilded Age, journalism's rising fortunes offered a dispensation from party duties and provided an impetus for independence, rather than an inexorable logic leading to independence.

The "first revolution" of 1873

In the years after the Civil War, manufacturing burgeoned in the industrial heartland of the Northeast and the Midwest. The US had entered its own "Age of Capital."[3] The population too increased at an exponential rate as immigrants flocked to the developing industrial cities in search of work. By and large this mass of poor workers and immigrants was not part of the newspaper-reading public. In 1870, Detroit's daily papers circulated to only 30 percent of the English-speaking population, while in New York City distribution remained confined to under 40 percent.[4] Workers were unexploited by the established partisan and usually conservative journals. Such dailies counted among their subscribers the social and economic elites, and biased their news accordingly.[5] In the recollections of James Scripps' younger brother Edward, "The well-to-do were instructed by their press in all matters political and economical, while the poor were left in dense ignorance."[6]

A central obstacle to attracting new readers, beyond politics, was price. All Detroit's dailies, whether they were Republican, Democrat, or pro-labor, (for example, the Detroit *Union*) were five cents, a hefty share of the average wage of a dollar a day. Yearly subscriptions, which were much more common than street sales, ran from twelve to eighteen dollars per year. As one author observed: "At that time newspapers were luxury items . . . People to whom the humble nickel represented butter if not bread thought twice before buying a newspaper and then usually bought butter."[7] Price, consequently, was a major barrier to the expansion of newspaper audiences. Until the launching of the *Detroit Evening News* in 1873, this fertile field of potential readers and consumers lay fallow.

A number of media historians have described the dynamic, novel economics that supposedly overcame this barrier to newspaper expansion and profits in the late nineteenth century. Harry Baehr Jr., for example, writes that the new journalism of Pulitzer and Hearst "was founded on cheap, mass circulation with advertising footing the bill."[8] Richard Ohmann gives a more precise picture of this dynamic model in reference to an analogous revolution in magazine publishing. According to Ohmann, three interlinked processes explain the explosive growth in the mass market for magazines in the 1890s. First, lower magazine prices encouraged an expanding circulation. This growing readership, in turn, produced an increase in advertising revenue. The newly generated funds (along with a reduction of the per unit costs of magazine production) were then employed to slash further subscription prices, which once again sparked a growth in circulation.[9]

In the early 1870s two obstacles prevented newspapers from implementing such a "dynamic" economic program. To start with, the high cost of newsprint paper blocked a cheap mass circulation newspaper.[10] For newspapers, "variable costs" (that is, costs that vary directly with the volume of production, such as ink or paper[11]), are a disproportionate share of the costs of production. And the largest single source of such variable costs resides in expenditures for paper. In the 1870s, paper stock commanded high prices and consequently only limited economies of scale could be derived from any increased output. Reducing a journal's price to capture a larger audience might well result in a collapse in profits.

The second difficulty confronting journalism in the post-bellum era, as Scripps emphasized, was that "advertising patronage of the country fell far short of the capacities of the papers to accommodate it."[12] Plenty of available newspaper space, but limited demand, resulted in a "demoralized" advertising market. In such a market, advertisers could dictate the terms of trade to publishers. Prices remained low and journals printed columns of antiquated advertising with little hope of collecting the fees.

Confronting these barriers, Detroit publishers had scoffed at the possibility of ever issuing a cheap, popular paper. In 1872, however, James E. Scripps outlined a new model for dealing with the limitations of the market. As business manager of the morning Republican organ, he first presented his plan to the *Advertiser and Tribune*'s board, which promptly rejected it as not feasible.[13] In place of a dynamic model of publishing based upon a continued cycle of expansion of production and popular consumption, Scripps proposed an alternate strategy for circulating the news to all Detroit citizens. His model was premised on an all-around cutting of production costs. By implementing strict economies, Scripps would revolutionize the news market.

Within a year of his rejection by the *Advertiser and Tribune*, Scripps scrounged the necessary capital to independently launch the *Detroit Evening News* priced at a mere two cents. The key to Scripps' effort was a reduction in the size of the printed page and as a consequence a cut in paper costs. In the immediate post-war period, all Detroit journals had remained four-page publications. Gradually they had expanded in size, not by printing supplementary pages, but by annexing more and more columns to the page. They metamorphosed into huge "blanket sheets," with each page spreading out to eight, nine, or ten columns of print.[14] In contrast, Scripps distributed his *Evening News* in a greatly reduced format. The new daily was approximately one sixth the size of other papers with its four pages measuring eighteen by twelve inches. And its columns were shaved to 2 inches, saving an additional 8 percent on composition and paper costs.[15]

In additions to cuts in paper and printing expenses, Scripps instituted other money-saving procedures. He sliced frills and extravagances out of the newsroom; and he insisted there was no need for a "lavish expenditure for telegraph [news] and $35–a-week writing."[16] Scripps enlisted the capital and labor of an entire clan of family members in his enterprise, thus economizing on wages and gaining longer work hours.[17] Memoirs often recount how the publisher, in the midst of an editorial conference, would continue his labors of slitting open envelopes, smoothing them out in preparation for their reuse as writing paper.[18]

This austere economy of scarce resources even entered into the paper's official writing style: "condensation." After all, less paper should mean less space for the news, yet the *Evening News* was dedicated to providing its readers with a full news report. Condensation resolved this contradiction. News stories, especially those copied from the morning journals or taken from the wire, would be rewritten in the briefest possible form. Half-brother, Edward W. Scripps, recalls how the idea of condensation animated James' dreams of a cheap paper years before the founding of the *Evening News*. One day, the normally distant James approached the younger Edward in their Illinois family home.

It was in "the boys' bedroom" that he narrated to me the whole plan of that little newspaper which he was later to found in Detroit and which was the kernel of the Scripps newspaper concerns . . . Now the great idea my brother submitted to me was the publication of a daily newspaper very small in size with large type, and which, by reason of having condensed writing, would contain all the news . . . and even the love stories that could be found in any of the large "blanket sheets" that were being issued as newspapers.[19]

The condensation of stories into news briefs enabled the journal to print all the news of the day, to be exhaustive in topics if not in detail.[20]

The newspaper that Scripps planned would be democratic and austere, in a word: republican.[21] Democratic since Scripps' cheap paper would allow all citizens to join the public-political dialogue of the community. In addition, with its condensed stories, Scripps' small newspaper would not only supply working-class readers with the information they needed, it would also be a publication they could read in their spare time. Previously, periodicals had been sprawling sheets. Perusing such a journal "was a task for long hours of leisure, an article that was lacking in homes where the working day was from sunrise to sunset."[22] Now, with the *Evening News*, all Detroiters – rich or poor – could read the news even if their time and money were limited.

Scripps desired to expand the circle of newspaper readers, but more than that it was an austere, disciplined consumption of the news that he envisioned.[23] Nineteenth-century republicanism (as against today's post-modern emphasis on social diversity) stressed the cohesiveness of the body politic and its political discussion. Debate was mandatory not only for the purposes of establishing agreement, but for integrating the peripheral, marginal parts of the population and teaching them civic virtue. For republicans, the press should be a unifying strand in the citizenry's discussion of the commonweal. The *Evening News*'s limited size ensured that all would read the same news stories. There would be no consumer choice among the news items.[24] The newspaper was not a vast smorgasbord or giant menu, to use the later metaphors of Edward Scripps, where the heterogeneous readership could pick and choose items of news it found most delectable. In this sense, the *Evening News*'s lack of headlines and the absence of introductory summarizing paragraphs become comprehensible. There was no need for such guides to enhance the readers' choice, nor to advertise the merits of each news story. Instead, the whole of the newspaper was intended as an expression of dialogue between editor and reader. The paper was meant to be read from cover to cover.

An ascetic vision also informed the paper's literary style. Working-class readers would receive the bare-bones of the story without any elitist literary flourishes. Stories were modeled on the "austere brevity" of E. L. Godkin's *New York Post* in opposition to the style of the blanket sheets which "carried copious dull reading . . . turgid in style and over-heavy with essays and sermons."[25] The condensed news was stripped of the extravagance and ornamentation of genteel rhetoric. In addition Scripps (in typical Liberal Republican fashion) planned to remove the biases of partisan opinion and subjective voice that usually mediated between the reader and the facts.[26] Lastly, in expanding the universe of readers to incorporate the previously dispossessed, Scripps would do without the element of human interest typical of cheap newspapers up until then. No sensationalism would pander to the corrupt tastes of the masses.[27]

The Detroit *Evening News* did not turn out exactly as James E. Scripps planned. In the words of former *Evening News* editor Malcom Bingay, the *News* was born "in a war of clashing personalities."[28] Brother Edward Scripps, a young bohemian rascal, joined with the leading reporters to battle against the conservative, status-conscious James for the paper's soul. The editorial staff quickly trespassed upon the ascetic vision of the publisher and produced a sensationalist paper. Indeed, according to Bingay and Edward Scripps, the success of the *News* derived precisely from this sabotage of James Scripps' journalistic ideals.

In part, the *News*'s sensationalism consisted in publicizing the peccadilloes and malfeasances of Detroit's middle and upper classes. Edward Scripps boasted: "Rich rascals found that . . . they were living in glass houses, and that they had no means of protecting themselves from public exposure. This applied to rich men . . . men in political offices . . . doctors, lawyers and even judges . . . The News gained a reputation almost nationwide for its attitude."[29] This invasive journalism first resulted in a series of libel suits including a judgment of $20,000 against the newspaper. Second, as Edward suggested, the sensationalism produced a wave of public attention and a rising circulation. Later, in an 1889 letter, Edward recalled how the Scripps papers had taken a less than respectable road to prominence. In both Detroit and in Cleveland, "we fought our way to prominence through the courts [i.e. libel suits] and by means very disagreeable to all of us [i.e. scandalous articles]."[30] In the end, James Scripps found the lure of profits too powerful and he turned away from his high-minded vision. In a celebration some twenty-five years after its founding, he spoke about the birth of the *Evening News*. Scripps did not so much disown his journalistic child as acknowledge that he was not its legitimate father:

Something really meritorious and elevating, but in small compass and at a cheap rate, was the ideal I set myself. But I soon found I had journalistic genius on my staff, and I was quick to see that true policy demanded that it have a fair scope. Had I held everything down to my own views, I should have produced a good, but dull newspaper . . . [31]

By 1878 the *Evening News* was a roaring success, and Scripps applied his talents to broader fields. In conjunction with Edward Scripps, he established a chain of five papers in the Midwest. In each case the Scripps journal was a cheap, down-market, afternoon sheet which held down expenses through tight economies and which appealed to an untapped market by a mixture of sensationalism, an abbreviated but complete news report, and greater sympathy for the issues and struggles of urban, immigrant workers.[32] In this sense, as the press historian Edwin Emery rightly points out, the Scripps brothers were forerunners of Pulitzer and Hearst's new mass journalism.[33]

After 1889, when the two brothers broke off all personal and business ties in a huff of recrimination and litigation, Edward Scripps cultivated an extensive newspaper chain in the small, bustling industrial cities throughout the West between 1892 and 1923.[34] Despite the anger and the competitiveness he displayed towards his older brother, in his various autobiographical accounts Edward recognized the roots of his many papers in the model and the fiscal resources of the Detroit *News*.[35] Writing in 1919, James Scripps' son-in-law, George Booth summarized Scripps' achievements:

From the unusual enterprise established [at] 65 Shelby Street have sprung some 49 newspapers. Several were directly attributable to James E. Scripps, others to the enterprise of the men whom he trained in that first property where they learned the ropes: still others flowed from the encouragement the Scripps brothers gave young men . . .

James E. Scripps was a revolutionist of his day or at least a pioneer in the small daily newspaper field.[36]

The accomplishments of 1873

James Scripps and the *Evening News* fundamentally reshaped the newspaper market in Detroit. As an innovator Scripps mapped out a market niche unexplored by his competitors, the five-cent blanket sheets. Between 1873 and 1882 the *News*'s circulation expanded prodigiously. Already by 1876 its readership equaled that of all other Detroit papers combined. Scripps' recognition of such opportunities reaped for him great financial rewards and opened a path for entrepreneurs in other cities. Within six years he could proudly rest on his laurels and lecture the Michigan State Publishers Association on the ingredients for success.[37]

Table 4.1. *Circulation*

	News	Free Press	Tribune	Post	Union	German Papers
1870	–	6,000	4,500	6,300	2,300	4,900
1874	6,100	5,300	4,500	3,300	2,100	4,600
1878	15,600	6,400	(merged):[4,000]	(folded)		4,700
1882	40,000	9,000	6,750		*Journal*	5,700
1886	37,800	20,000	16,000		21,000	6,500
1890	40,300	30,300	20,900		20,000	9,100

Scripps' innovations can be analyzed as part of a second "expansion phase" typical of all developing industries. According to the Norwegian press analyst, Svennik Hoyer, newspaper markets typically undergo three stages in their economic development. After an initial introduction of a commodity into the urban centers, a second stage ensues where the commodity is diffused across the nation. In this period of growth, the number of both newspaper producers and consumers rapidly multiply (see table 4.1).[38] Hoyer sees this expansion as spreading from the societal center "along both geographic and social dimensions to incorporate farmers in rural areas and lower-classes."[39] Industrial entrepreneurs conquer new markets in part by creating journalistic products for previously untouched market niches. Thus, the growth of newspaper circulation is accompanied by a segmentation of the reading audience along political and class lines. Eventually, says Hoyer, this expansion phase is followed by a third "consolidation phase" as the market becomes saturated and newspapers enter into close competition.

Hoyer's theory assumes a natural process of economic evolution.[40] Circulation expands as increased productive efficiency and other market factors make newspapers economically accessible, and as publishers transform their journals to attract new audiences. This theory takes demand as a constant, and neglects the diverse social, economic, and cultural barriers to the growth in newspaper circulation. Nevertheless, Scripps' efforts in 1873 largely fit this model of expansion through market-niche innovation. Scripps' genius was to confront the economic barriers to a lower-class audience and circumvent them, even without the introduction of new, more efficient publishing technology and without a reduction in the costs of other production factors. In this manner Scripps recognized the existence of previously excluded social groups and altered his paper in order to seize this audience.

Scripps' paper increased the accessibility of the press through a price reduction, just as had the penny press back in the 1830s.[41] With its price

Table 4.2. *Detroit papers as a percentage of the daily wages of a worker*

Daily price	1865	1870	1875	1880	1885	1890	1895	1900	1905
most costly	$.05	$.05	$.05	$.05	$.03	$.03	$.03	$.03	$.02
least costly	.05	.05	.02	.02	.02	.02	.02	.01	.01
Daily wages	$1.54	1.47	1.27	1.16	1.34	1.43	1.32	1.45	1.68
Paper price	3.2	3.4	3.9	4.3	2.3	2.1	2.3	2.1	1.2
as a percentage			1.6	1.7	1.5	1.4	1.5	0.7	0.6
of wages									

of two cents, the *Evening News* took a significantly smaller share of the worker's daily pay. In 1875 the *News* cost 1.6 percent of the average daily wages of a worker compared to 3.9 percent for the nickel journals (see table 4.2).[42]

Scripps' daily paper interjected a new class perspective into the Democratic and Republican viewpoints dividing up the newspaper market. As Baehr and Richard Slotkin demonstrate for New York City, until the introduction of a new, cheap press by Pulitzer and later Hearst, the poor and workers lacked a public, journalistic voice.[43] Previously, newspapers – tied to parties, owned by the wealthy, and with a circulation limited to the upper third of the population – tended to ignore the interests of the mass of workers, poor, and immigrants.[44]

The *Evening News* made its daily pennies from this lower-class audience, and often pushed issues that had symbolic appeal to those just scraping by. Between 1888 and 1920, the *News* incessantly harped on the need for municipal ownership of utilities and especially public transportation. Street-railway conditions eventually provoked a public riot in 1892. These issues became symbolic touchstones for the paper,[45] and the *News* pressed these policies with all its resources of publicity and repetition. For example, in what amounted to the newspaper's motto, the *News* regularly emblazoned the editorial page with the slogan: "No more Street Railway franchises on any terms. Restoration of government by the people, not by private corporations."[46]

In 1913 the upper-class weekly *Detroit Saturday Night* dissected this editorial policy as a standard "corrupt" commercial tactic of the *News* management (then under George Booth):

Like most Booth newspapers, the *Evening Press* has been a conspicuous financial success. Like all of them, it has achieved the feat of remaining financially honest while developing a highly effective community of interests between policies and pennies. It was discovered, for instance, by the *Detroit News* . . . that corporation baiting was . . . popular, and that large circulation was to be won that way even

though political battles might be lost. Large circulation meant large advertising
. . . [which] meant, of course, large revenues. So all the little *Newses* have
followed the corporation-baiting as a worthy profession ever since.[47]

In this fashion, the *News* duplicated the class crusades of Hearst and
Pulitzer, famous for their attacks on monopolies and corporate control
of city utilities.[48] It initiated a long-term strategy of cheap journals, of
issuing populist appeals that sensationally highlighted issues outside of
the two-party elite consensus.[49]

Of course, there were significant limits to this class politics of the
Scripps paper. Historian James Bow provides the appropriate character-
ization; the *News* was not so much a labor or working-class paper as a
"popular" paper.[50] The limits to the *Evening News*'s support for any
labor agitation were exposed in 1877. That summer a general strike of
railroad workers threatened to paralyze the nation. Violence spread as
state militia attacked strikers and workers rioted. The *News* rushed to
join the country's other dailies in a virulent, hysterical denunciation of
the workers.[51] On July 24, 1877, it characterized the rioters and strikers
as a "criminal class per se, that swell every mob, throw the first stone,
fire the first piston, and ignite the first house in every riot, whatever may
have been the original cause." The proper remedy for the social
disorder: let it "be distinctly understood that bullets and steel are to be
used."[52] Edward Scripps, for one, believed that his brother James
possessed no feelings of sympathy for the laboring classes. He recalled
how James once observed a strike from his hotel window and remarked
in anger, "[If I were Mayor . . .] I would sure teach these fellows a
lesson that they would remember, as would every other workingman in
the city."[53] Similarly, Pulitzer's new journalism withdrew support for
workers whenever they engaged in strikes or violence flared.[54]

Instead of a sense of sympathy, the Scripps management introduced
class issues into the paper as part of a conscious economic strategy. In
the years 1894–1904, for example, Scripps' son-in-law George Booth
attempted to break into the Chicago market. While using (and losing)
approximately a million dollars of his father-in-law's money, Booth
prescribed a pro-labor editorial policy for the *Chicago Journal*. He
pragmatically designed his paper to appeal to workers and the popular
classes, in the manner of Pulitzer's great New York paper. Writing to his
Chicago manager, Booth declared:

As to the style of paper desired . . . my ideas may be summed up by reference to
New York World. The general style and method of handling news and the
editorial style and sentiment . . . are such as will be applicable to the situation in
Chicago . . . [C]ircumstances now seem to make it necessary not to delay efforts
to secure circulation among the general masses of people . . . As to editorial

policy on general matters . . . I have felt disposed to go as far as seems wise on the side of the workingmen. Be honest with them and ourselves, and yet calculating to please and to win them by securing their confidence with the methods we may adopt. We are not in a position to be very dignified as yet. We must get right down with the people.[55]

The *Detroit Evening News* crested a wave of cheap evening papers in the US. The explosive growth of these one- and two-cent dailies captured a major share of the population that previously stood outside the domain of newspaper subscribers. Scripps followed his Detroit venture with papers in Cleveland, Cincinnati, St. Louis, and Buffalo. Meanwhile, other entrepreneurial publishers such as Victor Lawson in Chicago and William Nelson in Kansas City launched their own cheap afternoon sheets. In each case, the journal was a short, scrappy bulletin paper, supplying an abbreviated but complete news report, and distributed to the urban working populations. The rapid proliferation of American papers at century's end rested on this expansion in afternoon publications. Between 1870 and 1910 (the high-water mark for US dailies), the number of journals increased almost four-fold, from 574 to 2,600. By 1910 evening sheets comprised 74 percent of the daily press.[56]

Throughout the late nineteenth century and into the early twentieth, Detroit's population, like that of the US as a whole, grew at a fierce rate. Buoyed by the "second wave" of immigrants from Southern and Eastern Europe, the city more than doubled every twenty years and increased twelve-fold between 1870 and 1920.[57] Despite this spurt, Detroit papers more than matched the population explosion. In 1870 the press reached only a minority of Detroit's inhabitants, with about three papers produced for every ten citizens. But in the next two decades circulation doubled to approximately six papers for every ten Detroiters.[58] Similarly, New York City saw a boom with distribution surging from about four copies per ten inhabitants in 1870 to slightly more than nine for every ten in 1910.[59] In the Gilded Age, newspapers as a whole, and cheap journals in particular, shifted from a class to a mass audience, almost saturating the population with sheets (see table 4.3).[60] The growth in one- and two-penny papers was accompanied by expansion of elite papers, who likewise lowered their price to capture more readers.

By the early twentieth century, taking the paper was a daily routine among workers in Detroit and in the nation. In the early 1920s, Robert and Helen Lynd surveyed the consumption expenditures of blue-collar households in *Middletown*. One hundred percent subscribed to a daily journal.[61] Indeed, other studies in that decade reported that "news-

Table 4.3. *Circulation compared with population*

	Detroit's population*	Circulation of Detroit's dailies	Circulation compared to population (%)**	NYC's circulation compared to population (%)***
1860	46,000	NA	NA	30
1870	80,000	27,000	30.0	38.8
1880	116,000	40,800	35.2	42.3
1890	206,000	120,600	58.5	72.8
1900	286,000	154,400	54.0	81.7
1910	466,000	292,200	62.7	92.5
1920	994,000	523,000	52.7	86.2

* Bureau of the Census 1972.
** Circulation taken from Ayer & son 1880–1930; and Rowell & co. 1870–78.
*** Lee presents New York City's population as derived from the US Census (Lee 1947: 730).

papers were by far the most common reading matter of young workers, followed by fiction magazines, the 'pulps.'"[62] Even later, in the 1930s and 1940s, with the arrival of radio as principal home entertainment, a close scrutiny of the paper remained a required evening ritual. On average, readers devoted twenty minutes to their reading, with the radio supplying background noise.[63] Such habits persisted until the 1960s when newspaper reading began a long-term, persistent drift downwards among the middle and lower classes.[64] For the first half of the twentieth century, social reality in its official narratives and rites was daily defined and delivered by the press.

In the realm of formal politics the *Evening News* pursued an independent political posture.[65] The *News*'s non-partisanship, in fact, was unique and cannot be found in Scripps' journals in other cities, nor in the down-market papers of Pulitzer and Hearst. They were all advocates of the Democratic party.[66] Don Seitz, business manager for the *New York World*, bluntly explained the reason for this political slant: "The city papers securing the most success are those of the independent Democratic type. Cities are usually Democratic."[67]

What accounts for the *Evening News*'s independence, however transitory? By virtue of their price differences, Scripps' afternoon paper and the morning papers addressed virtually separate audiences. Until the mid-1880s, the *News* was insulated from significant competition and, consequently, Scripps pursued a non-partisan, generalist marketing strategy. However, once Detroit's other dailies recognized the *News*'s success with its implicit threat to their own fortunes and futures, they encouraged a variety of cheap rivals to the *News*. These proved ephemeral until the founding of the *Detroit Journal* in 1883.[68] Initiated as a Republican paper, the *Journal* represented serious competition for Scripps. With sufficient capital and an advertising manager who had previously been in charge of the *News*'s own advertising department, the *Journal* threatened the *News*'s premiere position. In response to this Republican bisection of the cheap afternoon market, Scripps' paper turned Democrat.[69]

Throughout the Gilded Age, the managers and publishers that made up the Scripps clan approached the issue of "policy" (as the politics of the press was then labeled) from the angle of profits. They exhibited a pragmatic economic calculation in their selection of the political ideas to be propagated through their editorials and news. As chapter 3 argued, not strong convictions but the profits to be earned by appealing to one market segment or another determined their political opinions. For the sake of increased circulation, they compromised their political integrity, just as James Scripps had surrendered his journalistic integrity and accepted the sensationalist antics of his yellow baby, the *News*.[70] For instance, during the 1896 election James Scripps counseled his son-in-law to entice readers by supporting the radical silver Democrats and their presidential nominee, William Jennings Bryan. "I believe it will be a great hit giving us a chance for once to be on the popular side. It may be the [Chicago] Journal's interest to join us especially as all the other papers will be on the other side. It may be your opportunity to rival the [Chicago] Daily News in circulation."[71] Booth apparently concurred. He informed his editors: "I have favored an inclination to the side of free silver, because it has seemed a large proportion of the Democratic population of Chicago are free silverites, and because this field does not seem to be covered by other evening papers."[72]

Or more absurdly: in 1883 in the early days of Scripps' Cincinnati paper, Edward Scripps guided the penny *Post* in a program of advocacy and partisanship that infected both the editorials and the news. But, instead of the Democratic or Republican party, Scripps' paper subscribed to the party of the Lord. The *Cincinnati Post* was conducted as a proselytizing organ in an evangelical campaign.[73]

We belong to the Lord's party, and the partisans of the Lord are having a great rally down here in Cincinnati . . . Column after column and page after page was devoted day after day to this great religious revival. The boy preacher and the little *Penny Post* were vying with each other and co-operating with each other in saving souls . . . Some of the editorials of the Post were prayers; some were sermons. But the effect on the circulation was remarkable. It grew rapidly; doubled, trebled and quadrupled.[74]

For the sake of profit and for a lark, Edward Scripps continued the campaign until there were no more pennies to earn. He later confessed, "It was all the worse hypocrisy and meaner lying, because I was doing it for the money."[75]

How did the birth of cheap, down-market competition and a general market expansion affect the traditional party newspapers? However much the *Evening News* might diminish the other papers' circulation, it did not necessitate a change in their tactics. The *Free Press*, *Tribune*, and *Post* all maintained their profitability if not their readership. The upscale papers were, like the *News*, insulated from direct competition. The *News* was protected by price, while the elite journals, for their part, constructed barriers to competition based upon greater news coverage (including a monopoly of Associated Press wire services which the *Detroit News* lacked), partisanship, and a more elevated, less sensational tone.[76] As John Lodge, city editor of the *Free Press* in the 1890s, noted, his paper took as its "chief rival" the other elite, partisan paper, the *Tribune*, while ignoring the *News*.[77]

This opposition between morning and afternoon papers, subtended by distinctions of taste and social class, persisted well into the twentieth century, and not just in Detroit. For instance, Walter Dill Scott's careful 1908 study of the reading patterns of Chicagoans noted that the newspaper market was sharply bifurcated along class lines. Consequently he advised: "If [an advertiser] wanted to reach the better classes, he would use the morning papers; if he wanted to reach the laboring class, he would employ the evening papers."[78] For workers, evening papers were the papers of choice because, as the Lynds observed, "[W]orkers rising and getting to work an hour or two before [businessmen] seldom have time to read papers in the morning."[79]

Elite newspapers stagnated in market share until the mid-1880s when they too increased their subscriber base. This growth corresponded to their price cuts in 1884 and again in 1886.[80] In fact, "a conservative, well-edited and responsible [partisan] newspaper could find a sustaining audience" in the face of downmarket, sensationalist competition.[81] Despite their smaller circulation, upscale papers had a better profit margin for each individual paper sold. While the *News* grossed about one cent from each copy, the *Tribune* and the *Free Press* made three.[82] In addition, demographics aided in attracting advertising. Then, as now, advertisers preferred upper-class readers with their greater discretionary income and their control over corporate purchases.[83] Furthermore, both the *Tribune* and the *Post* could count on their status as the state's premier Republican journals to bolster their sales upstate and in campaign seasons. However, such economic advantages would be insufficient to sustain partisan journals when confronted by cheap popular competition. Partisan papers needed to cultivate their news coverage and not simply rely on partisan appeals. A conservative tactic of simply relying on political prestige and party loyalty to attract readers was inadequate. According to ex-editor Stocking, the floundering Republican *Post* displayed precisely this failing. It neglected the hunt for news leads: "[Editor-in-chief] Colonel Morley was economical to the point of parsimony and did not appreciate the opportunities which a modern news field affords."[84]

The "second revolution" of 1888

Despite their innovations, the first cheap afternoon sheets of the 1870s and 1880s maintained the conservative business orientations of traditional nineteenth-century entrepreneurs. The *Detroit Evening News*, for instance, was a family company, built with family capital, and staffed and controlled by Scripps' siblings and cousins. The paper adopted a limited market-niche perspective; instead of dynamically competing against other publishers for a mass audience, it sought out those segments of the market previously unaddressed.[85] In addition, the publishers distrusted all dependence upon advertising and banking capital as a potential threat to the autonomy and purity of their enterprise. Penny-pinching in production allowed newspapers to subsist on subscriber pennies for their income.

Developments in the late 1880s rendered obsolete James Scripps' model of a small, cheap newspaper. The first revolution in newspaper economics was overthrown by a second revolution sweeping American cities. This upheaval reflected not so much the newspaper industry's "natural evolution" towards "maturity" and concentration, as general transformations in the American economy – specifically a shift towards a corporate-organized consumer society. As newspapers profitably met the novel challenges of their economic environment, they radically incorporated the pluralism, the pizzazz, and the distractions of civil society. Their content focused less narrowly on the pronouncements of official speakers and on the affairs of parties. Journals supplemented politics with the spectacles and diversity of consumer society.[86] Ineluctably the press acceded to a dynamic commercial logic of profit-seeking, audience-maximizing, and market concentration.

These new economic pressures fueled the final angry split between the Scripps brothers, Edward and James. In 1887 with an attack of gallstones and presentiments of an early death, James Scripps had retired from business to tour Europe. He called in brother Edward to manage the Scripps Newspaper League. However Edward's management policies in 1888 soon sparked James' criticisms. In 1889, in an angry climax to the growing dispute over the appropriate policies, James returned to the US and abruptly fired Edward. From that time onward the two brothers went their separate ways, pursuing their distinct journalistic destinies.

George Booth, James Scripps' son-in-law, reminisced over these events some thirty years later in a manner seemingly calculated to please the social historian. In his essay "Looking Backward" he wrote: "As I look back upon this era, I am much impressed with the belief that these contentions, which lasted for many years, were more natural than the participants supposed. They were attributed then to personal reasons when in all probability they were rooted in the newspaper revolution begun at this time."[87] What appeared as a personality conflict between brothers was actually a personalization of abstract forces, a reflection of the changed economic constraints confronting the operation of daily newspapers. Booth wrote with an element of reflective pathos, since he was tied by familial bonds and economic dependence to James, while recognizing that Edward better understood the demands of the market. Booth joined the management of the *News* in 1888 at the time of this upheaval and with the ouster of Edward soon became heir apparent to Scripps' journalism kingdom.

As with all sibling rivalries, the dispute between James and Edward featured a melange of grievances, suspicions, and misunderstandings. First of all, James feared for the future profits of the *Evening News*. He desired regular dividend payments yet Edward Scripps was investing the paper's income in a rapid-expansion program with questionable chances of success. Besides increasing the printing-production capacity of the newspaper plant in Detroit, he was subordinating the *Evening News* and its profits to continued investment in an expanded chain of papers. In effect, Edward's business decisions threatened to destroy Scripps' ideal form of a small, independent and profitable newspaper.[88] Lastly, Scripps feared Edward's ambition for dictatorial power. Edward innovated and changed the *News*'s traditional financial policies in ways that enhanced his own power while neglecting to gain James' approval in London.

From Edward's point of view the *Evening News* needed to increase its daily pages. He predicated this project of expansion upon a rapid decline in the price of paper and the likely response of the journalistic competition. Explaining his analysis to the new business manager in Detroit, George Booth, he wrote:

The cost of paper is racing down hill . . . I prophesy that very little paper will be sold during 1890, at a higher price than three cents. This means that the competition will require larger papers . . . I believe that the time is shortly coming when the [Cincinnati] *Post* will print for a cent an eight page paper as big as the [two cents] *News* is now.[89]

Edward also reasoned that a massive increase in advertising justified a program of speedy growth in both newspaper size and production facilities. On May 30, 1889, Edward typed:

[The *News* must enlarge] sufficient to monopolize the advertising business that can be gotten, [otherwise] some other papers must take it and over the profits grow rich and hence a powerful competition for the News . . . We have been leaving advertising out of the News at a rate of $1,000 a month. That money which advertisers are willing to spend in Detroit or at least a portion of it is going to *The Journal*, *The Free Press* and *The Tribune*, making them stronger financially and more fashioned for advertisers.[90]

Seeking to make the expansion of the *News* an irreversible fact (and to respond to the exigencies of the market) Edward Scripps committed funds to the purchase of new printing presses. Accompanying his unilateral actions was a barrage of arguments from Edward in Ohio to James in England.[91] But James remained unconvinced by Edward's pleas, and held onto his ideal of smallness. In a letter that survives only in a summarized form, James adamantly rejected the path of expansion:

Brief review of newspaper experience and policy – counsels small paper for reasons – have yield[ed] to enlargement owing to inability to get right men – upon my return and renewed health and vigor will endeavor to infuse my ideas – a paper to be read in one-half an hour and 12 columns of reading matter enough – Is still an open question as to what relation advertising will bear to the paper of the future . . . Has horror of changing News to quarto [eight pages length] . . . the News' circulation is its strength – circulation can grow as to make advertising unprofitable.[92]

On May 28th, 1889 reflecting the rapidly deteriorating relations between the two, the younger Scripps wrote:

Dear James, – yours of the 10th inst[ance] at hand. Some day, I hope you will learn to address me in a different tone, and from a different standpoint. Then there will be more pleasure for me, in working with you, and much more profits to you.

It seems to me, that you should have learned by experience, that if you wish to produce any effect on me, you will have to avoid such foolish tirades as these . . .

Do I understand you when you say, "That you will refuse to permit any press now in the News' office to be taken from it, also to accept from any source any seven column presses"; that you propose to invalidate contracts made by the Evening News Association with other parties?[93]

Seeking to convince James where it counted – in the pocket book – Edward contended:

However much you may [be] prepossessed in favor of the small paper, you will find yourself gracefully submitting to circumstances, especially when circumstances [that] compel enlargement of the paper will also compel enlargement of your profits . . . I am only looking facts in the face, knowing full well that we have not the power to resist temptation of sacrificing our theories to our great personal interest.[94]

Meanwhile, James Scripps was still envisioning a newspaper which would be priced at one cent, no more than four pages in length, and absolutely independent of advertising – in his proposal "the newspaper of the next 25 years."[95] George Booth later speculated:

It is . . . not unreasonable to suppose that a man like Mr. James E. Scripps of the old school of journalism and in a condition of poor health, felt it quite impossible [to] comfortably to enter upon this new era which meant a permanent discarding of his own ideal of a four-page daily newspaper . . .[96]

As letters crisscrossed the Atlantic, tensions heightened until James felt compelled to return to the States and the *Evening News*. Upon his arrival, Edward was deprived of all rights to run the *Detroit News* and the *Cleveland Press*. Deposed from power, Edward was greatly aggrieved. In his own words he was "very sore and very hurt," raging inside for the next two years.[97] In the split between brothers, Edward retained control over the *Cincinnati Post* and, with the connivance of brother George and sister Ellen, eventually managed to seize the stock of the Cleveland journal.

In essence, Edward Scripps asserted that fundamental characteristics of the economic environment had changed. Consequently, the Scripps newspapers must modify their tactics. These shifts were not just a matter of bigger or smaller profits for any individual journal, but were obligatory for the newspaper that wished to survive. Collapsing newsprint prices and rising advertising revenues rendered the small, well-trimmed, penny paper of James' dreams irrelevant, even dangerous, in the contemporary market. If the *Evening News* did not expand its pages, printing capacity, and paper purchases, so as to be able to encompass a proliferating demand for advertising space, then rival journals would seize this advertising revenue. These competitors would use the income to improve their product, increase their journal size, and reduce their prices – all potentially grabbing readers from the *Evening News*.

By and large, Edward Scripps correctly assessed the new, looming economic forces confronting the daily press in the late 1880s. These market forces destroyed the original premises for the afternoon papers' ascetic strategy of a reduced price based on lowered production costs. Starting in 1886, advertising revenue at the *News* rose as a share of the paper's profits, rocketing from 38 percent of the gross profits to 58 percent in 1889. These changes, in fact, paralleled developments in advertising across the country. Census data for the nation show that advertising as a proportion of all periodical income climbed from 44 percent in 1879 to 49.6 percent in 1889 and continued in a steady upswing to 54.5 percent in 1899 and 60 percent in 1909.[98]

The increase in ad linage rested on a tremendous rise in "display" advertising. Department stores in the 1880s, following the lead of Wanamaker's in Philadelphia, began to use full-page ads to lure customers into their stores in large numbers. They strove to attract customers from throughout the streetcar city, thus creating high-volume sales.[99] For these stores, such as J. L. Hudsons and C. Mableys' in Detroit, the old static advertisements of a business card left unchanged for months would no longer suffice. Henceforth advertising copy should be changed daily and large enough to draw notice.[100] In the 1890s, this mutation in the retail trade was followed by a push for publicity by national brands. In fact, the US was shifting from an era of family firms serving local markets with a highly segmented demand to an era of corporate mass production for mass consumption. Corporations risked ever-increasing amounts of capital in fixed productive facilities, capable of high-volume manufacturing of cheap goods. In order to make a profit from these investments, firms needed to stabilize consumer demand and construct national markets. The advertising boom enriching newspapers (as well as magazines) emerged as a key part of their strategy.[101]

The explosion in advertising undermined the first premise of James Scripps' original ascetic program for a cheap, mass circulation newspaper. Falling paper prices challenged the second. To recall, Detroit's "first newspaper revolution" of 1873 responded to the difficulties that high paper costs and limited advertising posed for a cheap newspaper. With expensive paper pushing up the variable costs of production, there could be very little per unit reduction of costs with increased press runs. However, after 1873, the use of woodpulp in the manufacture of paper initiated a long-term national decline in newsprint prices. At the *Evening News*, even after a decade of falling prices, spending on paper still made up 31.4 percent of the expenditures for 1884. But by 1889 paper costs had fallen to 19.4 percent of the annual budget. Precisely as Edward Scripps was pointing out, the years of management conflict at the *News* in 1887–89 (and indeed the entire decade of the 1880s) corresponded to a massive decline in paper prices extending into the twentieth century. In response to shifts in paper costs, daily journals across the nation cut their prices.[102] Falling paper costs made James' original, conservative savings tactics irrelevant in the late 1880s.

In the end, newspapers adopted the dynamic competitive strategy outlined by Baehr and Ohmann: in a continual cycle of expansion, journals slashed their prices to entice new subscribers. With an increase in circulation, newspapers gained new revenues from advertisers and, in turn, expanded their news sections and cut prices once again. They thus attracted more and more readers in an unending dynamic of expanding consumption and intensifying competition.

Consequences of the "second revolution"

The 1888 revolution fundamentally altered the economics and circulation of Detroit's daily papers, and consequently the politics of the press. Turning again to Svennik Hoyer's stage model of economic development, Detroit's second revolution can be classified as part of the third and final "consolidation" stage of the newspaper market. In the second "expansion" phase, the number of newspapers grows along with an increase in readers. But, as manufacturers augment their productive capacity, the third and final consolidation period ensues. Publishers' enhanced productive output draws them into more strenuous competition. In place of the cheap self-sufficient bulletin sheet that aimed at a limited market-niche, there flourishes a new dynamic, expanding newspaper – hunting for ever more news, readers, and above all advertising. Eventually, says Hoyer, after a series of mergers and bankruptcies, publishers create an oligopoly or monopoly media market.

Indeed, by the 1890s the US newspaper industry in general and the Detroit press market in particular were entering a "mature stage" where the growth in readership was accompanied not by new production units, but by rising circulation in existing papers.[103] According to Hoyer, the actual onslaught of newspaper consolidation in the US as well as Western Europe ensued in the early 1900s, after an immense proliferation of papers and readers in the second half of the nineteenth century. American press historian Edwin Emery roughly concurs with this timing, stating that in the US, the First World War "only accentuated trends which were developing as early as 1890."[104] Already in 1902, Milton McRae excitedly wrote to James Scripps and expounded on the shifts in the press business. From his vantage point as manager of the national (Edward) Scripps–McRae (later Scripps–Howard) chain of newspapers, he observed a rage of consolidation. "Everywhere it seems that the force of money has been used to crush out competition as far as it could do so." "What does this all mean? It simply means the centralization, consolidation and concentration idea which is sweeping this country, has been applied to newspapers as everything else. The stronger papers are becoming stronger and the weaker papers are having a hard time to exist . . ."[105]

From this consolidation stage of press markets, Hoyer deduces certain political consequences for the partisan press. Consolidation means reduced press competition and consequently fewer incentives for newspapers to segment the market. Newspapers in competitive struggle for circulation and advertising drop their old "specialist" strategies of appealing to a delimited political community and adopt a more neutral political attitude to attract a broader, general public.

However, the Detroit (and indeed the American) press market presents a more complicated picture – both politically and economically – than that delineated by Hoyer. Economic historians like Hoyer often treat the consolidation stage as the natural product of an industry's internal evolution. They remain captivated by the cultural spell of the "Fordist Age of mass production," even as the world economy is increasingly characterized by more flexible firms serving ever-smaller, more specialized, and more transitory taste markets. From a traditional "Fordist" perspective, industries naturally evolve towards the ever more efficient supplying of standardized goods to a mass market. Economic rationality seems to pose only one solution towards providing society with consumer goods: the large-scale national corporation with its high-volume, assembly-line production, that in turn creates the goods for an integrated system of distribution, marketing, and sales.

This deterministic economic theory abstracts from the historical conditions necessary for mass production. Unless there exists a relatively stable mass consumer demand, mass production and consolidation will not occur. Entrepreneurs will not risk the large sums of capital required by mass production's fixed machinery and inflexible organizational forms. Yet a mass demand is neither natural nor automatic. Given distinctions in public tastes, consumers will not necessarily choose a generic form of a product, even if cheaper. Indeed, as long as differences in journalistic interpretations and tone remain salient, readers will not inevitably purchase the cheaper paper. They will not necessarily buy a uniform apolitical news. With the news, as with other commodities, a homogenized mass consumer taste is not automatically given, but must be politically and culturally constructed.

Certainly, the US, as Charles Sabel and Jonathan Zeitlin point out, has historically been the country where mass taste has most fully predominated. In contrast to the old world of Europe, the US lacked aristocratic traditions of specialized tastes and regulated, guild-controlled markets of skilled artisan labor. Consequently, the Fordist model was invented here and has continued to hold sway.[106]

In the specific case of journalism, the questions arise: what accounts for the relative homogeneity of the US media market? Why does a generic commodity called "the news" – coming in only one package and uninfluenced by competing social interpretations – dominate the press? As a glance at other early-twentieth-century capitalist democracies would readily show, often a society is so contested and polarized along class, religious, or ethnic lines that there exists no single social interpretation that can be unproblematically packaged and distributed to the whole nation as "news."[107] In contrast, in the US, after the crash-up of the Populist party in 1896, sharp social divisions were missing from the public realm. The two major parties did not articulate significant social cleavages, thus creating an implicit social consensus. Journalists could draw upon this consensus to present "impartial and factual" news accounts that seemed to contain no point of view or interpretation. In sum, to explain the rise of non-partisan papers, this chapter's economic discussion needs to be supplemented by a political and cultural analysis of consumer demand.[108] Such a political explanation for why both American news producers and consumers preferred a politically denuded, unified news is advanced in the next chapter.

We can note, however, that even prior to political changes at the turn of the century, Detroit and American publishers were guided by the Fordist imagery of an undifferentiated news product supplied to an inclusive mass audience. They were influenced by the cultural mythology of an American society made uniform and harmonious through standardized mass production and consumption.[109] James Scripps, for instance, argued already in 1879 for a consolidation of the market around the production of a standardized news product. Consolidation, he argued, would enhance economic efficiency and news quality, but he studiously ignored the consequences of a loss of diverse political perspectives:

I believe there are too many newspapers, not alone for the good of their publishers, but for that of the community. With two rival grocery stores the public gets its tea and its sugar at cheaper rates. It is not so with its newspapers . . . the expense of printing two newspapers . . . is double what the costs of a single paper would be . . . With the diminished patronage both papers must be inferior in quality to what they would otherwise be, and their circulations being smaller, advertisers, of course, must receive correspondingly less benefit . . . The remedy for supernumerary papers is consolidation . . .[110]

Similarly, Edward Scripps in 1902 argued for a uniform factual notion of the news that would satisfy a variety of people despite the disparity of their personal beliefs. "[A]ny city had enough people of differing points of view to justify an equal number of newspaper exponents, but when it came to news one paper was as good as a dozen; the public only expected truthfulness, enterprise and industry in printing the news, and did not care what the editor's views were."[111]

However, even if we ignore cultural and political developments and focus on economics alone, Hoyer's model needs to be rendered more complex. The revolutions in the Detroit newspaper business were propeled not just by automatic economic processes specific to the industry, such as increasing printing-plant efficiency: the industry's competitive hunt for readers and its subsequent consolidation also reflected the US's broader economic turn to mass production and mass marketing.[112] As already noted, advertising emerged as a central component of the industrial transformation. This commercial publicity entailed numerous consequences for the journalistic trade. With advertisers filling their coffers, journals advanced towards a dynamic economic strategy; newspaper production costs were underwritten by advertising income, thus spurring price cuts and the pursuit of a mass undifferentiated audience. With rivals too reducing prices and offering more pages packed with journalistic attractions, the urban newspaper market turned dynamic and competitive.

In such a dynamic market, publishers confronted heightened barriers to the founding of new journals. On the one hand, the requisite start-up costs and capital investments multiplied. Increased competition for news entailed a multitude of expenditures: a larger editorial staff to cover local news and sports, and the subscription to wire services and syndicate features. Soaring circulation necessitated the purchase of the newly invented typesetting machines and the latest model of Hoe cylindrical printing press.[113] As McRae observed in 1902, "The fact that so many presses are being built with no new papers starting is conclusive proof, that the old papers are improving their plants, enlarging their papers, etc." On the other hand, the number of readers needed to break even at competitive prices increases. New publishers must struggle against the entrenched position of established papers before they can secure a large enough share of the market to return a profit.[114]

Newspapers struggle, fail, or more typically are bought out by rival papers, because of heightened competition and production costs. Indeed, consolidation makes increased economic sense once market barriers insure that the elimination of any individual paper will not spur the entrance of new ones. At the turn of the century, newspapers, especially chains, commenced buying out market rivals. At the forefront of this merger mania were the newspaper leagues of Hearst and Scripps–McRae.[115]

Advertisers constituted an additional force for the transformation of the newspaper field. They recognized, as Scripps contended in 1879, that fewer newspapers meant increased economies of scale and hence cheaper rates for advertisers. In city after city, advertising consistently patronized the circulation leader in a manner disproportionate to its actual number of readers. The better-off papers thrived while the poorer journals were forced into "oblivion."[116]

The subsequent history of the daily press in America and in Detroit suggests the consequences of these pressures for consolidation. Between 1879 and 1909 new dailies proliferated across the US, peaking at 2,609 in 1909. But thereafter the number of newspapers rapidly dwindled, falling to 2,441 dailies in 1919 and 2,080 by 1932.[117]

Detroit's long-term drive towards a monopoly market dates from 1891 when *Evening News* publisher, Scripps, bought the *Tribune*. The final entrant into the metropolitan newspaper field occurred with the founding of the *Detroit Times* in 1899. Priced at a penny, the *Times* was cheaper than the *News* and perpetually struggling until 1922 when it was bought by the Hearst chain. The *Times* grabbed a market niche that Scripps had long recognized as vulnerable.[118] Thus, at the start of the century, four publishers owning five papers fought for the attention of the Detroit public. In 1905 Scripps began negotiating with Quinby for the purchase of the *Free Press*. The deal was queered by fellow Detroiters, Col. Hecker, Freer, and McMillan. They feared Scripps' too-great influence on city politics if he acquired a third paper. In 1906, these three sold a share of the *Free Press* to Edward Stair who already owned the *Journal*. As a result, Detroit possessed five papers but only three managements. In 1915 the *News*'s owners shut down the *Morning Tribune* which by then was a mere appendage to their evening paper. Four years later the *Journal* was purchased by the management of the *Evening News* and closed. Three dailies remained alive. From here Detroit followed the usual scenario for American cities in the second half of this century. The *Times* lasted until the 1960s. In the 1980s, Detroit's final two journals, the *Free Press* and the *News*, adopted a joint operating agreement which merged their operations.[119] The nineteenth-century world of a multitude of contending, opinionated, political journals had long departed.

Advertising portended other consequences for the burgeoning metropolitan journal beyond increasing competitive pressures. In their hunt for customers, and to clothe their added girth in commercial publicity, journals expanded their pages. For example, in the course of the 1880s, Pulitzer's *New York World* jumped from four to eight to fourteen pages, reaching sixteen in the 1890s, while Detroit papers too doubled and tripled in size.[120] As McRae mused, "Where is the ideal [four] page paper we used to talk about? The Evening News was the prototype of an [four] page condensed newspaper for all at one time. Take a glance at the News today and note the change."[121]

Following Pulitzer's lead, the press added new sections, catering to an array of advertising interests and customers, most notably: sports, comics, and a woman's page.[122] With such an assortment of topics, the newspaper became different things to different people, mimicking the consumer economy of which it was both product and chief organ. Journalism thus abandoned Scripps' nineteenth-century republican ideal of a unified community engaged in reasoned, political dialogue. Instead, in the imagery of Edward Scripps, the newspaper was a great big restaurant, filled with bustle and noise, and tantalizing the customers with a jumble of smells.[123] Others likened the press to a "department store," or a "dime museum" filled with sights varied and bizarre. As these metaphors of the new consumer society suggest, the reader was no longer addressed solely as an engaged citizen or partisan, but also as a consumer, customer, and passive spectator.[124]

This increasingly heterogeneous content helped free the paper from the political demands of its readers. If the paper offended a reader because of a divisive political position, then there existed other, perhaps more important and cross-cutting, bases of subscriber loyalty.[125] Perhaps nothing dissolved the traditional republican political associations of the press as much as the inclusion of women in the reading audience. Publishers catered to women readers who they considered an attractive demographic draw for advertisers. The Gilded Age press, like the department store, evolved into a new public space suitable for the promenading of middle-class women down its columns.[126]

In many ways advertising induced a reconstruction of the reigning notions of journalism. Newspapers, as Edward Scripps averred, needed to be "fashioned for advertisers." In the perhaps naive assessment of E. L. Godkin, a leading public intellectual, publishers now quaked and cowered before the power of advertisers. Godkin's pronouncement constituted standard criticism in the early 1900s. Progressive reformers often feared the ability of concentrations of wealth and power to corrupt the public realm.[127] But, in truth, advertising worked in more subtle ways than Americans with their republican fears suspected. As Paul Weaver argues, advertising shifted the very size and definition of the audience to which a journal was responsive. With advertising's growth, readers' pennies no longer directly counted. The individual paper stopped emphasizing a core community of readers especially interested in the news or tied to a shared public identity. Instead, with their prices falling, "the media began to focus on the marginal customer, who, despite little interest in the news and little willingness to pay for it, was the building block of the ever-bigger audience sought – and paid for – by advertisers."[128]

Conclusion

In conclusion, the years 1870 to 1910 were the boom years, the "expansive phase," of American print media. Late nineteenth-century newspapers underwent a tumultuous economic revolution which touched and tinged every facet of the journalistic enterprise – from the heft and hew of the daily paper, to the content and form of the news story, to the size of the audience. On the backs of corporate and retailer demand for a mass audience, Detroit newspapers reached out to the previously ignored and excluded mass of the working population. The press enlarged to incorporate the vast majority of Americans into its reading audience. The interests of corporate America in reaching all potential consumers fortuitously coalesced with democracy's ideal of including all citizens in the nation's cultural and political dialogues.[129] In this process of expansion and commercialization, the pull of politics and parties was everywhere diminished. Coverage of politics declined.[130] Papers averted their eyes from the affairs of state, lowered their gaze from the concerns of the commonweal, and most of all shifted their focus from the dramatic spectacle of partisan combat.

As they expanded their circulation and their revenues, and as their investments multiplied, journals increasingly shifted from a political enterprise to a big business. The constraints of the market and the incentives of profit-making weighed ever more heavily on the conduct of journalism.[131] With large sums of capital potentially at risk, newspapers had to be treated as a serious business in their own right; a charity, a political platform, a public service – only secondarily. Newspapers became progressively less beholden to politicians. Rising market barriers and financial risks deterred politicians from investing in newspapers purely for the sake of punishing enemies or gaining a sycophantic mouthpiece. Party leaders could no longer discipline wayward partisan sheets by establishing new, rival organs more committed to political orthodoxy. Thus, the journals of this era were more secure from the wrath of disgruntled political leaders.[132]

These economic transmutations created both a motive and preconditions for the press's general divestment of its public, personal partisanship. However, despite the weakening pressures for political advocacy, partisanship remained the norm in the final years of the nineteenth century. Both popular and elite papers, such as the *Detroit Journal* and the *Detroit Free Press*, as well as journals of a national stature, for example the *New York Times* and the *New York World*, maintained a public partisanship, and often found this public identity economically advantageous. Urban press markets remained highly competitive and dailies continued to appeal to audiences defined by their party attachments.

From the Reconstruction Era to the political upheavals of 1894–96, the press watered down its biased political content. But, like good Scotch, partisanship apparently could be diluted with more and more columns of human interest stories without destroying its political flavor, without weakening the paper's formal and public political affiliation. Partisanship remained as salient among journals as among readers. Only significant upheavals in the system of party power and massive disruptions of popular political loyalties would permit the American press to break from its bonds of political allegiance and adopt a pose of disinterested impartiality.

NOTES

1 White 1888: 691; and cf. Emery 1972: 292, 393.
2 McGerr says that late nineteenth-century journalism was wrenched by revolutions in economics, news, and professional organization. He provides no strong description of these changes. This chapter focuses on the economic revolution and to a lesser degree the news revolution. For McGerr, none of these transformations was adequate to explain the cessation of partisanship (McGerr 1986: 111 and ch. 5). I agree, although I present a different how and when for this change.
3 Foner 1988: 260–9.
4 That is circulation rate as compared to size of the population. Strictly speaking, this does not tell us what percentage of the population read papers, since one journal was likely read by more than one person. However, by 1910 New York newspaper circulation equaled 92.5 percent of the population. Figures for New York taken from Lee 1947: 731; for Detroit, George P. Rowell & Company, *American Newspaper Directory*, and Bureau of the Census 1972.
5 Baehr 1972: 182, 232.
6 Scripps 1966: 317–18.
7 Britt 1960: 29 and 61. Also see McCabe 1951: 47.
8 Baehr 1972: 234. Similar changes in England are known as "the Northcliffe Revolution." See Seymour-Ure 1968: 22, 32, 98.
9 Ohmann 1981: 89–90; also see Norris 1990: 31, 35–7.
10 On paper costs see the informative article, Smith 1964: 328–45.
11 Udell 1978: 118 and in general 118–25.
12 Scripps, untitled essay beginning "In April 1871 . . ." in "James E. Scripps

Letters, etc. 1906–7" (Cranbrook Archives). Internal dating suggests the essay was written in 1875.

13 Pound 1964: 98.

14 Catlin, "Detroit Journalism," (manuscript) 18 in George B. Catlin Papers (Burton Historical Archives) and cf. James Scripps, "In April 1871 . . ." 1–2.

15 Gardner 1932: 26.

16 Letter, James Scripps to Edward Scripps, Sept. 18, 1884 quoted in Scripps 1966: 53.

17 Gardner 1932: 26–9; Britt 1960: 36–7; McCabe 1951: 48–50.

18 Ibid., 26; McCabe 1951: 48.

19 McCabe 1951: 40 and see 60.

20 Condensation as a journalistic practice spread to all the Scripps papers. See the letters Edward Scripps to George Booth Aug. 18, 1891 and Edward Scripps to James Scripps Nov. 11, 1887 both in George G. Booth Papers (Burton Historical Archives), and Scripps 1966: 38, 43.

   Even editorials under the pen of Michael Dee partook of this more condensed but lively style. They "seldom exceeded a paragraph in length," and Dee "avoided the heavy, ponderous, prosy style of the prevalent political editorials" (Catlin 1926a: 29).

21 Scripps makes a statement for inclusiveness in "Why I Started the Evening News," published in the first issue of the *News*, Aug. 21, 1873. For a discussion of late nineteenth-century cultural categories such as consumption and production, asceticism and hedonism, character and personality, see Susman 1984: ch. 14; and Kaplan 1988: ch. 1. On the republican ideal in newspapers see Schiller 1981.

22 Britt 1960: 33.

23 Publisher Scripps can be compared to another Detroit innovator and entrepreneur: Henry Ford. Ford, according to Susman, expanded the possibilities for mass consumption. He elaborated an efficient, standardized production of cars that reduced costs even as he paid higher wages. All should have the opportunity to consume. But Ford's Model T represented an ascetic form of expanded consumption; for the sake of efficient production all Model T's were the same, standardized, black box. Everyone could now consume the new mass car, all could participate in a consumer culture but only in a limited, disciplined form. Ford resisted efforts to multiply the styles and colors that would allow "individual choice" and personality to be expressed through the purchase of a car. And he had a life-long hostility to the market which was manifested in a perverse form in his anti-semitic attacks. Only belatedly did Ford learn "a fundamental fact about the new and affluent mass society . . . price and efficiency alone would not dictate consumer choice." He acceded to multiple car styles and color shades only in the face of competitive pressure from General Motors. See Susman 1984: 131–41.

24 We may say that Scripps, like Ford, was intrigued by the social utopia or social imaginary of mass, standardized production. Cf. Sabel and Zeitlin 1985: 172–4. Part of this utopian imagery, says Fisher, was the notion of a "transparent democratic social space"; through standardized mass consumption, the diversity of the American population would be disciplined

and regulated, thus creating the social homogeneity necessary to sustain a nation-state; See Fisher 1988.

25 Pound 1964: 104. The *Libel News* (April 9, 1894, Burton Historical Collection) quotes Scripps: "I started out to make the *News* a clear, able and reliable paper, and have always kept that object in view: the *New York Post* was taken as my model." Godkin's *Post*, however, could not be the inspiration for the *News*, since Godkin took over the *Post* only in 1880, after the founding of the *News*. Perhaps Bowles's *Republican* is the more accurate source for this model of journalism. In any case, both Godkin and Bowles were leaders in the Liberal Republican movement which spoke to a genteel elite and attacked current journalism as too partisan and sensationalist. The *Tribune*, for which Scripps had been business manager, flirted with the Liberal Republican movement of 1872.

26 On the Liberal Republican ideal in journalism see Curl 1980: ch. 3.

27 Edward Scripps wrote to George Booth, "The New York World – a paper which I know he [James Scripps] despises both as a journalist and as a gentleman" (letter dated June 7, 1889 in George G. Booth Papers, Burton Historical Collection; and see Pound 1964: 99; Gardner 1932: 32).

28 Bingay 1949: 134.

29 McCabe 1951: 64, 98; and cf. Catlin 1926a: 29–30.

30 Letter, Edward Scripps to James Scripps, May 22, 1889 in George G. Booth Papers (Burton Historical Collection).

31 Quoted in Britt 1960: 40. Or, as Scripps wrote, "[S]oon enough the publishers of these [one-cent] papers learned that their prosperity depended upon their catering not only to the interests of, but to the prejudices of, the vulgar crowd" (Scripps 1966: 317–18).

32 On the *Cleveland Penny Press* see McCabe 1951: 94–101; the *Cincinnati Post* (1883) ch. 14; the *St. Louis Chronicle* (1880) see Scripps 1966: 45–6; the *Buffalo Telegraph* (1880). Scripps asserted his sympathy for workers in McCabe 1951: chs. 12–13.

33 Emery 1972: 292, 296–7, 393.

34 Britt 1960: 61; Emery 1972: 296–7, 393–7; and the list in Scripps 1966: 766–8.

35 Cf. Scripps 1966: 80.

36 Booth 1919: 4, manuscript in George G. Booth Papers (Burton Historical Collection).

37 Scripps 1879.

38 Rowell & co. 1870–78; Ayer & son 1880–90. The circulation numbers reported by Ayer generally correspond to those reported in business papers of the *News* management.

39 "As the market expands towards the middle and working-classes, political and social differences make it increasingly difficult to balance the diverse interests of readers within one journalistic product" (Hoyer, Hadenius, and Weibull 1975: 12 and 26–7). The number of producers expands along with the number of consumers, in part, because of the publishers' limited printing capacity.

40 For example, he invokes "the basic laws of market concentration" and says they apply to journalism. Elsewhere, he recognizes the variable cultural

definition of newspapers. Between different social groups the definition of a newspaper and the types of needs it satisfies changes. However, Hoyer fails to consider what this means for the different phases of first newspaper expansion and later paper concentration. See Hoyer, Hadenius, and Weibull 1975: 9.

41 In the words of Scripps: "Without exception the daily papers of my youth were all selling for five cents. A dollar a day was the common wage of my time. A five-cent paper cost five per cent of the workingman's daily wages, whereas a one-cent paper cost only one percent of his wage" (Scripps 1966: 317 and see 316). Along with a reduction in price, street sales, instead of subscriptions and home deliveries, made the *Evening News* accessible. Catlin notes, "At first the circulation of the Evening News was mostly in the form of street sales as the price of two cents enabled the average person to gratify his curiosity very cheaply" (Catlin 1945: 375).
    On the economics of the penny press, see Crouthamel 1989: 19–21, 44, 51–2; Schiller 1981: 12–14.

42 Worker wages taken from US Bureau of the Census, *Historical Statistics* tables D-735, D-738, D-740 for all non-farm employees. For further discussion of workers' standard of living see Zunz 1982: 227–40. It should be recalled that most of the working class in the nineteenth century lived on hand-to-mouth budgets, where all family members pooled their income, and children most often also worked.
    A number of simplifying assumptions plague this chart: (a) worker families typically could consist of a number of wage earners, often including children; (b) such a chart of wages gives no clear picture of how much discretionary income workers possessed, nor how important they conceived newspapers to be; (c) the proportion of newspaper costs to wages assumes workers are employed throughout the year; (d) if one subscribed for a month or a year the price of the journal was reduced, but this required more ready cash.

43 Baehr 1972: 182; and more generally on the upper-class bias of the old partisan press see pp. 175–82. Also Slotkin 1985: 333, 437–8, chs. 15 and 18; and again see Scripps 1966: 317–18; and Curl 1983: 93–4, 142.
    Herbert Gutman adds an important qualification: larger cities in the Gilded Age, but not towns, were likely to be anti-worker in politics and press. See Gutman 1963; 1977: chapters 5, 5a.
    On Hearst and his working-class views see McGerr 1986: 127–8; and also Yellowitz 1965: ch. 9: on Pulitzer 126–7, 136; and Swanberg 1967: 122–3. On the Scripps' *Cleveland Penny Press* see Scripps 1966: 41–3. For all three see Emery 1972: ch. 20; and 296, 312–15.

44 In Woodward's famous accounting of the "compromise of 1877," elites in South and North were confronted by labor unrest. They consequently dispensed with their mutual hostilities, and established a *modus vivendi* that allowed each to consolidate control of their internal region. Parties turned right and internal factional splits, such as the 1872 revolt by Liberal Republicans, were quieted. The laboring man was denied a space at the political dinner table (1966; and Bender 1987: ch. 5).

45 Lutz 1973: 183, 186.

46 See the *News*, Feb. 11: 1907.
47 *Detroit Saturday Night*, Nov. 29, 1913, newspaper clipping in Booth Newspaper Letters, 1911–19 (Cranbrook Archives).
48 Cf. Villard 1918.
49 See Baldasty 1993.
50 Bow 1992: 5–6, 22; and 1989b: 8–12.
51 On the "great railroad strike of 1877" see Bruce 1959. On press reaction to the strike see Baehr 1972: 179–182; Slotkin 1985: 478–84. The *News* condemned the strike in editorials on July 23–8, 1877. Detroit's Democrat daily, the *Free Press*, denounced the strikers as mobs of criminals and communists July 21–31, 1877. On Chicago's press reaction see Nord 1984.
52 *Detroit News*, July 24, 1877: 2. At times, the *News* did equivocate on who was to blame for the national conflagration.
53 McCabe 1951: 70. James Scripps can probably be classified as a middle-class reformer, caught between the conflicting forces of a developing working-class and an emerging corporate capitalist society.
54 Cf. Swanberg 1967: 122, 173–4, 187–8
55 Booth letter quoted in Pound 1964: 162–3. No date is given but it is probably about 1895.
56 Lee 1947: 65–7, 82, 271, 278–9. And see Smith 1964: 341–3. Lee tells us that most of the massive growth in late nineteenth-century circulation occurred with the introduction of evening papers.
57 Zunz 1982: 106.
58 Despite the *News*'s rapid rise in circulation in the late 1870s, daily newspapers did not capture a larger share of the Detroit population for their readership – hovering around 30 percent of the population. The other newspapers stagnated in their market share until the mid-1880s when they too grew in subscriber base as they reduced their prices. However, in the 1880s the circulation of the *News* hit a plateau that the publishers and editors repeatedly lamented. Only in the late 1880s and 1890s did total circulation of the dailies increase as a percentage of the population.
59 For the US in general, see Smith 1964: 341–2, 345.
60 Some potentially distorting assumptions are built into table 4.3: first, a good share of the rapidly rising population was ethnic immigrants with limited command of English. If we factor in this share of the population, the circulation of English language dailies rises from approximately 5 to 10 percent as compared with the English speaking population for the years 1880–1920. (A break-down of the relative ethnic background of the population can be found in Zunz 1982: 106.) Second, I neglect what amount of the circulation went to readers outside the city of Detroit (and New York). Over time the circulation of dailies probably became more centered in the metropolitan area. Third, more than one newspaper may have been bought by any individual.
61 Lynd and Lynd 1959 [1929]: 514.
62 Drawing upon library reader surveys of the period: Denning 1987: 220–1.
63 Baughman 1992: 11.
64 By 1990 only 62 percent of the adult population said they had read the day's paper. Cf. Leonard 1995: 178–9; Baughman 1992: 187–9.

65 See Bow 1992.
66 The Scripps paper in Cincinnati was Democratic. So was Edward Scripps'
    chain of newspapers, at least until the Progressive Era. Early on in the 1880s
    Edward Scripps had political aspirations. See Emery 1972: 297; and Scripps
    1966: 57.
        Hearst's first newspaper, the *San Francisco Examiner* was a Democratic
    party organ. It was purchased in order to support Hearst's father's successful
    drive for election to the US Senate. Hearst maintained the *Examiner* and
    later the *New York Journal* as Democratic papers until the early twentieth
    century, when his political aspirations took him out of the party and into his
    own third party. See Swanberg 1961.
        Pulitzer similarly maintained his papers as Democratic and into the
    twentieth century was a powerful force within the party. His power was
    magnified by the lack of alternative public voices after 1896 in a weakened
    Democratic party. Cf. McGerr 1986: 123–4, 129, 257; and Emery 1972:
    320.
67 Seitz 1916: 48. Seitz's practical judgment is confirmed by the political
    historians of today. By and large people in the poorer sectors of the cities,
    including Detroit (those who bought the cheap afternoon press), were
    Catholic, immigrant, workers. These Detroiters voted overwhelmingly De-
    mocratic for both class and ethnic reasons; see Jensen 1971: 309–15.
68 Catlin, "Story of the *Detroit Journal*, 1883–1892," in George B. Catlin
    Papers (Burton Historical Collection), 1, 4–5.
69 From 1888 through 1904 the *News* advocated Democratic candidates and
    policies. Cf. the *Free Press*, Jan. 4, 1891 on the *News* as a Democratic
    paper.
70 Examples of this policy of the Scripps to change and shape their newspapers'
    politics in order to enhance their profits are contained in: Letter, Edward W.
    Scripps to James Scripps, Feb. 18, 1889; Letter, Edward W. Scripps to
    George Booth, Feb. 20, 1889; Letter, Edward W. Scripps to George Booth,
    Feb. 25, 1889; Letter, Edward Scripps to James Scripps, May 22, 1889 (all
    four letters are in George G. Booth Papers [Burton Historical Collection]);
    and McCabe 1951: 161 and ch. 14.
        Still, the Scripps newspapers responded to the fundamental partisan
    divisions in American nineteenth-century politics. Despite (or because of)
    their pragmatic, profit orientation they were obliged to respond to the
    partisan loyalties of their readership, and also the way in which the news-
    paper market was divided up into segments based on reader partisanship
    preferences.
71 Letter, James E. Scripps to George G. Booth, June 17, 1896 (Cranbrook
    Archives). Actually, Scripps was an ardent supporter of Bryan; here, he was
    disguising his wishes in pragmatic economic rhetoric.
72 As quoted in Pound 1964: 162–3.
73 Letter, Edward Scripps to James Scripps, May 22, 1889 in George G. Booth
    Papers (Burton Historical Collection). On the *Post* and the Cincinnati
    market see Curl 1983: 91–4.
74 McCabe 1951: 161 and ch. 14.
75 Letter, Edward Scripps to James Scripps, May 22, 1889 in George G. Booth

Papers (Burton Historical Collection). For other examples of policy guided by profits and political market segments of partisans, see Letter, Edward W. Scripps to James Scripps, Feb. 18, 1889; Letter, Edward W. Scripps to George Booth, Feb. 20, 1889; Letter, Edward W. Scripps to James Scripps, Feb. 18, 1889; Letter, Feb. 25, 1889 (all in George G. Booth Papers [Burton Historical Collection]).

76 Schudson describes status distinctions among papers in the 1830s and late 1890s (1978: ch. 3).

77 John Lodge 1949: 58–9.

78 Scott 1921 [1908]: 382.

79 Lynd and Lynd 1959 [1929]: 471.

80 This price reduction was typical to upscale papers across the country in the 1880s. See Smith 1964: 343–5.

81 Cf. Curl 1983: 141–2; Baehr 1972: 265–7; and Catlin 1926: 529.

82 Cf. Baehr 1972: 238.

83 Ibid., 237. Cf. Seymour-Ure 1968: 99–101, 111.

84 Stocking 1915; reprinted in Fuller 1928: 891. In all games of power in state politics, most heatedly in the contest over the legislature's election of senators, the *Tribune* was an involved player. It is no surprise that the *Evening News* would reprint excerpts from the *Tribune*'s editorials as relevant news items.

85 Letter, James Scripps to Edward Scripps, Sept. 18, 1884 quoted in Scripps 1966: 53; and see Leach 1993: 17.

86 Cf. Paul Weaver's interesting if flawed analysis: Weaver 1994: ch. 2; also Scripps 1966: 60, 68–70, 200–1.

87 George Booth, "Looking Backward" (1919, manuscript) in George G. Booth Papers (Burton Historical Collection). On Booth's life see the biographies by Pound 1964; and McCabe 1951: 188–9.

88 Besides the documents already referred to and those below, other sources for this account are Pound 1964: 112–13, 123–30, 136. McCabe 1951: ch. 18. Regarding James Scripps' fears of Edward Scripps, see Scripps 1966: 70–2; and George Booth, "Looking Backward," 3 (1919, manuscript) in George G. Booth Papers (Burton Historical Collection).

89 Letter, Edward W. Scripps to George Booth, April 19, 1889 in George G. Booth Papers (Burton Historical Collection).

90 Parts of this letter are incoherent. Letter, Edward Scripps to James Scripps, May 30, 1889; also relevant is Edward Scripps to George Booth, May 22, 1889 both in George G. Booth Papers (Burton Historical Collection).

91 Letter, Edward W. Scripps to James Scripps, May 23, 1889 in George G. Booth Papers (Burton Historical Collection).

92 Letter Extract, James Scripps to Edward W. Scripps, May 14, 1889 in George G. Booth Papers (Burton Historical Collection).

93 Letter, Edward Scripps to James Scripps, May 28, 1889 in George G. Booth Papers (Burton Historical Collection).

94 Letter, Edward W. Scripps to James Scripps, May 23, 1889 in George G. Booth Papers (Burton Historical Collection).

95 Mentioned in Letter, Edward Scripps to James Scripps, Oct. 11, 1887, George G. Booth Papers (Burton Historical Collection).

96 George Booth, "Looking Backward" (1919, manuscript) in George G. Booth Papers (Burton Historical Collection).

97 Letter, Edward Scripps to George Booth, Sept. 12, 1889, George G. Booth Papers (Burton Historical Collection).

98 Percentages calculated from business statements for 1881–1906 in the "Quadrapartite folder," George G. Booth Papers (Burton Historical Collection). Source for the years 1873–76 is Pound 1964: 108. See also Kaplan 1995; national figures include magazines and come from the US census as reported in Lee 1947: 748–9; and cf. Ohmann 1981: 96. See the description of the impact of new advertising revenues on the *Emporia Gazette* in White 1946: 377, 401. Griffith 1989. Griffith 1984 focuses on the 1920s.

99 See Leach 1993: ch.1, 61–2, 123.

100 Pound 1964: 113; George Booth, "Looking Backward," 1 (1919, manuscript) in George G. Booth Papers (Burton Historical Collection). Presbrey 1929: chs. 37, 38; Schudson 1984b: 161–8.

101 In general see Ohmann 1981: 93–4. Also Chandler 1980.

102 Prices paid by the *NY Tribune* as reported by Lee 1947: 743–5. Jon Udell presents the price for newsprint from 1925 to 1976 in his *Economics of the American Press* (1978: 125). Lee 1917: 346–7; see also Smith 1964.

Booth writes in "Looking Backwards": "[In 1888 change] was taking place in almost every department. Print paper at that time was costing $3.60 per 100 pounds and from almost the very day I went into business there came a steady reduction in cost which continued until print paper was to cost less than 2 cents a pound. In 1917 it again reached the old time price."

103 Smith 1964.

104 Hoyer, Hadernius, and Weibull 1975; Emery 1972: 442.

105 Letter, Milton McRae to James E. Scripps, Jan. 2, 1902, James E. Scripps Newspaper Letters, 1892–1910 (Cranbrook Archives). McRae apparently also wrote to Edward Scripps about these market developments at the time. Knight makes reference to Edward Scripps' reply in Scripps 1966: 201.

106 Sabel and Zeitlin 1985; and see Sabel and Piore 1984: 40–2.

107 On comparative cleavage structures of the polity, see Lipset and Rokkan 1967; Alexander 1981: 31.

108 I am referring largely to the "fourth party system," 1896–1932. Most specifically, the lack of a working-class party and its affiliated newspapers, as was often found in European countries, in part accounts for the greater homogeneity in demand in the US press market.

109 On the long-term dominance of visions of America as a society of uniform visible equals, disciplined and made the same through standardized consumption or via participation in the public realm, see Carey 1989: ch. 5. Also see footnotes 24 and 26.

110 Scripps 1879; and see Scripps 1966: 201.

111 Scripps 1966: 201.

112 See Sabel and Piore 1984: chs. 2–3; and Ohmann 1981. Scripps' turn to increased mass circulation paralleled the national turn to mass production and national markets.

113 See Salcetti 1995: 51, 53. Curl discusses the increased economic costs for the *Cincinnati Commercial* in the competition to obtain the news in the 1870s (Curl 1983: 91–2 and esp. 141).

114 Cf. the general discussion of barriers to market entrance in Caves 1977: 24–8; On comparable press dynamics in Great Britain see Seymour-Ure 1968: 105–8, 114–15.

115 Emery 1972: ch. 22.

116 Hoyer, Hadenius, and Weibull 1975: 20–2; Scripps 1966: 201, 68. Compare Seymour-Ure 1968: 107–9.

117 Lee 1947: 723.

118 Among other letters see Edward Scripps to James E. Scripps, January 22, 1889 in George G. Booth Papers (Burton Historical Collection).

119 Angelo 1981: 3–20, 115–6, 120, 143; Ferman 1963; Louis L. Richards, "History of the *Detroit News* and its personnel between 1891 and 1931" (N.D., manuscript) 18–19 (Cranbrook Archives); Franklin 1993: 15–16.

120 Detroit papers on average moved from four pages in the late 1870s to eight and twelve pages in the early 1890s. More elite papers, for instance the *New York Post* and the *New York Tribune*, doubled their pages to eight just when they reduced their price to three cents in the early 1880s. See Smith 1964: 342–3, 345; Lee 1947: 322–6.

121 Letter, Milton McRae to James E. Scripps, Jan. 2, 1902, James E. Scripps Newspaper Letters, 1892–1910 (Cranbrook Archives).

122 Griffith 1989: 215–16. The Lynds in their survey of Middletown's newspapers measured shifts in the press content between their two dates of 1890 and 1920. See Baldasty 1991.

123 In the eyes of the genteel elite, this commercial press was escaping the control of the legitimate cultural arbitrators and catering to the undisciplined tastes of the masses. See Kaplan 1988: ch. 1, and especially 29; cf. Seitz 1916: 93.

124 See Seitz 1916: 93; Baldasty 1991. Baldasty, among others, sees the change as one from citizens to consumers. While certainly it is true that the press in a capitalist society comes to the reader via market exchanges, it is not the case that consideration of profits and audience maximization, and selling to consumers ever fully define the press's content or its modes of addressing its audience.

125 No individual audience segment is so large as to impose its political agenda (or any politics at all) upon the paper. In other words, the pluralization of the audience increases the autonomy of the newspaper from the demands of its (political) environment. See Alexander 1981.

126 On the gendered nature of nineteenth-century public space, see Ryan 1990. On the press see Leonard 1995: 19–28. On changing notions of the public with inclusion of women see Schudson 1978: 128–31. On the orientation to women as readers see 99–101; and Baldasty 1992: 126–7, 153–5. On advertisers' desire to reach women see pp. 117, 65. Baldasty notes that society and women's sections filled 2.5 percent of the news space in the early 1800s, and 6.3 percent at century's end.

127 Godkin 1898: 195; and Ross 1918.

128 Weaver 1994: 46. Leonard in his important account of the expansion of the

audience for newspapers discusses a variety of "low-minded" commercial inducements – prizes, special discount offers, the razzmatazz of newsboys in the streets – as necessary supports for the press expansion. This "cornucopia of the market" most fully comes into play when the press is motivated by the advertiser's dollar to focus on the marginal customer (Leonard 1995).

129 Cf. Leonard 1995: pt. 3. During the next half century this fortuitous coincidence appeared as journalism's necessary and natural ideal state. For Progressive historians, this ideal of an independent, commercially supported, professionally governed press addressing a mass-universal audience was the goal to which the press had always been slowly and surely progressing. Cf. Hallin 1994: ch. 9.

130 See chapter 5.

131 Seymour-Ure 1968; Howells 1957: 209, 155–6; Baldasty 1991: 408; Emery 1972: 332–3.

132 Compare Seymour-Ure 1968: 97–8, 22.

5   1896 and the political revolution in Detroit journalism

1896 was an epochal moment in the history of American journalism. In that year Adolph Ochs, a stalwart Tennessee publisher, journeyed to New York City, bought a minor straggling daily, and transformed it into the leading national paper for the twentieth century: the *New York Times*. Ochs' rejuvenation of the *Times* into the most prominent elite paper blithely ignored the historic newspaper battles occurring down the street. As Ochs labored to raise the *Times*'s circulation from a mere nine thousand copies sold a day, William Randolph Hearst and Joseph Pulitzer were waging journalistic war for the hearts and minds of America's immigrant and working masses.[1] The circulation fights of these masters of sensationalism were the historical culmination to an economic strategy of a cheap, down-market sensationalist newspaper. James Scripps' *Detroit Evening News* had prefigured this strategy two decades earlier, but Scripps had never imagined that his model of a cheap, condensed news sheet could find a daily audience of a million readers.

But more importantly, 1896 shook the world of American journalism because of the drama of the fall presidential election. The election race pitted populist reformer William Jennings Bryan against the self-declared establishment defender, Republican William McKinley. The campaign blew across the political map like a seismic twister, and blasted apart the political system of the Gilded Age. When the election storm subsided, the American political landscape was no longer recognizable. Newspaper politics too fell victim to the tempest of the campaign season. In the gale winds of political passion stirred up by Populists, Democrats, and Republicans, the nation's dailies were buffeted, battered, and blown every which way across the political map.

This chapter argues that Detroit newspapers, like their counterparts across the country, broke from traditional ties of party commitment only in the context of this political upheaval. The "critical realigning election" of 1896 upset the steadfast political loyalties of millions of Americans. The election campaign, and the reform movements that

140

followed in its wake, initiated fundamental changes in the US polity, most importantly the displacement of political parties from their nineteenth-century centrality. With this collapse in the power and prestige of parties, America's daily journals boldly issued their declarations of independence.

In their fight for political independence the daily press joined forces with the early twentieth-century Progressive reform movement. Together, reporters and reformers articulated a vision of a reconstructed polity – a democracy purged of the corruptions, the strategic distortions, the emotional allegiances, and the expressive rituals of parties. As they worked to renew American politics, Detroit's editors and publishers also recast journalism's role in the public realm. They drew upon the political rhetoric and ideals of Progressives to elaborate a new public philosophy for the press. Instead of a committed partisan advocate no matter what their party's fortunes or follies, early twentieth-century journalism aspired to a new independent role in the arena of democratic discussion. The press proclaimed that henceforth it would publish only an impartial and factual account of the day's most important events. The daily paper would be guided by the ideal of "public service" without regard for any particular group's political or economic interests. Instead of personal views or political evaluations, journalists asserted that professional expertise would direct their news choices and interpretations. From avid party organ, the press supposedly became dispassionate recorder of American daily life and impartial arbiter of public debate. The press would insure that the public received "true," legitimate information, that is, facts undistorted by the propaganda efforts of large-scale economic or political interests. The news media would indeed be "mediators" standing between politicians and the public to guarantee that the populace would not be manipulated by the politician's cynical words.

To this day, the ideals and practices formulated by journalism in these early years of the century still grip the imagination of reporters, editors, and publishers. Even as their economic and political premises fade and crumble,[2] journalism's ideals of studied neutrality, technical expertise, and critical adversarial reporting hold the profession enthralled.

A political theory of press reform

Newspapers' abrupt departure from past patterns of exuberant partisanship cannot be explained by alterations in the urban newspaper market, as the previous chapter demonstrated. Nor is the journalist's desire for professional autonomy and prestige able to account for the press's revolt from political control. In the late 1800s, working journalists struggled to gain decent wages and job security. Failing to win such basics as a respectable standard of living, they certainly lacked the power to define the nature of the press's political commitments. Rather, as this chapter suggests, the reorientation of journalism's highest ideals from political advocacy to neutrality occurred at the behest of newspaper owners and managers.

Against the emphasis on markets or reporters' occupational ideals, this chapter argues for a political theory of press reform. The work of historian Michael McGerr offers an important precedent for such a political explanation. His analysis crucially directs our attention to the nineteenth-century press's strong cultural allegiances to parties and to its forceful advocacy of political goals. Before the press could depart from the ranks of party faithful, McGerr reasons that its cultural ideals would have to be modified. However, McGerr only focuses upon the changing political ideals of a limited upper-class elite – the Mugwumps – and cannot explain wholesale shifts in the political attitudes of average Americans. Mass institutions, such as parties and papers, are fundamentally dependent upon the resources of the many, and are not free to follow the whimsies of the few.

In contrast, this chapter maintains that journalism's changing politics reflects broader transformations in the press's political environment. Indeed, the press is permanently dependent upon the overarching institutions and political culture of the public sphere. What explains this dependence? Why is journalism not a self-sufficient institution? Why must the press continually rely upon the public sphere's cultural ideals and legitimate authorities to prop up its own journalistic observations, inferences, and reports?

The media's dependency derives from the type of authority asserted for its narratives. Far from being merely an interesting melange of facts and anecdotes, the press claims to provide an authoritative depiction of our social reality. Indeed, in some sense, journalism possesses special rights and exclusive privileges in recounting the life and times of American democracy. The news constitutes a public narrative of the nation. As such, the news commands the populace's interest and demands the citizenry's attention. In a democracy, however, all such rights of public representation stem from the broader ideals of the "public sphere." This more fundamental norm – the public sphere's cultural fiction – declares that the society's truths and values are the product of the collective deliberations of the citizenry. No one can permanently appropriate the right to name and define social reality. Instead, society's truths and norms rest upon the right of all to freely introduce their views, experience, and knowledge into society's debate.[3] The press always draws its justifications for the right to speak authoritatively from this broader democratic ideal.

Furthermore, the news as an authoritative public narrative becomes a "cultural focal point" and a crucial "symbolic resource" for contending social actors.[4] The news inevitably entails political consequences and confronts an array of critics and rival authorities in the public arena. These competing political speakers – whether they be the President, parties, individual politicians, or citizen advocates – often possess their own legitimacy and mandate to provide definitive interpretations of the day's events to the American citizenry.[5] In this overwhelming context of political dispute, the press seeks to ensure the cultural legitimacy and popular acceptance of its news reports.[6] To justify its particular narratives to mass public and elite alike, journalism draws upon the norms of the dominant political culture and defers to the issues and interpretations offered by "legitimate" political authorities. Consequently, any transformations in this broader public arena, with its distribution of legitimacy and power among rival public voices, will necessarily result in changes in the very definition of the news – in journalism's plots, in its rhetoric and narrative forms, and even in its public role in the political arena.

The emergence of an independent and impartial press in the early 1900s, thus, finds its explanation in fundamental disruptions in the American polity at the turn of the century. This political turmoil was rooted in the fiercely battled presidential campaign of 1896.

The battle of gold and silver

In 1893 an economic depression struck the US. From coast to coast factories shut down and workers were cast out onto the streets.[7] The Democrats, in control of both the White House and Congress, were blamed for the country's economic malaise. Public disapproval was already manifested in the election results of 1894. Meanwhile, the People's Party – the dissident movement of farmers – had been gathering strength since 1890 in the South and the West. In 1896 the weakened Democrats joined forces with these Populists. Uniting behind the presidential candidacy of William Jennings Bryan, the Democrat–Populist coalition immediately became the party of protest and reform. The long-standing grievances of farmers – oppressed by inequitable railroad rates, declining prices for agricultural goods, deflationary currency that increased their long-term debts, and inaccessible credit – burst into the two-party system.[8] The Democrats and Republicans absorbed these emotionally charged issues, but only at the cost of a reshuffling of their social bases of support. Furthermore, a widespread hysteria quickly overtook the Democrats' specific protest issues. The *Nation* declared, "Probably no man in civil life has succeeded in inspiring so much terror without taking life as Bryan."[9] The Democratic candidate was repeatedly denounced from the platform as well as the pulpit as a dishonest, dangerous demagogue, who would bring "repudiation, national dishonor and anarchy."[10]

Under Bryan, the farmers' diverse demands for economic relief and increased democracy were reduced to a plea for an inflationary silver currency. Standing before the Democratic national convention, Bryan famously attacked the nation's traditional monetary policy of a rigid gold standard. He vowed, "You shall not press down upon the brow of labor this crown of thorns, you shall not crucify mankind upon a cross of gold." The "battle between gold and silver" thus commenced.

The hysteria afflicting the country at large likewise inflamed the press. Reflecting the entrance of new class and sectional issues into the political realm, Detroit's newspapers waxed vastly partisan. According to my content analysis, in 1896, 85 percent of the editorials were openly partisan while biased reports filled 40 percent of the total news. In his diary the publisher of the *Detroit Evening News*, James Scripps, noted the passions provoked by the 1896 battle of standards, and he remarked on the consequences for all those, such as Scripps himself, who were pledged to William Jennings Bryan and the cause of silver currency. His entry for December 31, 1896 summarized the events of the year: "The campaign was conducted with a bitterness never before known and silver advocates are ostracized."[11]

As the newly charged party divisions of 1896 overturned the parties' traditional electoral coalitions, they necessarily influenced the parties' affiliated newspapers. The career of William Quinby, long-time proprietor of the state's major Democratic organ, the *Detroit Free Press*, illustrates these shifts in Detroit journalism. Quinby maintained strong links with the Democratic party establishment of Michigan.[12] But Quinby's political partisanship did not stop him from cultivating close ties to Detroit's elites, no matter what their political persuasion. In fact, Quinby was a conservative, "Gold Democrat," and when upper-class, good government reformers campaigned against Democratic corruption in municipal government, the *Free Press* joined the reformers. Similarly in 1895, when virtually the entire press and upper class mobilized against the provocative reforms of Mayor Hazel Pingree, Quinby's paper denounced the liberal mayor as ardently as the rest.[13] Thus it came as no surprise that Quinby broke with his party when the Democratic national convention nominated the populist Bryan and expelled Michigan's pro-Gold delegation. The typical integration of newspaper owners with party leadership and economic elites, described by Richard Slotkin, meant that papers were unlikely to follow the party into its reform alignment.[14] Publisher Quinby issued a "Declaration of Independence" renouncing all partisanship.[15] *Free Press* city editor and erstwhile Republican, John Lodge, read Quinby's editorial declaration "with a great deal of pleasure."

In fact, I had anticipated something of the sort, for Mr. Quinby had always been a Gold Democrat . . . When I had read it Mr. Quinby said: "John, does that satisfy you?" I said, "Of course it does . . . But do you remember what you have told me, not to inject my Black Republicanism into the paper? Does this mean the fetters are off so far as this campaign is concerned?" He smiled and said, "Maybe before long I'll be as black a Republican as you are."[16]

This departure of classic Democratic newspapers from the ranks of the party was typical for most daily Democratic papers throughout the nation.[17] Even liberal Democratic journals with a putative working-class audience such as Pulitzer's *New York World* or Edward Scripps' *Cincinnati Post*, not to mention conservative elite papers like the *New York Times*, fled the party in a mass exodus. At the close of the campaign, candidate Bryan remarked on this journalistic inequality between the two parties: "With all the newspapers of the country against us, our 6,500,000 votes is a vindication of which we have a right to be proud."[18] Earlier on the campaign trail he declared:

We do not have all the newspapers with us in this fight, but an editor only votes once and I have known some editors who have had so little influence that they could not even control the one vote which the law gives them. We would be glad to have the newspapers with us, but . . . we would rather have the people with us at the polls.[19]

The disparity nationwide between those journals loyal to the Democrats and those faithful to the Republicans decisively affected the campaign tactics of the two presidential candidates.[20] During the election season, McKinley never ventured far from his home in Canton, Ohio. However, he need not fear any lack of news coverage. Every day, as McKinley stood on his front porch and addressed a specially gathered crowd of well-wishers, his words were dutifully reported by the allied press. Bryan, on the other hand, could not count on reaching a broad public through the traditional means of party-affiliated papers. The man famed for his oratorical eloquence was forced to take to the stumps with a whistle-stop train tour of most of the country. About his Michigan tour Bryan wrote:

Friday was one of those long days. In order that the reader may know how much work can be crowded into one campaign day, I will mention the places at which speeches were made between breakfast and bedtime: Muskegeon, Holland, Fennville, Bangor, Hartford, Watervliet, Benton Harbor, Niles, Dowgaic, Decatur, Lawrence, Kalamazoo . . . [etc.]; total for the day, twenty-five.[21]

In Detroit and Michigan, Bryan at least gained the support of the Scripps' *News* and his *Tribune*. But he was still lacking in means of communication as Michigan's newspapers adopted the typical partisan tactics of grossly unequal coverage of the two sides' campaigns. As the *News* fretted in one editorial:

The *News* and the *Tribune* are the only papers in Detroit which are printing speeches delivered by Mr. Bryan in various cities in which he is visiting on his way to Lincoln. Why the other two dailies of Detroit should suppress these speeches is a mystery. Even the Eastern papers which are most vindictive in their opposition to the Democratic candidate, publish his speeches in full and allow their readers an opportunity to compare the arguments of Mr. Bryan with the editorial comments of the papers . . . [22]

Similarly, if less often, press loyalty to party was disrupted among Republican organs. As already noted in chapter 3, James Scripps took the *Tribune*, the official state Republican paper, out of the ranks of party faithful to the vociferous protests of leading Republican officials. Scripps had long been preoccupied with the issues of currency reform, corporate monopolies, and reduced import tariffs. In 1876, his paper had endorsed the Greenback candidate for president, while the 1880s brought the *News* into close alignment with the Democrats because of their shared positions on political economy. In 1896, in the words of a biographer,

James saw the silver issue as vital. It would not mean anything to him if he lost money through sticking to his principles, for in spite of his thriftiness no man had less hunger for money . . . When Detroit realized that Scripps through the columns of his papers was supporting Bryan and "Free Silver" the bank called his loan, advertisers dropped out and circulation of the *Tribune* dropped.[23]

Despite the break of two of Detroit's four newspapers from formal party allegiances, campaign reporting in 1896 fell into the typical forms of partisan news. Indeed, the new contentious class issues of the election infused established partisan genres with more than their usual energy. Reporters and papers elevated the two parties into potential savior and destroyer of the American nation. And the range of issues was seen as adequately contained in the positions and policies dividing the two parties. The news genres included standard morale-boosting articles focusing on the parties' campaign successes and, secondly, news reports that supposedly revealed the deleterious consequences of the opposed party's policies. In this case, the papers quoted the assertions of one factory owner after another that the country's continued economic prosperity was contingent upon the election of McKinley. Bryan's election, they proposed, would prompt an immediate resumption of the national depression that had struck in 1893. In addition, the journals published quips, editorials, and cartoons that aligned the newspaper explicitly with party in an active and evaluative, if juvenile, voice.

After 1896: disaffection and reform

1896 injected charged controversies and political passion into the polity. This outbreak of partisan fever naturally infected the political press as well as the electorate. In Detroit's dailies, political bias climbed to a feverish 85 percent of the editorial space and 40 percent of the news. The critical election, however, was immediately followed by a sharp decline in political passions, and the body politic enjoyed a respite from its political illness. Commencing in 1900, press political advocacy drastically decreased from its fairly constant late nineteenth-century levels. During the election seasons of the late nineteenth century, the majority of the sampled editorials had been explicitly partisan. In 1900 and thereafter, opinion pieces that explicitly evaluated the parties or their policies became a declining share of the editorial page. In the non-election periods, the fall in partisan editorials between the nineteenth and twentieth centuries was even more dramatic. From the Gilded Age's erratic 18–54 percent, editorials identifying with the fortune and fate of the party dropped to a minuscule 1–5 percent.

Turning to the news, the Detroit press typically filled about one-fourth of its news space with partisan articles during the presidential election campaigns of the late 1800s. In the early twentieth century, this evaluative and selective bias of the news decreased to 7 and then 5 percent. News in non-election seasons saw a sudden fall in partisanship to only trace elements in the early 1900s.

To summarize, in the early twentieth century overt, explicit partisanship in the news all but disappeared. Partisanship in editorials decreased to a small but still present amount. This continuing editorial partiality was however confined to the election season. The newspaper no longer engaged in a prolonged, year-round effort of proselytizing the voters or in a continual display of its formal allegiance to the party. Overt partisanship had disappeared. Covert bias had massively declined.

This sudden and complete eclipse of the fiery sun of nineteenth-century partisanship is explained by the ongoing transformations of the American polity in the early 1900s. The change unfolded in two stages,

Table 5.1. *Editorials in presidential election seasons*

	1868	1876	1884	1892	1896	1900	1908	1916
Partisanship as a percentage of editorials	81	78	62	52	85	29	28	17

Table 5.2. *Editorials in non-election seasons*

	1867	1875	1883	1891	1899	1907	1915
Partisanship as a percentage of editorials	54	40	18	34	5	1	3

Table 5.3. *News in presidential election years*

	1868	1876	1884	1892	1896	1900	1908	1916
Manifest bias (%)	9	12	17	9	30	12	7	0
Latent bias (%)	6	9	22	7	10	2	0	5
Total partisan news (%)	15	21	39	16	40	14	7	5

Table 5.4. *News in non-election years*

	1867	1871	1879	1887	1895	1903	1911	1915
Manifest bias (%)	2	0	2	1	8	0	0	1
Latent bias (%)	16	4	2	2	1	3	0	2
Total partisan news (%)	18	4	4	3	9	3	0	3

only slowly revealing the full consequences of the realigning election. First, the critical election disrupted traditional partisan identities. The election altered the social coalitions of voters supporting the two parties. As a result, the nature of the two parties' electoral competition changed. Secondly, while 1896 destabilized parties and modified the rules of the political game, political parties did not come under systematic attack until the early 1900s with the Progressive campaigns for political reform.

How did 1896 change the nature of American voting and parties? How did the election provoke the press's rebellion against all bonds of party servitude? In Michigan, as in the nation as a whole, the elections sparked a massive decline in voter participation. The 1896 "battle of standards" generated remarkable passions and interest, as well as a voter turnout of 95.3 percent in Michigan, substantially higher than the state's nineteenth-century average in presidential contests. But after this battle between gold and silver, Michigan's turnout immediately declined, reaching 78.9 percent in 1904, and continued falling in presidential elections to reach an abysmal 53.7 percent in 1924. Only in 1932 did the "New Deal realignment" initiate a temporary recovery in popular electoral participation.[24]

American historians variously explain the fall in voter participation by the dislocation of the conventional role of political parties. The upheaval of the 1896 campaign overturned years of steadfast party loyalties by millions of Americans. The *Detroit Free Press* and the *Detroit Tribune*, as official party organs for over thirty years, mirrored on a larger scale a multitude of individual decisions to break with one's party. Perhaps Detroit resident John Vallee Moran was typical of these traditional partisans. His son writes that this patriarch of a wealthy and prominent Detroit family was a well-mannered gentleman, polite to everyone. But every four years Mr. Moran was transformed: "[During presidential elections] father expressed his opinions freely, frequently, and pungently. A Democrat by heritage and early conviction, he remained one until 1896. After that and until his death he was a staunch Republican. He couldn't accept William Jennings Bryan and the "Free Silver – 16 to 1 – Platform."[25]

Furthermore, as Paul Kleppner tells us, parties after 1896 were less tied to particular ethnic–religious communities. Nineteenth-century parties were able to cultivate popular loyalty, in part, through their capacity to express the identity of ethnic groups seeking to maintain their cultural integrity against all external threats.[26] Moran, as an Irish Catholic, had been a Democrat "by heritage." However, in the early twentieth century, voting for a party no longer expressed an ethno-religious identity; the line between Republicans and Democrats no longer mirrored the divisions between major ethnic communities. In addition, unlike the political systems of most developed, capitalist democracies, American parties did not express pre-political, class-based identities.[27]

Secondly, the fall in vote reflected the decline in significant two-party competition throughout vast regions of the country.[28] In Michigan, as in the nation at large, the elections of 1894–96 durably shifted the relative electoral strength of the two parties. The Democrats were precipitated into a position of weakness throughout the "Fourth Party System" (1896–1928). For example, in the race for Michigan governor,

Democrats maintained a rough electoral parity with Republicans in the years 1874–92.[29] But after the depression of 1893, voters decisively repudiated the Democratic party (until the Progressive upheaval of 1912–18). In 1894 and thereafter the Democrats "were thrust into a virtually hopeless minority position."[30] As effective party competition died out in the state, the two parties no longer posed viable alternative policy choices to voters in elections. In response, voters stayed home in droves, failing to cast their ballots.

Political historian Walter Dean Burnham points to additional aspects of voting behavior that suggest the decline in the parties' capacity to package relevant political identities and choices for the electorate. The amount of split-ticket voting versus a straight-party ballot measures the extent of popular partisan loyalty. Michigan again was typical of Northern states in the electoral "System of 1896." Ticket-splitting, or variance between party votes for different state offices, was minimal in the nineteenth century, indicating that citizens were casting their votes for the party's entire slate of candidates. In 1904 variance jumped exponentially from the nineteenth century's minimal rate.[31]

What consequences did this political realignment have for Detroit's journals? The altered political constellation of this Fourth Party System of 1896–1928 (as evidenced in declining voter rates and increasing split-ticket voting), made politics in general, and partisan identities in particular, less salient for citizens. Consequently, political stories became less of a dramatic, gripping narrative for readers. Political news declined as a percentage of the total number of articles in the Detroit papers in election years from a high of 58.8 percent in 1880 to 23.8 percent in 1916.[32]

The nineteenth-century incentives that had worked to enforce partisan correctness on competing Detroit dailies passed out of existence. Parties no longer possessed the capacity to define the political identities and loyalties of the populace. Ritual affirmations of party fealty would only hinder, not help, the journal expand its market share. Newspaper promises of political advocacy would be a weak inducement to the reader to subscribe. In the previous century, parties had occasionally called for boycotts of press organs that bolted from the party, selectively endorsed the party's slate of candidates, or displayed other signs of disloyalty. Such punitive threats would have little force when the party lost its command over voter sympathies. In addition, the new electoral context also provided incentives for newspapers to abandon the sinking party ship. As the following section shows, Detroit newspapers joined the Democrats in advocating anti-party reform.

Michigan's path to reform

How did political reform come to Michigan? How did voters attack the diverse set of political ills represented by political parties? While historians have focused on Republican and independent voters as the active carriers of reform elsewhere in the nation, reform in Michigan followed a distinctively Democratic path.[33] In 1904, the already-weakened mechanisms of party organizational power were assailed by a coalition stretching from the Michigan Democratic party through independent reformers to insurgents within the Republican party. Detroit's Democratic papers took up the crusade of anti-party reform. While the crusade was initially adopted by the Democratic party for propaganda purposes, the crusade itself disseminated and legitimated anti-partisan sentiments. This movement for reform, part and parcel of the Progressive Era movements, found both true believers, such as George Booth, the publisher of the *Detroit News*, and opportunistic supporters in the ranks of the press. The anti-partisan campaign in the name of the public good exploited the growing weakness of parties and allowed newspapers to break decisively from the old party rituals.

In 1904, Michigan Democrats, confronting sure election losses, shifted their political tactics. With increased numbers of independent voters and the Democratic party severely discredited, the strategic electoral calculations for the two parties were fundamentally altered. The nineteenth-century's close electoral competition and fixed voter loyalties had turned the two parties into voter-mobilizing machines. The parties' chief task had been to rally their "troops" for maximum voter turnout at election battles. But now, voter allegiances were weakened and election victory margins were significantly larger than a few percentage points. Insisting on the old party loyalties of the voters would not ensure election victory. Morale-boosting in the press and rallying the troops in campaign tours would not suffice, even if numerous journals had not already repudiated their Democratic allegiances. In this electoral context, the Democratic party had less invested in the electoral game as it was played by nineteenth-century rules.[34] Therefore, they sought new issues, new policy divides, that would expand their electoral appeal. As Richard McCormick notes, the minority party is the traditional voice for innovation.[35]

Thus, Democrats in Michigan hooked up with insurgent Republicans to make broad public appeals for political reform.[36] The Democratic party launched its own attacks against the "party machines" and pushed for political reforms, notably election primaries and the direct election of senators. In their clamor for political renewal, the Democrats nominated for governor an outspoken reformer: Professor Woodbridge Ferris. And, the party's state platform was notably more Progressive than that of the national party, headed by conservative, business candidate Alton Parker.[37] *News* publisher, James Scripps, bluntly characterized the divergence between the state and national nominees: "Judge Parker is the nominee of the interests which use money most largely in the control of governmental affairs, while in this state the [Democratic] ticket and platform are squarely for the restoration to the people of the powers of nomination."[38]

In this election contest of 1904, gubernatorial candidate Ferris gained the support of Detroit's Democratic newspapers, the *News–Tribune* and the *Times*, and was opposed by the classically Republican *Journal*. The papers joined standard partisan press tactics to several innovations. As in the past, the press published partisan jibes, partisan editorials, and partisan letters to the editor purporting to represent the spontaneous and unadulterated sentiments of voters. In addition, in their opinion columns as well as in the news, the papers insistently interpreted the issues of the campaign through the stereotyped frame of "the people" (as Democrats) resisting the blandishments of the Republican party machine.

In their coverage of the campaign, the journals engaged in typical overt partisanship: the preferred gubernatorial candidate monopolized the news, while his opponent was unaccountably invisible. Coverage consisted of two parts rallying to one part verbatim reporting of the candidate's words and arguments. This rallying news sought to demonstrate that the preferred candidate, whether Ferris or his Republican opponent Fred Warner, enjoyed a ground-swell of popular support. The percolating popular acclaim would be sure to overturn all age-old partisan loyalties and expert predictions.

This partisan bias operated through the newspaper's standard division of political labor. In this distribution of tasks and authority among journalists, the papers assigned their regular state political correspondent the job of traipsing after the candidates on the campaign trail. As the politician hopped from town to town, each locale was the occasion for another rally and another news story (which were printed sequentially for one to three columns in the daily edition.) The journalist was a past master of the art of applying the proper amount of political spin to each story, and he warmly praised the candidate's performance and his enthusiastic reception by the crowd. The reporter's narrative voice freely decorated the news report with interjected evaluations and arguments. His sanctioned right to speak authoritatively for the paper was indicated by the byline credit he received.[39]

The sampled issue of the *Times* supplied the following rhapsodic description of Ferris' tour:

Northville, Mich., Oct. 15. – Prof. Ferris and Judge Cahill were given the most enthusiastic and promising reception here that met their tour in all its daily chapters of warm greetings and friendly hearers. The audience which jammed the opera house was made up in large degree of Republicans . . .

The township of Northville is politically Republican in the proportion of about two to one. Nevertheless, the fair-minded Republicans themselves admit that the township will be carried by [Republican] Warner by a fearfully reduced majority if at all . . .

A big delegation came over on an excursion to hear the speeches and to pay their respects to the candidate and the Republican leader who had independence enough and the good of his own party enough at heart to stand outside the reach of the party lash and fight for political honesty and cleanliness . . . [40]

John Fitzgibbon, long-time political reporter for the *Evening News*, contrived the following picture of a Republican party overwhelmed by the appeal of Democratic reformer Ferris:

At the close of Mr. Ferris' speech scores of republicans, some men who have been high in the councils of the party for the last 25 years, flocked to the platform, and, grasping the hand of the candidate, pledged him their support in his magnificent fight for the salvation of Michigan from a rule of machine corruption. The history of politics in this county never witnessed such an upheaval. For months there has been unrest and an undercurrent of protest against the machine . . . but with the arrival of Mr. Ferris the storm broke. The lieutenants of Warden Vincent in this county are amazed at the defections in the ranks of their party.

"Honest John" Lane . . . introduced Mr. Ferris to the cheering hundreds and at the close of the meeting, in his enthusiasm, he proposed three cheers for the next governor. [etc.] [41]

For all the emphatic exuberance of the newspapers whooping it up in the election campaign, newspaper politics in 1904 were strikingly different from previous years. The avowed campaign program for the previously Democrat papers – the *News*, the *Times*, and the *Tribune* – consisted of political reform. They were breaking free from the power of "party machines."

Indeed Ferris along with his applauding mouthpieces in Detroit conducted the campaign as a general assault upon the entangling webs of partisan commitments. The crusading reformer declared that the issues of the campaign were too important to be judged by traditional political allegiances. In fact, the very crux of the campaign was a fight against the corruption that followed from such ritualistic partisanship. In part, Ferris' proclamations reflected the typical political ideals of Progressive reformers: voters should independently and privately deliberate over the important campaign issues, uninfluenced by habitual bonds of allegiances and affective ties to groups, whether they be to party, class, or ethnic group. In part, the attack on partisanship was a useful strategy when the Republican party and especially President Theodore Roosevelt possessed an almost overwhelming hold on popular affections and votes. Any Democratic campaign for state office could hope to succeed only if it separated the state contests from the national, and if it divorced the campaign issues from questions of party loyalties. Accepting Roosevelt's reelection, the *News* editorialized:

Intelligent observers must concede the state to Mr. Roosevelt by a plurality which promises to be unprecedented, if a full vote turns out.

If it were strictly a party contest there would be no enthusiasm, because in such a case the result would be fore ordained by the power of the natural majorities. Michigan is under rational conditions a Republican state by an overwhelming majority . . . in this year . . . a strictly democratic campaign would have been ridiculously impotent.[42]

With all opposition to the incumbent President rendered futile, Roosevelt became the leader of the nation united, the representative of the country beyond all political division or conflict. In the midst of the campaign the *News* offered its readers a special premium: a colored lithographic portrait of "Our Popular President."[43] And the papers instructed voters how to prepare their ballots in order to split their votes between Roosevelt for the presidency and Democrat reformers for Michigan offices. In order to ease the heretical practice of ticket-splitting, the *Evening News* stated that "many republicans are bolting for Ferris, though naming Roosevelt as their presidential choice."[44]

Other tactics of the Democratic papers, beyond accepting Roosevelt's election as inevitable, undermined traditional conceptions of loyalty to party. The *News*, for instance, crossed party lines and endorsed candidates without regard for their formal party affiliation. Their only relevant criteria in evaluating candidates, declared the *News*, was whether the candidate "may be depended upon to advocate the principles [of reform]."[45]

In addition, Ferris tried to divorce his issues from traditional Democratic or Republican associations. Not surprisingly, the Republicans responded by seeking to invoke the old issues and allegiances that had forged their overwhelming majority in Michigan. But the Democrats asserted that the campaign of 1904 was "not in any sense a contest between the two great political parties, but a revolt of the people of Michigan against an evil system which has deprived them of the powers of government." It was "a grand awakening of the public conscience."[46] For the Republicans, this "grand awakening" figured more as a nightmare. And they continually attempted to raise a Democratic bogeyman to chase its members back to the party fold. Republican State Senator William A. Smith argued:

Cleveland's last administration put factories out of business; the Democratic campaign of 1896 drove money into hiding: Parker's name has not been heard in Michigan this campaign; the party led by the intrepid Roosevelt can always be depended upon to do the right thing: let's give three cheers for Roosevelt." The crowd responded. William Alden [Smith] fired this shot: "The platform Mr. Ferris stands upon denounces protection policy as robbery. A vote for Ferris is a vote for free trade . . . [etc.]⁴⁷

In turn, the Democrats mocked the Republicans' defensive election rhetoric:

Here lies the power of the machine. Pretty soon you will hear [Republican Senator] Burrows, Young and other high-power teat suckers, telling you how much they love you, and how the grand Republican party (tears) wants to protect the poor but honest laboring man . . . Now, gentlemen, after you have listened to this kind of dope for a few weeks, you will say to yourself, "Oh, this is a presidential election and I must vote straight."
    . . . As for your humble servant, Roosevelt and Ferris is a good enough combination for him.⁴⁸

However strategically useful, the rhetoric and tactics of nominee Ferris and the Detroit journals constituted more than a clever gambit for a Democratic party desperate for power. Their generalized attack on partisanship would be sure to redound on the Democrats too, hindering continued party loyalty and organization. For example, the *News* published one slogan of Ferris against continued partisanship, boxing it as a quote. The box with its bold, enlarged type is a typical device used by papers to endorse the quoted sentiments and to suggest that the words are worthy of the readers' attention. This quote was illustrated with an engraved, hagiographic portrait of the speaker, Ferris: The headline read "Principle Above Party," as Ferris preached, "You voters have got to stand on principle. You can be either republican or democrat but IF YOU ARE SLAVES OF EITHER PARTY WITHOUT PRINCIPLE YOU ARE PART TO THE WORST KIND OF MACHINE . . ." Such arguments ended up attacking all party ties. This kind of publicity popularized the reformers' criticisms of parties in strong rhetoric and simplified demonological terms. The *Evening News* published similar slashing attacks on "blind loyalty" to any party. Here the *News* typically invoked Progressive Era ideology of the purification of democracy which opposed pure party line voting. Against such blind obedience "they extolled independent voting as the mark of the educated, intelligent class."⁴⁹

The inflated rhetoric of political reformers and reform journalism points to their attachment to the Progressive movement. True believers or merely willing foils, they happily drew upon the Progressives' imagery of democratic revitalization. Yet, this Progressive program of political reconstruction cannot be directly deduced from the altered political conditions that followed the 1896 critical election. As political historian Stephen Skowronek explains, the realignment merely released the major political actors – parties, politicians, and press – from the cost-benefit calculus specific to nineteenth-century politics, with its emphasis on party organization and party loyalty. Without the pressures of perennially close elections, the Republican Party was not compelled to press all governmental (and journalistic) resources into the service of the party's electoral efforts. The new opportunities, however, did not dictate the shape of the emerging political world or the new journalism.[50] Only the elaboration of a novel political culture and a new occupational ethic could establish journalism's proper political role. Only a new public philosophy of the press would permanently sever the newspaper from all political alliances and party relations. Such a newly forged cultural model was necessary to stabilize the press's new function in a transformed public sphere. In the end, reformers in the polity and in the press interacted to forge a new political universe.[51]

The fall elections of 1904 revealed the political fruit of all this attempted sabotage of partisanship. As already noted, variance or ticket-splitting (that is, the practice of dividing one's vote between candidates from both parties) escalated in 1904. Detroit papers predicted Roosevelt's victory and, indeed, he achieved a landslide in the state as in the nation. In Michigan, Roosevelt garnered 361,000 votes compared to the Democrat Parker's 134,000, an extremely lopsided vote. However, the gubernatorial race ran much closer. Reformer Ferris lost with 223,000 votes to the Republican machine's 284,000. In voting for president and governor, approximately, 78,000 voters (or 16 percent) split their ballots between the two parties while another 11,000 balked at voting for any presidential candidate after having registered their choice for governor.[52]

Throughout the following decades the Republican party would continue to be convulsed with factional and sectional disputes over the issues of reform and tariff.[53] Most famous was the party division occasioned by ex-President Roosevelt's disavowal of his Republican successor, William Taft, and Roosevelt's subsequent capture of the Progressive party presidential nomination in 1912. Michigan's Republican party too was the scene of Republican defections to the state Progressive party.[54] By 1912 all this party fractiousness ushered in the election of a Democratic governor – the perennial campaigner Professor

Ferris. The political turmoil perpetuated the attacks on partisanship and the confusion of traditional party allegiances.

In this Progressive environment, newspapers for both pragmatic and ideological reasons campaigned for political reform and independence from strict party lines. The papers' vitriolic rhetoric dissolved the political ties that had united Gilded Age papers and parties in kindred political pursuits. Their campaigns, with all their strident exhortations, continued aspects of past partisan practices, and yet also reconstructed the political universe and redefined for citizens what it meant to participate politically.

The new structure of primary elections

Other changes in the polity more directly undermined the continued relevance of parties and partisanship in 1904. For the first time new primary elections prefaced Detroit's fall campaign season. Detroit had obtained a "local option" to hold primaries in 1903, even if the Republican party was unwilling to extend such legislation to the state as a whole. Within Republican and Democrat parties, candidates jousted for the right to be nominated to a whole gamut of local offices, running from Mayor on down to city coroner.

Primaries made a number of notable changes in the political universe. In V. O. Key's famous interpretation, primaries fundamentally weaken the minority party. The smaller party loses control of the right of opposition, as primaries allow political competition to migrate into the dominant party which ultimately holds every real chance of winning a political office.[55] In Detroit's 1904 primary, however, a more specific shift occurred in the interaction of voters and politics that also attacked the relevance of parties. Most notably, the parties could no longer act as a cue for the mass public. They could not guide voters in their choices among the multitude of candidates in these nominating elections. The cluster of traditional associations, policy positions, and governing consequences that voters attached to parties were not available as a basis for discrimination between the different office-seekers.[56] The problem became the public's familiarity with, and knowledge of, candidates when party labels disappeared. One "expert politician" pondered the implications of the 1904 primary with its bewildering swarm of politicians:

The scramble [of candidates] furnishes considerable humor to the onlookers though the principals cannot find it so very funny. The scratching and leg-running of the candidates for coroner, for instance, to let even a small section of the public know who they are and what they want . . . has become the joke of the campaign. It is a very clever citizen who will know his own candidates when he comes up against a three-foot city ticket . . . The big guns running for mayoralty . . . and other important offices have completely overshadowed the field, and what extra public mental energy is left is mostly taken up with state and national politics.[57]

Of course, the dissolution of all ties of party loyalty has been diagnosed since 1950 as a general failing of the American polity, a deficiency that seriously disrupts the government's capacity to generate coherent policies and to be held accountable.[58] However, for reformers such as publisher Scripps the 1904 replacement of corrupt party conventions by primaries would purify democracy. The individual voter's rational deliberations would replace blind party loyalty and the secret influence of money. To educate voters in the performance of their democratic duties, new responsible, civic-minded advocates were needed. Without parties, other agencies stepped in to bridge the gap between citizens and politicians. Civic organizations and interest groups sought to steer voters past the potential mishaps of primary elections and all the tricks and ruses of the scheming party machines.

Hence, Scripps' evening paper gave extensive space to the Municipal League for an exhaustive list of candidates and their summary evaluations of the candidates' qualifications. This civic group, which variously judged the candidates as "well-qualified" or not, was an independent, non-partisan group. Its evaluations presumably did not reflect any political agenda except "efficient" government. In the *News's* judgment, "the Municipal League is one of several agencies through which the general public may obtain reliable and unprejudiced information."[59] Other intermediaries found entrance into the pages of the press. For instance, the *Times*, in its news column entitled "Political Straws," reported the endorsements of various civic groups along with those of local party clubs.[60] In addition, the daily journals themselves surveyed the candidates on the vital political questions of the day. The *News* polled politicians on the contentious issue of municipal ownership of the city transportation system so "that the people might understand the views on this question of the men who ask their votes at the primaries."[61] All those who refused to answer the *News's* queries in the name of the people were assailed:

[I]t is a deliberate insult to ask men to vote for you if you are unwilling to tell them not only where you stand and what you intend to do, but where you have stood and what you have done in the past . . . Our whole political system necessarily presupposes the right of the meanest citizen to question any man who solicits his vote for any place of power and the candidate who refuses to answer becomes by that very fact unfit for any position of public trust.[62]

Newspapers, both as collectors of information useful to voters and in their editorial endorsements, sought to assist the voter in his choices.

Just as in the previous century, the press aspired to be the chief public adjudicator of the people's will. However, now journals were not supplying cues to voters as representatives of the party. Separated from political organizations but still central vehicles of public communication, the papers gained an enormous power to arbitrate the words and recommendations that reached the citizenry. The *Free Press*, the *Journal*, the *Times*, and the *Evening News* built up an autonomous cache of legitimacy as a trustworthy representative of the public interest (and, in turn, they were subject to attacks that tried to impugn their impartiality and political independence).[63]

As a last practical consequence of the primary elections, the pages of the press became pluralized. The political space was filled with more voices than just the parties and their disputatious factions. Any speaker, given adequate money or legitimacy as a civic group, could gain entry into the supposedly neutral medium of mass publicity, that is, the press. Michigan publisher Edmund Booth wrote about the press's role as an open medium for diverse political voices: "We must not forget, however, that a daily newspaper is a kind of public trust and that the true publisher is the one that tries to handle the thing impersonally – equal rights for all, special privileges for none."[64]

Given this new openness of the press and the lack of party markers to guide voters in primaries, political candidates flooded the papers with advertisements. The sampled 1904 edition of the *Detroit Times* printed nineteen columns of political advertisements or 23 percent of its available space.[65] The politicians tried to mobilize a mix of appeals to capture the vote. The advertisements mostly consisted of candidates' photos with short captions. The publicity remarked upon the politician's upstanding character or briefly mentioned policy positions, but made little or no reference to party affiliation. In effect, candidates were forced to market themselves as individual personalities without reference to party positions and without the use of the party organization. In Richard Jensen's terms, a new candidate merchandising approach superseded the party mobilizing of voters.[66]

News publisher and state senator Scripps had hoped that the new primary laws would eliminate the growing problem of money in politics – the threat of "plutocracy."[67] Despite this belief that primaries would block the role of money in corrupting democracy, dollars became crucial in buying public attention and potentially obtaining public support. Already the *News* saw the specter looming and they asked with apparent bewilderment, "Who opened the [money] barrel?" "Everywhere men are asking each other who opened the barrel for Truman H. Newberry? The primary law was enacted to discharge the influence of money in politics, and it may be that enemies are endeavoring to injure him by making it appear that he is insulting the sentiment that gave rise to this legislation."[68]

The power of parties, both in controlling nominations and in guiding voters' choices, was under siege in the new primary system. Party identification, as an ongoing symbolic system that directed voters through the maze of choices, was irrelevant in selecting a party's nominees.[69] Those seeking office were forced to go it alone, unable to command party symbols or organization in fighting their fellow Republicans or Democrats. The novel tactics of candidates in primaries and the new openness of newspapers undermined the dominance of parties in the public sphere and weakened the salience of party to the mass electorate. Thus, primaries, with their admixture of reformer propaganda touting the virtue of independence, effectively constituted an attack on party power.

As already mentioned, the pages of the press as a central medium of public communication were made available to diverse organized voices in civil society. The pluralization of the medium of public communication represented both an opening for new voices in the public realm and a displacement of parties. Previously parties held an automatic right to speak directly to the public. Now, the press arbitrated such rights for all political actors; the independent press chose whose words and deeds merited public attention. Parties, however, had been the central vehicle for thematizing public issues and uniting governmental policy with the will of the electorate. In the analysis of Walter Dean Burnham, parties were attacked in the Progressive Era for precisely this reason; they rendered the government's policy decisions too public. In the new political order a more privatized political decision-making process would insulate capitalist industrialization from redistributive efforts by farmers and workers, as manifested in the mighty struggles of the Knights of Labor and the Populist movement in the 1880s and 1890s.[70] Furthermore, such privatized legislative procedures would allow powerful economic interests to achieve results more favorable to them without the counter-balance of organized public opinion. For Burnham, only parties succeed in turning policy contentions into full-fledged public battles for the voter's favor. With the weakening of party discipline and the elaboration of more privatized arenas for political decision-making – such as – congressional committees, governmental commissions, the executive branch of government, or the federal administration – politics becomes ritualistic. The legitimated powers of political representation make a show of control over important governmental affairs and of submission to the public will, but the relevant decisions occur elsewhere.[71]

Reporter cynicism and the crusading narrative voice

The *News*'s and the *Times*'s attacks on Republican political corruption were tales of both cynicism and sentiment.[72] These crusading narratives reconfigured the reporter's relationship to reader and political society, even as the newspaper's stories re-envisioned the nature of society's problems, the protagonists involved, and the reforms necessary to resolve the conflicts. The narratives of the daily news unfolded in the form of a "republican plot."

The republican cultural imaginary perceives society as beset by political corruption; private powers have gained public privileges and government no longer serves the commonweal, but instead is diverted to private ends.[73] The population, too, has acquiesced to this political decay, content to abdicate their public responsibilities in favor of private pursuits and pleasures. The solution to such political vice is a revitalized citizenry, vigilant in the protection of their political virtue. It is journalism's exposure of the hidden political wrongdoing that awakens the citizenry, stirring them to action.

As cynicism, the journalistic crusade negates the politician's words, dismisses his flowery speech as mere window dressing to the real machinery of power. The press crusade seeks to expose political and social problems previously obscured by the regnant political rhetoric.[74] But, as sentimentalism, the news sidesteps deep social divisions and offers simple solutions to regenerate the moral, social order. While moralizing over the threat to political virtue, this journalism asserts that democracy can be reestablished through the painless means of an awakened citizenry. As literary critic Amy Kaplan remarks, "To allay fears of powerlessness, [the reformer] identifies with the public" and casts the social problem as "an external disruption imposed on the community instead of an articulation of fundamental social relations."[75]

In this republican theater, the reporter necessarily assumes a central dramatic role in the workings of reform. The journalist stands in for the public and assumes responsibility for vigilant political action, bringing to the citizenry's attention dark political disorders. In mediating between public and politician, individual readers and political organizations, the reporter stakes out a new occupational role. These changes are reflected in novel forms of narrative address. In journalism's reform crusades, the reporter's narrative voice – speaking directly to the readers

– overshadows the reported speech of others, most specifically of party officials. No longer is the reporter the passive bearer of words from party official to party member, from American leader to American people. Instead, the journalist reveals, explains, and denounces the political reality behind the polite professions of the professional politician.[76]

Illustrating this new political posture was an entirely original journalistic vernacular. Political correspondents, in common with the muckraking writers so prominent in national magazines, adopted a new political jargon. Words, such as "boodle," "graft," "boss," "machine," and the like, rolled off their pens. By this contrived language, journalists represented the corruption, both political and linguistic, of political insiders. The slang supposedly duplicated the politicians' own speech behind closed doors, behind the facade of surface gentility. The phrases signified the triumph of personal greed, money and power over democracy and ethics. By echoing the insider's slang, the reporters displayed their own hard-boiled realism; they were not fooled by the politicians' linguistic niceties. The jargon was the souvenir the reporters brought back from their journey into the political underworld. They had explored how the political other half lives and returned bearing tales to their readers, who were safe and secure, but naive, in their middle-class homes.[77]

Reform rhetoric constructed an opposition between crusading reporter and immoral politician. Journalists, who were aligned with genteel, middle- and upper-class readers, stood against the supposedly ethically deficient, lower-class denizens who had captured politics. Some of these poses and political operations are on display in this local news story:

The man with the "job" almost invariably was the leader of the applause at the [Gubernatorial candidate] Warner meetings on the west side Tuesday night. He was assisted by those, who think they "have something comin" and correspondingly enthusiastic . . .

At Oasis Hall, Myrtle street candidates were denounced by one man who stood in the doorway after they departed. "Not a drink!" he muttered. "Now what do you think of that for hard luck? Politics is on de bum for sure . . . Those guys goes 'round in automobiles and hacks, but they don't buy [drinks]."[78]

The reported speech is blunt and pockmarked with grammatical errors. The quotes mark out the speaker as one of the ethnic lower-class who lack the upper-class's concern with moral appearance and developed sense of ethics. Progressive journalists drew upon generalized, derogatory stereotypes of immigrants and the lower-class. Such social groups supposedly upheld the rule of party bosses because they lacked the ethics and rationality to exercise independent judgment.[79] By this narrative operation, political relations were regrouped: the political class was defined as far different from the public, which purportedly consisted of refined, virtuous middle-class citizens. Through these early 1900 crusades, journalists greatly increased the distance between genteel public and corrupt politicians, and at the same time they drew the genteel readers and themselves into close fellowship. In this exposé, journalists stood with the citizenry in a new relationship of intimate communication and trust. As representatives of the public, journalists were given a new autonomy to investigate and to purge party organizations of their corrupt operations. Thus, this new, crusading politics of the press moved the reporter to center stage. By negating the value of the politician's words, by undertaking the rigors and dangers of a voyage into the dark hidden world of politics, and by standing as representative of the public interests, the journalist became a central actor in the news and a prominent player in politics.[80]

The pragmatic actions of newspapers as crusading protagonists of the Democratic party and the narratives of republican exposure worked together to forge a new political universe. In this new-born world, newspapers supposedly stood as the central independent and impartial intermediaries for a revitalized public. The citizenry would no longer be dominated by the machinations of parties, no longer divided by the pursuit of private interests, no longer confused by the partisan biases and misrepresentations of the press.[81]

The new journalistic ethic of independence and public service

Journalism's new ideals of independence and non-partisanship were a positive project, articulated forcefully by newspaper publishers. The ethic was not just a passive adaptation to the new opportunities opened up by the political changes of the Fourth Party System (1896–1932), Progressive Era reforms, and the new economics of the retail revolution. Detroit publishers, like other journalists across the nation, were driven by a vision of a new ordering of society.[82] James and Edward Scripps, James Schermerhorn, publisher of the *Detroit Times*, and George Booth, director of the *Detroit News*, were advocates for the movements of social reform of the Progressive period.[83] Yet, the new occupational ethic, despite all its noble and elevated pronouncements, established no independent standpoint from which journalists could criticize American society. When the passions of the Progressive reform movement ebbed, journalism quickly retreated from its reform stridency. The new ethical posture of public service and impartiality transmuted into a simple conformism with mass sentiment and a submission to the viewpoints of legitimate political representatives and the economic elites.

The pronouncements of Michigan publisher George G. Booth provide a useful case for examining in detail journalism's new public philosophy. In 1906, Booth ascended to general control of Michigan's largest paper, the *Detroit Evening News* after the death of his father-in-law, James Scripps. In conjunction with his brothers, Booth also controlled a string of eight smaller papers throughout the state.[84] Booth had drunk deeply from the fountain of journalistic independence, imbibing a strong draught of the ethic of non-partisanship from the teachings of Scripps. His profession of a high-minded ethic of press independence revealed his appropriation of Progressive cultural motifs. And, Booth's editorials, his public proclamations, and his private correspondence also indicate the possibilities as well as the limits – the legitimating utilities and the political liabilities – of journalism's new occupational ideals.

The most prominent theme in George Booth's reform ideals was "public service," a note repeatedly touted in his private and public statements. Booth asserted his devotion to public service in public platitudes:

A newspaper desiring a position of prominence, influence and profit in its field must learn to serve. The more thoroughly and efficiently it serves the uplifting of constructive life of the community, the greater its financial reward and the longer it will enjoy life.

. . . Make your newspaper SERVE, constructively serve the public interest first; your reward will come without great effort.[85]

He also declaimed on public service in private correspondence with his brother Edmund: "We are conscious that we have no other ambition in a newspaper way than to do those things that mean success, the main purpose in such efforts being to insure good government and to encourage anything that tends to the welfare and happiness of the people in general."[86]

In Booth's letters, such journalistic devotion to public service was united with the Progressive reform tradition. He believed that journalism played an especially crucial role in the movement's efforts to uplift and improve society. For example, in 1906 Booth offered his brother Edmund guidance upon entering into the world of newspaper publishing. He declared there was a continuity between Edmund's past labors with the Young Men's Christian Association and his future tasks as a newspaper manager:

[Y]our new work [as journalist] . . . has in it the spirit which aims to lift people up, to help towards progress, improvement, improvement in the social and moral conditions, that it is the enemy of crime, public and private sins, etc. That it is itself the very spirit of the people yet may in its direction do much to show the way to higher ideals in personal, civic and national life, etc.

He added that in the current era, "Nothing is feared so much as publicity by the wrongdoer, and by the free publication of all kinds of news the people of this country have become enlightened and do not act in the dark. The tremendous upheaval going on at present . . . [is] in a sense chargeable to the press."[87]

In this model of devotion to the public good, an ethic of journalistic autonomy guided Booth. He emphasized that neither his own interests nor those of his partners and staff were involved in the selection of the paper's editorial content. The newspaper should guard its virtue so as to avoid all suspicions, eschewing all entangling and incriminating economic ties. Newspaper workers, in fact, had to observe a rigorous code of behavior. Owners, editors, and reporters must resist the blandishments offered by political and economic powers. Booth saw, as did Edward Scripps, the intertwining of the press with powerful interests as a permanent difficulty for newspapers in the early twentieth century.[88] These fears corresponded to those of middle-class Progressives who were embroidering such stitches into a worrisome tapestry of a corrupt society seduced by the wealth of monopolistic corporations.[89]

Perhaps economic incentives offered the strongest personal temptation to the modern business publisher. The letters among the men of the Booth chain repeatedly refer to their ethical stand in this regard. Edmund Booth writes that in conversation with a major local bank director, "I . . . very good naturedly informed him that you and I in our code of ethics for an independent newspaper did not permit ourselves to be bank stockholders."[90] Two weeks later Edmund contrasted the actions of Booth managers with those of a local priest who had a finger in every local economic pot: "We even set a standard for our reporters and say that they shall have no outside affiliations because such relations are contrary to our ethics of independent journalism."[91] George Booth summarized their position, "[The newspaper man's] money must flow only in those fields of business which cannot be construed as prejudicing or tainting his convictions."[92]

The Booths' code of ethics extended to the realm of political payoffs. Favors from the political system could take the form of patronage to individual newsworkers or profits to the newspaper as a whole. Booth newspapers forbade employees from accepting any political positions. When Michigan governor Groesbeck considered appointing brother Ralph Booth to a vacancy in the Senate, George Booth stepped in and vetoed the offer.[93] More importantly, political independence implied that the newspaper had no permanent ties to any individual, group, or party and that general principles, not particular interests, governed its editorial columns.

Our own men, the managers and others, are certainly conscious that we have no political ambitions, that we have never tried to use the paper to further any particular political party or individuals from any political standpoint. We believe it our duty as a newspaper to see that public offices are not private scraps, and that is about all the interest we have in any political office.[94]

Booth asserted that in the contemporary era it was not particularly advantageous for any journal to receive political patronage or to be identified with particular causes. On the one hand, such "public pap" would deter the partisan paper from pursuing the rigors of real competition. Living on political easy street, it would pose less of a competitive threat to a Booth paper. On the other hand, Booth believed the public was less tolerant of newspapers that twisted the news to promote private purposes. A permanent attitude of suspicion guided the modern reader. Educated by the persistent anti-monopoly propaganda of the Progressives, the public perused the columns of the news for signs of concealed political interests. The *News* publisher wrote, "It is not a bad thing to have the local business atmosphere permeated with the idea that the other paper is a machine paper supported by public pap and is largely operated for private ends and . . . for private advantage."[95] Booth was implicitly pointing to the broad institutional supports for non-partisanship: expanded advertising and a public adverse to the promotion of particular political views and party interests.

Booth so seriously professed belief in the journalistic ideals of public service and not private gain that he argued for public ownership of the press. In the privacy of his letters to his brother he stated that he wanted to go "on record" in support of municipal ownership of papers as feasible and desirable.[96] "At this stage," writes Booth's biographer, "its publishers considered the *News* a semi-public institution, operating under a tacit franchise from the people."[97] Booth's service ethic was in part a reaction against what he saw as the corrupting power of commercial trusts, the degraded quality of industrial society, and the loss of moral purpose in work.[98] Booth, like the Scripps brothers, held on to the republican ethic of individual moral worth established through labor, an ethic threatened on many fronts.

Such were the ideals that Booth vigorously upheld and that guided Detroit papers in their onslaught on partisanship. In the early Progressive era, this journalistic ethic helped the media to sever permanently their formal ties to parties and to repudiate all the obligations and duties incumbent upon a partisan journal. Public service and impartiality became the rhetorical mainstay of journalism's self-conception and a defense against all external criticism and political pressures. Journalists used the idea of public service to deny that the individual publisher, editor or reporter gained any particular remuneration or advantage from specific news decisions. Rather, the journalist, as a professional, was devoted to the higher public interest and was rewarded only for serving that public good. As Booth defensively wrote, "Our policies in the conduct of the *News* are not private policies . . . We have no ulterior motive, no private axe to grind."[99] Booth's strategy here in replying to the criticisms of a prominent businessman points to the general role of such journalistic ethics. They are designed to insulate the newspaper from political attacks and they represented a fundamentally reformulated basis of public legitimacy for newspapers after the previous century's justifications of explicit, formal, press partisanship.

The language of public service along with assertions of technical expertise have been employed by different occupations and professions for a variety of purposes.[100] Magali Sarfatti-Larson emphasizes the economic advantages for professions which are able to achieve "market closure" through requiring formal training and accreditation to aspiring professionals. She also points to the status and prestige granted to those claiming to be professionals and to serve the public interest. More applicable to journalism, Terence Johnson's model emphasizes the power that occupations achieve relative to clients by asserting their professional status and invoking a devotion to public service.[101]

In fact, public service rhetoric in journalism accomplishes three such "political" purposes. First, public service ideals and assertions of independence from all social interests help to legitimate the newspaper's construction of news stories and, also, to insulate the press from external critics. It guarantees journalism a degree of autonomy from outside criticism, intrusion, and control. In Gaye Tuchman's words, it is a "strategic ritual."[102] Like all "professional altruistic codes of ethics, [they] are defenses against the potential distrust of their clients."[103]

Secondly, the rhetoric hides from reporters themselves the political biases of their choices. Notions of impartiality and expertise assure journalists of the purity of their motives and the truth of the knowledge they create, even as they disguise the politics involved in the news corporation's decision-making procedures.[104] The news selections of the editorial staff come to be justified and negotiated through a language of professional values, likely audience appeal, and commonsense understandings of the nature of the world.[105] Such naturalistic criteria hide the values and power – the politics – entailed in choosing the news. The sociologist Warren Breed in his famous study of "social control in the newsroom" saw reporters as pressured to bias the news. They were forced to fit the news to the views of those higher-up in the newspaper bureaucracy. He believed that owners and editors effectively steered the paper away from objectivity. But actually, it is precisely through the language of objectivity – professional assessments of what is fair and what is factual – that the newspaper's management is able to impose its "policy choices" upon the reporting staff.

Lastly, the new legitimacy masks which social interests gain a hearing from the press.[106] The newspaper claims to be impartial. Its selection of the news does not privilege one social class over another. No group because of economic wealth, political power, or ethnic heritage has any special ties to the media or in the determination of what is newsworthy. In fact, Booth implicitly linked the ethic of public service to the new worries over the power of the press occasioned by the decline of newspaper competition and the abandonment of explicit partisanship.

Elimination of competition puts an end to the miserable wrangling that once characterized so many newspapers. It assures a community of steadiness of purpose on the part of the publisher; poised in the representation of news and opinion; greater efficiency in operation; reduction in expenses . . . It tends also to reduce contention in the community. On the other hand, the paper which is fortunate enough to occupy a field alone where once it had competition must beware smugness . . . of employing its strength unjustly . . . [etc.][107]

We might say that under conditions of monopoly or oligopoly, newspapers were open to more serious charges of bias. To escape accusations of bias and illegitimate monopolization of the public arena, newspapers had to avoid all evidence of partiality. They could no longer justify representing merely one political opinion when they had no competition or were, indeed, actively seeking to reduce their number of competitors. In situations where the public had an active distrust of monopolies, newspapers devised justifications drawing on governmental and professional notions of public service to insulate themselves from criticism and from charges of merely serving their own interests. In the era of reform they appropriated (and subscribed to) the new political cultural ideals of public service as against any type of partisanship. Such occupational ethics secured a place for their particular function free from immediate suspicion by the populace.[108]

Publishers no longer affirmed the old, partisan justifications for a newspaper's freely expressed point of view in opposition to other viewpoints. In the nineteenth century, newspapers had possessed a right to explicit political speech. They had such rights both as adjunct to that popular political representative – the party – and as equal political citizens engaged in public dialogue. They were participating members of the public sphere. In the twentieth century, however, the press claims to be above the "wrangling" and conflict of the public–political arena. Independent and unconnected to any fixed political point of view, the paper's news floats above political contention.[109] It is not part of the swirl of opinions and partisan preferences. It no longer aspires to serve one particular segment of public opinion, and does not possess ties to any political organization in its advocacy of policies or in the pursuit of political power. If a journal adopts an active, evaluative, crusading voice, it is in the name of the shared, unimpeachable public interests of the entire community. Newspapers thus define themselves as specifically not part of the public sphere. They stand above politics. In Jeffrey Alexander's analysis, the media no longer "produce sharply divergent perspectives of public events." They avoid the self-conscious, explicit articulation of norms in conflict with other perspectives.[110] As bearers of political speech, they are a neutral medium of communication. Their words fall from the lips of impartial technical experts or non-political representatives of the community's will.

Newspaper reformers such as Booth and his father-in-law Scripps or the later Walter Lippmann saw themselves as escaping from any social partiality. Typically, science, as a dominant cultural ideal, was invoked to justify this vision of the news as "monological," as a technical issue for professionals, and as free from social divisions and conflicts.[111] Scripps, in his proposals for a penny paper, daydreamed about unbiased news and editorials that would be penned by only the foremost experts. In his "model one-cent paper": "Popularity should be cultivated and personal assault avoided as far as possible. News matter should not be colored to favor any opinion. Entire impartiality and absolute correctness should govern the news columns. The single leading editorial should be by the work of one expert in the subject it deals with."[112]

Booth too repeated this fantasy of conflict-free journalism, a news without any politics. As he proclaimed in one editorial, "[T]he News will tell faithfully all that is true so that the public will know."[113] In his letter proposing the public ownership of newspapers, he wrote:

In the first place the primary thing is the publication of news and it seems to me that it ought not to be difficult for a public institution running a newspaper to control the news. I assume that it is just as easy to find an honest editor drawing pay from the public to handle the news as that we can . . . find an honest judge or an honest city treasurer.[114]

The ethics of George Booth and his brothers were part of the Progressive Era's political vision. In the early twentieth century, at the height of the movement's power, newspaper publishers and reformers articulated a new vision of American politics and of the arena of democratic discussion. The polity would be purged of all private interests, hidden deals, and corrupt powers. Without the influence of party machines, city bosses, corporate payoffs, ethnic groups looking for governmental handouts, and biased partisan papers, the citizenry supposedly could examine political issues openly and freely come to agreement on policies reflecting the public good. A newly purified public opinion would function without the previous distortions, misrepresentations and manipulations. More specifically, with partisanship and corruption banished, the "intelligent and educated classes" could unite and guide public opinion to proper policies.[115] This utopian project assumed the existence of an "underlying harmony of social interests" that would allow public opinion to reach an open and rational agreement. No deep and enduring social divisions, nor accumulations of social and economic power, prevented the triumph of persuasive, rational speech. In more bureaucratic–professional variants of this political project, politics would be transformed into technical decision-making under the province of experts and managers.[116]

This Progressive cultural vision joined with the altered political situation after the 1896 election to reconstruct the American political universe. The reformation of American newspapers from partisan to impartial and independent was part and parcel of this historical dynamic. The journals responded to the decreased power of parties and joined reformers in attacking all partisan affiliation as blind and corrupt. Newspapers' strategic ethic of neutrality – designed to secure a measure of autonomy for the reporting of the news and to free the press from the ubiquitous contention of the public sphere – participated in this more general, ideological movement of society. Numerous historians have noted that the Progressive upheaval along with other political institutional changes of the early twentieth century encouraged a privatization of politics and a segmentation of society. Newspapers' claims of autonomy, of specialized technical expertise, of disinterested, impartial reporting of the news, paralleled the general expansion of specialization and technical decision-making, of which the eclipse of parties in American politics was the most prominent form. The expansion of such technical decision-making processes reduced "the scope of political conflict" (Schattschneider) by eliminating the open, contentious, collective deliberations of politics.[117]

Denouement: 1908

After 1904, the Detroit press dispensed with much of the limited, overt partisanship that had colored reporting efforts in the previous national elections. Certainly, the dailies still sided with one party or the other.

However, this partiality (which may have been necessary to reassure readers that their paper stood on the side of right and common decency) was largely confined to editorials, and a reduced number of partisan editorials at that. The exuberant, explicit declarations of loyalty to party vanished. And the news itself took on the explicit appearance of neutrality in all political conflict. All newspapers avowed their independence from partisanship. This change in the politics of the press both mirrored and reinforced the weakened role of parties in American public life.

A closer scrutiny of campaign coverage in 1908 will reveal the particular nuances and textures of this political reporting. In general, the protagonists featured in 1908's news stories evolved from parties to candidates, from legislatures to the executive, and from the citizenry to politicians. Instead of the previous century's practice of printing the complex schedules of party rallies throughout the state and then reporting on the hundred and one rallies in each small town, the news trailed the individual nominees on their Michigan campaign tours.[118] More specifically, daily stories detailed the activities of the Democratic and Republican candidates for the executive offices of President, Governor, and Mayor. The press slighted other races, especially those for the local, state, and national legislatures. While an increase in press attention to the office of the President in the twentieth century has long been recognized, 1908's coverage shows that this mutation extended also to state and local executive offices.[119] In Michigan, candidates for executive offices eclipsed all city council and state legislative races.

In McGerr's analysis, nineteenth-century election rallies had constituted a ritual of partisanship. The party gatherings with all their parades and festivities were a celebration of collective political identity, an opportunity to participate in a public display of commitment and belonging. While twentieth-century election rallies similarly displayed popular support for the office-seeker – a showing of committed voters that the candidate represented – it also shifted the emphasis from the collective entity of the party with its members to the individual candidate. The rallying audience had no collective existence outside their support of the individual politician.

Instead of the evident bias of the partisan press's one-sided coverage, 1908 papers covered all sides of the political campaign, that is, the two major parties. Journalism in 1908, as today, adopted the simplifying assumption that the activities of the Democrats and Republicans exhausted the political spectrum. Michigan's Prohibition party and Socialist–Labor party with their slate of candidates for state offices in 1908 did not merit paper or ink.

In 1904 political coverage had been devoted to one side to the neglect of the other. One party was praised and quoted; the other ignored or ridiculed. The press had no independent place outside the jousting of the parties. In 1908 this adoring publicity, so typical of the partisan press, was transferred to both parties' candidates. The coverage of 1908 adopted a sort of parallelism between the two parties, a political balancing act. This balance was achieved in a manner quite unlike that of our contemporary news media. The press of today covers political controversy by quoting the two rival sides, that is: both the legitimate political authorities involved in the dispute.[120] One quote rebuts another as the journalist assumes a relatively effaced narrative stance. The news, by this juxtaposition of views and its own narrative distance from either side, turns the views and assertions of the two sides into matters of dispute and uncertain truthfulness. The press in 1908, instead, balanced the coverage of the two parties' candidates by publishing doting, deferential articles for each candidate's campaign tour. For example, in the local Detroit contest, the Democratic incumbent faced a Republican challenger. The Detroit *Journal* printed accounts of the Democratic and Republican campaigns for mayor in side-by-side columns:

DISCUSSIONS AND
ISSUES IN THE LOCAL
MAYORAL CAMPAIGN

Thompson Tells What He "Has Not Done"	Ald. Heineman Talks For Mr. Breitmeyer
With the Cubs on their way to Chicago with the [Detroit] Tiger pelts cached in their grips, Mayor Thompson last night swung into the campaign with a chance of getting some attention. The mayor addressed five meetings, all of which were well attended. Three were in good Democratic territory, one was in a church bazaar, where politics was tabooed, and the last was in a Republican bailiwick. The first stop was at Perkins Hall, Twelfth and Grand River, where the parish of St. Leo is holding a church fair. The mayor escorted by Fr. Meathe, visited the various booths [etc.] . . . The last stop was at Ellery and Arndt in the Thirteenth ward, where the best crowd of the evening was found, about 300 being present. This was in the	Philip Breitmeyer's campaign tour last night began at 6:30 in the Epiphany church, and ended at 11 o'clock in the order of Amaranth meeting in the East Side Bohemian Turner hall. In these four and one-half hours the campaigning party flashed through 10 different gatherings, and heard 10 varieties of applause. The street car question was not discussed by the candidate, except when he mentioned Thompson, or when the Rev. Mr. Locke asked him in the Epiphany church whether he stood for three-cent or five-cent fares. "Emphatically for three-cent fares," said Mr. Breitmeyer. In Kawecki's saloon on St. Antoine Street two boys were singing a song, "Breitmeyer," to the tune of

fourth precinct of the Thirteenth ward in a strong Republican district.

The mayor wandered from his set speech last night, warming to his subject . . . "The Wayne County Republican club offered a prize of $50 for the best essay on why I should be beaten," said the mayor. "That is a high compliment because it shows the opposition is hard put to find reasons for not re-electing me. Also, I can remark that thus far the effort to find reasons does not seem to have been very successful and I advise them to raise the price to $100 . . . Perhaps it would be well for these people who are asking: 'What has Thompson done,' to learn what he has not done. Thompson has not received any punch bowls of dubious origin: no official appointed by him has been sending in bills to be paid twice or padded bills for crushed stone, or has been knocking down money at the rate of a dollar for every electric sign put up in the town. Thompson has not been wined and dined by the D[etroit] U[rban] R[ailroad] lobbyist . . . [etc.]"

"Harrigan." Breitmeyer made a speech from a chair . . . "I want to tell you gentlemen why you should vote the Republican ticket," said Mr. Breitmeyer. "If there are Democrats here, I want to change your votes. (Cries of 'Hooray.') I am not asking you to vote for a man who will promise things he can't do. Thompson said he would give three cent fares in three months or in two years. Has he? No; and he won't in two more years if you elect him. He has done nothing but four-flush. He monkeyed with the gas company, but you are paying more for your gas . . . [etc., etc.]"

The coverage of the national campaign exhibited a similar balance. An article describing the electioneering of presidential nominee William H. Taft mirrored a story on the Democrat Bryan. The quoted statements of the Democratic National Committee provoked an article on the Republican Committee's reply. Most of the national news was transmitted to the Detroit papers by the Associated Press news service. However, the narrative form of parallel praise and deference to the candidates was not dictated by the Associated Press's wire copy, nor by the need of the AP to supply impartial and objective accounts that would not offend any potential customers.[121] Rather, the wire service had been producing this type of "balanced" news coverage for thirty to forty years. In the past this balance allowed the partisan papers to trim and tailor the wire service to their political needs. The party sheet could print the wire copy that praised their own party, while dispensing with that which lauded the opponent. In addition, the organ could supplement the wire reports with partisan analyses by special correspondents. Thus, the Associated Press did not dictate the political bias or balance of local papers. As the local reporting on the mayoral race indicates, newspapers deliberately chose to exclude their old formal, overt display of partisanship for the sake of a new impartiality.

The Gilded Age press had proudly demonstrated its commitment to a single party and its principles. The resulting news devoted vast amounts of space to the words and deeds of the party leaders. This deference to the party reflected the legitimacy of the politicians as representative of the citizenry, as recipients of a democratic mandate to speak and act for the public. The 1908 coverage similarly deferred to the statements and political agenda of the candidates. Reporters followed the campaign and recorded the speeches without initiating new topics or issues for debate. As in the prior century, the 1908 coverage not only reflected this democratic legitimacy of the politician, it also participated in the rituals of conferral of political power. In 1908, as previously, newspapers publicized the candidate's every rally, speech, and gesture as newsworthy. The Detroit *Journal*'s daily reporting of mayoral candidates Thompson and Breitmeyer was not predicated upon the occurrence of an important development in the election race or some novel statement by the office-seeker. Rather, it was the whole campaign that commanded news attention and the individual daily story was only one part, one ritual enactment. Each day's account was an aspect of the ritual ceremony of American democracy in action – the process of candidates presenting themselves to the public for judgment and electoral approval. The leader bowed down to the citizenry before picking up the scepter of political rule. This explains the journalists' rigorous following of the sequential actions of the campaign and the repetitious reproducing of the politicians' words day in and day out. The news worker was chronicling for the public the workings of democracy and, at the same time, allowing its extended operations.

The narrative structure of the news echoed this logic. The reporters did not employ the modern narrative news form of a "summary lead paragraph" and "inverted pyramid narrative." Such a summary introductory paragraph emphasizes a single topical event as the focus and content of the story. It points to the occurrence of some new and important event which supposedly justifies the news coverage and journalistic attention. Instead, in 1908, the lead paragraph sets the scene, the characters, and the geographic locale, without summarizing the highlights or the central important event of the story. No single event justified the decision to include news of the campaign in the paper. Rather, it was the more important right to publicity for the candidates who were conferring with the citizenry that automatically secured its space in the paper. In addition, the 1908 chronological narrative, with its extensive verbatim quotes, duplicates and respects the original integrity – the ritual nature – of the campaign rallies and speeches. The journalist did not intervene in the communion of political representatives and the assembled public.

In 1908 the dueling duet of the two parties and their candidates monopolized public-political speech during the campaign. News reporting produced a highly stratified public sphere. These stratified rights of public speech duplicated, to some extent, the rigidity and exclusions of the nineteenth century. With only weak legitimation for including alternative perspectives beyond the boundaries of formal political society, the print media deferred to the dominant social consensus on who constituted a legitimate political speaker in the election process.[122] The press treated the election campaigns as best befits a sacred ritual in the self-definition of American society.

The liberation of the press from the constraints of partisan correctness did not expand the content or quantity of political discussion, at least in early twentieth century. No longer partisan, the press provided only minimal recounting of the political debates of the two parties. The news media avoided the prolonged discussion of political issues that had characterized nineteenth-century papers with their partisan axes to grind. Instead of the extensive dissection of the Republican positions on tariff, the formerly Democratic papers, the *News* and the *Times*, supplemented their political news with stories of crime, murder, and tragic tales of divorce. They digressed at length on the Detroit Tigers' chances in the baseball pennant race. They devoted ever-expanding news space to the harrowing details of the latest natural disaster, whether flood, fire, or earthquake. Increasingly, political coverage was displaced by "social" stories that aimed at entertaining and informing, not persuading, readers.

NOTES

1 In general see Schudson 1978: ch. 3.
2 Hallin 1994: ch. 9; James Carey's "Afterword," in Munson and Warren 1997.
3 Lefort 1988: ch. 9.
4 Schudson 1986b.
5 Cf. Bourdieu 1991: ch. 9.
6 Alexander 1981: 34.
7 On the depression in Detroit see Holli 1969: ch. 4.
8 Goodwyn 1978; Schmitz 1989.
9 As cited in Baehr 1972: 255: and see Wiebe 1967: ch. 4.
10 Bryan notes the various bitter attacks in his speeches and in his campaign retrospective. (Bryan 1896: 467, 471, 474–5, 493, 603; and see Baehr 1972: 254–5).

11 James E. Scripps, Diary, Dec. 31, 1896 (Wilkerson negatives, Cranbrook Archives).
12 Pound 1948.
13 Holli 1969.
14 Slotkin 1985: 332–69.
15 See the *Free Press*'s "Declaration of Independence," July 12, 1896: 12. The *New York Times* issued its own declaration.
16 Lodge 1949: 60.
17 On the nation's papers leaving the Democratic party in 1896 see Jensen 1971: 272–5; Sarasohn 1989: 10–11; Baehr 1972: 254–5. Hearst was one of the few publishers to stick with Bryan. Even newspapers in the solidly Democratic South left the party.
   On Michigan politics in 1896 see VanderMeer 1989 especially pages 69–70 on newspapers.
18 Livingstone 1904: 501.
19 Bryan 1896: 447 and see 628, 612–14.
20 On the differing campaigns see Josephson 1953; Croly 1953. On Bryan's eloquence see John Lodge's account of Bryan's famous Cross of Gold speech (Lodge 1949: 59–60).
21 Bryan 1896: 561; and for total number of miles traveled and speeches given see pp. 604, 618.
22 As quoted in Cyril Player "The Story of James Edmund Scripps," 307 (Cranbrook Archives). John Fitzgibbon recalls reporting for the *News* as the only Michigan paper to cover Bryan's Michigan tour (*News*, Dec. 30, 1927: 17).
23 Ibid., 36.
24 Burnham 1970: 114.
25 Moran 1949: 65. Cf. Baum 1984: ch. 1.
26 Kleppner 1980: 93–9, 102–5; Kleppner 1987: 170–1, 220–5.
27 Lipset and Rokkan 1967; Alexander 1981: 29–32; Burnham 1982: 142–3; Kleppner 1982: 148–50.
28 Other alternative explanations for the decline in voting are: (1) the limited thematization of salient issues between the two parties after the failure of the Democratic–Populist fusion party in 1896; (2) The legislation of various rules governing election procedures operated as barriers to voter participation; (3) The decline of parties as mechanisms supporting voter turnout (see McGerr's analysis of the displacement of a public, demonstrative, partisan culture, manifest in the partisan rituals of newspapers); (4) Muckraking journals' pervasive cynical discourse with an emphasis on the exposure of politics in early twentieth century (Leonard 1986).
29 Michigan, as with other Northern states, saw a long-term secular rise in Democratic support in 1874–92. This reflected general demographic changes in the population make-up. Many Midwest states saw an in migration of the ethno-cultural groups typically supporting the Democrats, most specifically Germans; cf. Jensen 1971.
30 Burnham 1970: 114.
31 Burnham 1970: 111–12 and in general 111–20, 195–203. Variance for the nineteenth century was below one. In 1904 it jumped to 18.60. Also see Burnham 1986: 293–6.

32 This is a percentage of the total number of newspaper articles. It does not count total newspaper space devoted to politics, but there is no reason to suspect that this difference introduces any bias into the measure. Secondly, this is the relative number of articles. The newspaper increased in size over this time period. Therefore, the absolute number of articles discussing politics may have remained the same. Still, the point remains that politics has become a less central focal point of the press. Generally, papers in the late 1800s election seasons focused on politics in 60 to 40 percent of their news stories. Compare Baldasty 1992: 153–7. References to parties in political news also suffered a long-term decrease from the 1880s to 1920.

33 Historians have elaborated three alternative paths to reform in this new political universe. Richard McCormick's analysis of New York State politics views independent voters and reformers as the carriers of anti-party reform. New York after 1896 retained relatively competitive parties. Democrats and Republicans used patronage and traditional partisan appeals to shore up their electoral support. However, independents were able to use their strength as the balance of power between the two parties to extract anti-party reform measures from the Republicans (McCormick 1981). A second pathway to reform emerged at the national level. According to Stephen Skowronek, the Republicans in the federal government, now freed from the political pressures of close elections, were no longer obliged to turn all governmental jobs into party-patronage. Party outsiders, like Theodore Roosevelt, expanded civil service to jobs previously taken as electoral spoils by the victorious party (Skowronek 1981: 167–71). In addition, the hysteria over lower-class threats from below, so commonplace in the 1890s, vanished with the decisive defeat of the "Popocrats" (cf. Haber 1964: 101, 134–8; and lastly, Sarasohn 1989).

34 Also, Sarasohn claims that the Democrats, with constituents on the outside of the establishment, were more hospitable to reform (1989: xi).

35 McCormick 1981: 104.

36 The Republicans, in turn, facing no substantial external threats, continued their own internal factional conflicts over reform. The pitched battles within the Republican party were a holdover from the days of Governor Hazen Pingree's tremendous fury against elite control of the machinery of government. Democrats in Michigan, like their fellow party members in the Congress, often played second fiddle to insurgent Republicans. Simplifying his agenda, in 1899 Pingree declared, "the two greatest questions of the day [are] the trusts and the popular elections of senators," in other words – the developing concentration of wealth and its control over Republican party policies. Despite Pingree's retirement, then death, in 1901, these reform battles continued throughout the Progressive Era (1900–16). See Catlin 1926: 636–40, 628; Holli 1969: ch. 9; cf. Campbell 1941.

37 See the Democratic National Platform in Porter and Johnson 1966: 130–5.

38 "The Great Political Issue of 1904," Detroit News–Tribune, Oct. 2, 1904: 2.

39 Bylines have multiple and sometimes opposing implications. In all cases they signal the article's enunciation – marking out the individual reporter as the narrator speaking directly to the reader. However, this narrative enunciation and the definition of the reporter's authority to speak takes different forms.

Sometimes bylines operate as a quasi-trademark proclaiming the author's individual personality. Here the byline points to the author's subjective evaluations, his or her particular literary skills, or the personal "intimate" relation being established between writer and reader. Alternatively, in the context of political reporting credit lines may point to writers' viewpoints as their own and independent of the newspaper's. Conversely, as in the case mentioned here, the byline indicates the reporter's sanctioned authority to speak for the paper. Lastly, the credit may serve to indicate the prestige and accomplishment of the reporter as an expert in the effaced factual reporting without voice.

	Byline as representing the delegated voice of the paper	Byline as representing the writer's voice as distinct from the paper
+ Voice	− Sanctioned Political Reporter	− Trademark personalities − Feature writers − Independent political commentator
−	− Expert neutral Reporter	

40 *Times*, Oct. 15, 1904: 2.

41 *News*, Oct. 3, 1904: 4. On reporter Fitzgibbon, see the *News*, Dec. 30, 1927 and upon his death Feb. 24, 1931.

42 *News*, Oct. 16, 1904: 2, col. 1.

43 *News*, Oct. 6, 1904.

44 *News*, Oct. 16, 1904: 1.

45 *News*, Oct. 10, 1904.

46 *News*, Oct. 16, 1904: 2.

47 *News*, Oct. 3, 1904: 10.

48 *News*, Oct. 3, 1904: 10.

49 Kleppner 1987: 170.

50 Skowronek 1981: 167–71.

51 Cf. Kleppner 1987: 226.

52 Compare Kleppner who says Republican voting was stable in the period of 1902–1904 (1987: 128–31). It is interesting to note that Ferris' vote count is close to the Democrats' total for the same office in 1902. This suggests that Roosevelt was able to draw Democratic votes, while Ferris only retained the traditional Democratic vote.

53 Kleppner 1987: 134–6.

54 Campbell 1954.

55 Key 1954.

56 In general on voting see Burnham 1987; Kleppner 1987. These issues of voter knowledge and guides in election campaigns when party salience declines continue to play out in contemporary American elections. See Wattenberg 1986.

57 *News*, Oct. 9, 1904: 13.

58 In 1950 the American Political Science Association issued its report "Towards a More Responsible Two-Party System"; see Fleishman 1982: 17.

59 *News*, Oct. 4, 1904.

60 *Times*, Oct. 15, 1904: 8. Other civic groups mentioned are the Independent Voter's Club and the Good Citizen's League. Also cf. the *News*, Oct. 15, 1904: 9.
61 *News*, Oct. 5, 1904.
62 *News*, Oct. 4, 1904: 2.
63 See, for example, the advertisement of Edwin Denby which cites various newspapers' endorsements of him (*Times*, Oct. 15, 1904).
64 Letter, Edmund Booth to Henry Booth, March 13, 1913 (Cranbrook Archives).
65 *Times*, Oct. 15, 1904.
66 Jensen 1969: 43–5; Burnham 1970: 95–7.
67 *News*, Oct. 2, 1904: 2; an opinion column with a Scripps byline.
68 *News*, Oct. 15, 1904: 1 and 2. After 1904, money continued to plague the primary elections. In private correspondence Booth in 1910 dismissed the problem raised by an employee's critique of primaries. See Pound 1964: 199; and Letters, George G. Booth to Edmund Booth, Oct. 31, 1910 and May 8, 1907 (Cranbrook Archives).
69 On the role of parties in rendering clear and comprehensible political programs, political responsibility and hence voter choices see Burnham 1987: 102–4, 123–4. He uses rational-choice, retrospective voting evaluation theories in his analysis.
70 Of course, Burnham also points to Republican party hegemony and the policy decisions of the US Supreme Court as effectively protecting the market from any political redress (Burnham 1981: 162–4; 1982: 47–50; and 1986: 269–74).
    While Burnham addresses the issue of redistributive governmental policy and the veto of such efforts by the Fourth Party System, Paul Kleppner and Richard McCormick discuss governance in the Fourth Party System when the question is the necessary governmental regulation of the economy. In the standard neo-Marxist analysis that they duplicate, at a certain stage of economic development and concentration, society attempts to rationalize the market and control some of the deleterious consequences of unregulated production and competition. The market is no longer sacrosanct and the government must intervene. For capitalists, the issue becomes how to ensure that this politicization of the market does not turn into a full, democratic discussion challenging corporate interests and even the presuppositions of private control and profit. Cf. Offe 1984: ch. 1; Vajda 1978: chs. 8–10; McCormick 1986: 19–25, 83–5, 222–7, 274–80.
71 Burnham 1982: 113–15. Of course, my account of party rituals in chapter 3 suggests that parties too are able to divorce governmental decision-making from public debate and general deliberation (Cf. Pizzorno 1993). The issue is, at least, two-fold, involving both publicity in governmental decisions and the organization of civil society. Civil society should be complexly organized and contain extensive public discussion so that the citizenry is not passive before the decisions and assertions of the government and the parties.
    A second set of questions are historical: when and why did these changes occur in the organization of the American polity? Here, I can only refer to various suggestive works: Bensel 1986: 26–30, 53, 56, 130, 139, 148–51;

Kleppner 1989: 166–75; Clemens 1993; Rodgers 1987: 199–201; and, for more general views, see Lasch 1967: ch. 1; Hofstadter 1955.

72 Cf. Ziff 1966: ch. 7. Also on the cynicism of reporters see Alexander 1981.

73 Cf. Kasson 1976; Schiller 1981.

74 On political reporting and exposure see Leonard's analysis of its historical evolution (1986). In his important account, Leonard largely focuses on the literary forms, the journalistic "vernaculars," the plots – in sum, the cultural perspectives – that facilitated journalism's growth as a mode of exposure and political muckraking. From the viewpoint of this book, Leonard's account of the genesis of journalistic crusades does not adequately situate the press among the contending voices of the public political sphere. He gives too much power (and blame) to the press without factoring in changes in the political institutions that the press confronts.

75 Kaplan 1988: 59–60, referring to the novels of William Dean Howells; Rogin 1967: 171. At the time, Michigan socialists repudiated political reform such as primary elections. They insisted class domination would continue nonetheless. See the *Times*, Oct. 15, 1904.

76 From the viewpoint of authorial enunciation, "discourse" takes a new prominence over "story." See the discussion in Morse 1985.

77 Lasch 1965: ch. 8.

78 *News*, Oct. 5, 1904: 7.

79 Therefore, Paul Kleppner sees the campaign for reform, despite its verbal professions of democracy as elitist and largely directed against the lower-class, immigrants, and blacks with anti-democratic reforms (Kleppner 1987: 179). Rogin, instead, says "Few Progressives . . . were consciously anti-democratic" Rogin (1967: 196–8).

80 Cf. Kaplan 1988: 32; 1990.

81 Rogin 1967: 197–8.

82 Cf. Hofstadter 1955: 186–98.

83 Cf. Stark 1943; Currie 1968; Tompkins 1969.

84 On Booth's life see Pound 1964; also Bow 1989a.

85 George Booth, "Notes for An Address" (Cranbrook Archives). Internal dating suggests the document was written circa 1920. A similar version was printed in Pound 1964: 233.

86 Letter, George Booth to Edmund Booth, July 30, 1907 (Cranbrook Archives). Other documents that sound the theme of public service are: document entitled "1913" (Cranbrook Archives) by Edmund Booth announcing the formation of a philanthropic fund in Grand Rapids; Booth 1918.

87 Letter, George Booth to Edmund Booth, April 19, 1906 (Cranbrook Archives); and cf. Pound 1964: 224–5, 234.

88 See Scripps 1966: 238–45 and also 215–18, 269–72. And cf. Letters, George Booth to Edmund Booth, July 9, 1908 and Oct. 8, 1907 (Cranbrook Archives).

89 On the fading away of such fears see Hofstadter 1967. In addition, as many historians have written, this period saw a massive rationalization in the organization of the market. Corporations were achieving a more coordinated control of production and distribution of goods. At the same time, the

capitalist class as a whole was establishing its own social, economic, and political organizations, thus producing a group cohesiveness and capacity to act as a coordinated ruling class. Cf. Kleiman 1986; Couvares 1984.

90 Letter, Edmund Booth to George Booth, Dec. 7, 1907 (Cranbrook Archives); and cf. Pound 1964: 217, 235–6. "[GB] would never permit a manager to be on the directorate of a bank or public utility, lest the connection prove embarrassing" (p. 217).

91 Letter, Edmund Booth to George Booth, Dec. 20, 1907 (Cranbrook Archives).

92 Pound 1964: 236.

93 Pound 1964: 458–9. Later Booth acceded to his brother's wishes and Ralph was elevated to the office of US Ambassador to Denmark.

94 Letter, George Booth to Edmund Booth, July 30, 1907 (Cranbrook Archives). And see Letter, George Booth to Edmund Booth, July 31, 1912 (Cranbrook Archives); Bingay 1949: 179–84.

95 Letter, George Booth to Edmund Booth, July 30, 1907 (Cranbrook Archives). And cf. Booth, "The Senatorship" (1918): 3 (Cranbrook Archives) on legitimate newspaper income.

96 Letter, George Booth to Edmund Booth, Nov. 11, 1914 (Cranbrook Archives).

97 Pound 1964: 191; and see the document by Edmund Booth titled "1913," on establishing a philanthropic foundation in Grand Rapids (Cranbrook Archives). Also see Bow 1989a: 2.

98 See Booth's lectures, "Art and the American Home" (1905); "Art, Sacrificed to War, Must Rise Again" (1917); "Industrial Art in Museum" (1918); reprinted in Pound 1964: 473–83. Also see Booth 1918.

In this sense, as James Bow has argued, Booth's journalistic ethic displayed an affinity with his Arts and Crafts aesthetic. Both, journalistic ethic and aesthetic, tried to recover a purpose for work from the dead instrumentality of commercialized production. Booth supported the local Arts and Crafts movement by establishing the Detroit Society of Arts and Crafts and the renowned Cranbrook School. However, Arts and Crafts tended to be backward looking, while journalism's ethic of public service looked ahead. The Arts and Crafts movement retreated from mass, industrial production to artisan handicraft, just as Booth established his refuge for aesthetic production, the Cranbrook School, in the suburbs far from the modern city of Detroit. Instead the new ethic of journalism sought a place in modern, complex, differentiated society for the news media's specialized social function. (Bow 1989a, b; also see Bingay 1949: 242, 176).

99 Letter, George Booth to H. Chalmers, Nov. 7, 1915 (Cranbrook Archives).

100 The rhetoric of public service, along with ideals of technical efficiency and social reform, were the three main cultural codes used by members of the Progressive reform movement. In the view of Daniel Rodgers, the movement, despite its bewildering complexity, found its unity in the appropriation of these three codes in the new political space opened up by the alteration of the party-political system after 1896. (Rodgers 1982; also see Samuel Haber on rhetorics of social efficiency: Haber 1964.) Magali Sarfatti-Larson traces out some of the genealogy of the rhetoric of service

ideals in Progressive professionalization projects. Claims of public service were usually combined with claims of technical knowledge by occupations seeking professional status. (Sarfatti-Larson 1977: ch. 5.)

Booth's invocation of public service instead of the other Progressive motifs may be attributed to the early time period; rhetoric of public service and moral uplift was more specific to the years 1900–10. The idea of public service may also have been more appropriate for a publisher, while "efficiency," with its connotations of technical expertise, was more suitable to the middle-class worker aspiring to the status and power of a professional. Indeed, Walter Lippmann in his arguments for the training of the reporter in 1918 clearly sought to give reporters added status through claims of special expertise and knowledge. Cf. Lippmann and Merz 1920; also see Lippmann 1965.

101 Sarfatti-Larson 1977; Johnson 1972.

102 Tuchman 1972; 1978b.

103 Collins 1979: 136.

104 Schudson emphasizes the psychological reassurance for reporters played by codes of objectivity (Schudson 1978: ch. 4). Collins charges that the rhetoric of a higher ethic conformed to upper class, native-born American prejudices. They served to draw invidious distinctions between the older Protestant Americans and newer immigrants from Southern and Eastern Europe (Collins 1979: 100).

105 Breed 1955; Tuchman 1972: 662–3, 667, 669; Barsamian 1992: 26–7.

106 I thank Arvind Rajagopal for this argument.

107 Pound 1964: 221; and cf. Booth 1918.

108 These issues were all described explicitly in the later Hutchins commission on press ethics in the 1940s (cf. Commission on Freedom of the Press 1947).

109 On differentiation see Alexander 1981: 23–39.

110 Alexander applauds this state of media affairs. In his illuminating interpretation, the media's special social function is to provide normative integration by the weaving of daily events into the flexible fabric of social norms. The media, thus, expand the societal resources of social integration. Alexander further writes that the differentiation of news from all political agencies and perspectives does not mean that a society will lack all substantive political debate. Rather, it is up to the political institutions, not the journalistic ones, to supply self-consciously opposed perspectives on the proper ordering of society. However, he paradoxically notes that for news to achieve its differentiated status, that is, for journalism to supply non-controversial, factual (and normative) descriptions of events, society must have a degree of depoliticized consensus. Society must not be polarized into sharply opposed political camps (ibid., 29–32, 35–7; also see the discussion of Hallin and Mancini 1984: 849).

111 Haber 1964 on the dominance of images of science in the resolving of social problems. Also see Schudson 1978: 71–6.

112 James Scripps, "The Model One-Cent Paper," labeled "about 1897," James E. Scripps Letters, 1883–1897 (Cranbrook Archives).

113 George Booth, "Again the Senatorship." George Booth papers, Editorials and Articles, 1903–1915 (Cranbrook Archives).

114 Letter, George Booth to Edmund Booth, Nov. 9, 1914 (Cranbrook Archives). And cf. Pound 1964: 191.

115 Haber 1964: 101.

116 Rogin 1967: 197–8. For example, the Progressive intellectual, George Herbert Mead is used by Habermas to develop a conception of communicative action. This form of social action would underpin the processes of democratic will formation that occur in the public sphere. But actually, Mead's writings are characterized by an uneasy mix of communicative action, technical reason, and expressive–aesthetic action. He even argues in standard Progressive manner that once parties are done away with City Managers can be appointed to resolve all political issues on the basis of technical expertise. See Mead 1962: 312–14.

117 For example, see Sarfatti-Larson 1977: ch. 9; Hallin 1985; Habermas 1970: ch. 5; Burnham 1970: ch. 4; 1982: 175; Schattschneider 1975: chs. 4–5; Hays 1964.

118 While party rallies continued in 1908, they did not make it into the press.

119 Cornwell 1959. In addition in the early twentieth century presidential candidates took to the campaign trail unlike the prior century. In the nineteenth-century they were generally secluded from the public. The change partly occurred in 1896 (see McGerr 1986: 36–7; and Tulis 1987). Tulis and Rogin describe the broader changes in political cultural and constitutional theory that, in part, account for alterations in presidential public performances (see Rogin 1971).

120 Daniel Hallin presents a topography of journalistic narrative styles depending on the degree of consensus by the elite over the topic. In contexts of elite controversy, the media adopts an effaced narrative posture and quotes the two sides' opposed viewpoints. In conditions of elite consensus, the press is free to add its two cents of evaluative editorializing into the news (Hallin 1986b: 116–18).

121 This argument is in opposition to Donald L. Shaw's view presented in his classic article of 1967.

122 Corporate ownership of newspapers and a mass audience also limited the inclusion of such diverse and potentially controversial views.

Conclusion

Between the nineteenth and twentieth centuries, the American press drastically revised how it reported the everyday dramas and rites of American public life. Journalists dispensed with the celebratory partisan rhetoric typical of the Gilded Age and proceeded to adopt a sober style of impartial, expert reporting. How did this radical transformation occur? Media scholars' explanations for such changes have most often focused on shifts in newspaper economics, or the emergence of a professional occupational consciousness among journalists. In contrast, this study has contended that an analysis of politics and the public sphere is essential to account for the press's altered public role. Far from constituting a secondary or extraneous factor, politics decisively affects the functioning of all other facets of the modern journalistic enterprise. From its corporate organization to the size and shape of its reading audience, from its highest professional ideals to the typography employed on page 1 – no aspect of the modern daily paper has remained free from the now forceful, now insidious, influence of politics.

Media historians greatly neglect this political dimension. Such disregard, in fact, attests to the pervasiveness of journalism's modern occupational ideal. According to this cultural image, journalism's only true duty consists in supplying factual and reliable information to the American citizenry. Its sole sustenance comes from selling news to private individuals in the market place. Inaugurated in the early years of the twentieth century, this contemporary ethic of objectivity led Progressive Era publishers to break from parties, disavow their past political entanglements, and cancel all old political debts and commitments. In this manner, the modern media vehemently deny that any political considerations enter into their daily litany of crime, crisis, and calamity.

The ideal of objectivity is a particularly refined and elevated philosophy of journalistic independence. With its attendant distinction of bias versus impartial truth, objectivity suggests that the news can be a transparent depiction of reality. The collection of facts, their interpretation and subsequent ordering into a narrative account, supposedly

184

require no literary craft, interpretive labor, or theoretical perspective. In objectivity's simpler form of "naive empiricism," facts and events are conceived as merely waiting to be uncovered and harvested by the working reporter. Alternatively, in its more sophisticated version, the news hound is a trained expert – a technical functionary who knows how to weigh competing versions of events in order to achieve a balanced news report. In neither case is journalism conceived as creative moral or political work.

The denial of all political entanglements, however, merely disguises the intrinsically political nature of journalistic muckraking. (Objectivity only allows politics to infiltrate reporting in a more disguised and unimpeded form.) As argued in chapter 1, the journalist's recognition of facts, demarcation of events, and articulation of social issues implicitly depend upon a theory and/or a moral point of view – in essence, a social perspective. Before a fact can be counted as news, that is, as a salient facet of social life because morally problematic or causally important, the journalist must possess an understanding of how the world works.[1] Indeed, far from floating above the realm of politics, each crafted journalistic story implies a particular political standpoint. The news as a construct of a detached professional is thus an unworkable illusion. The daily paper is not solely a scientific report, but also a moral proclamation, an aesthetic creation, and certainly a democratic document. Because the news is inherently a political and public account of our shared social world, it remains the concern of citizens and not just of news technicians.

Thus, this book argued that the press is inextricably entwined in the arena of public–political debate with all its disagreements over what is and what should be the proper ordering of American society. This political account of the press was intended as a two-fold diagnostic tool – first to describe the mechanisms determining the functioning of the press, and second to evaluate the press's performance in facilitating democracy's debates and deliberations.

A proper ethic for journalism?

What would a proper press ethic entail? In the classical model of democracy, the press was a crucial institutional support for public discussion. Its role was to facilitate the dialogue of citizens – flung far and wide across the broad continent – as they formulated a rational consensus on public affairs. In more anxious or more empathic republican versions, the press was the woof and warp of the country's frayed social fabric. The communication media would knit together a commonweal tattered by the heated conflict (or simply the cool indifference) of private interests.[2] In his famous meditations on American democracy, de Tocqueville proposed that the fourth estate "becomes more necessary in proportion as men become more equal and individualism more to be feared." "A newspaper is an adviser that does not require to be sought but that comes of its own accord and talks to you briefly every day of the common weal, without distracting you from your private affairs."[3] For de Tocqueville, the ideal daily paper should enhance public discussion's exchange of information and opinions without distorting the equality among speakers and without infringing upon the public sphere's openness to all disputes, grievances, and perspectives.

Such a classical conception, although crucial as a corrective to the infirmities of our present-day corporate-controlled press, inadequately thinks through the constraints and possibilities of democracy in the modern era.[4] The press constitutes a distinctive medium which adds its virtues and limits to society's face-to-face conversations, extending them in time and space, but also, and necessarily, mediating them. Journalism cannot reproduce the contents of civil society's deliberations without distortion. Indeed, the press as a specialized institution is inevitably selective in the publication of citizens' opinions. Yet, the news media can also play a positive role, providing crucial resources to overcome the otherwise overburdened cognitive and communicative capacities of individual citizens. The media can assist public dialogue with the refinements, deliberations, and extended reflections of experts, representatives, and independent thinkers. To be sure, the press's more elevated, more rarefied, perhaps more logical, discourses should be fundamentally open to the opinions, perspectives, and issues of the broader-ranging and more diffused discussions of civil society. Nonetheless, to its role as medium of public debate, journalism also needs to append the contemporary tasks of information collector, synthesizer, and interpreter.[5]

Drawing upon the work of Habermas, Schudson, Blumer, and Gurevitch, I argue that the modern news media are charged with five tasks in serving the democratic public.[6] Some of these duties pertain more to the press's role as an information gatherer; others function to bolster the nation's dialogues and debates. In democratic political systems, the media should:

(1) provide full and fair information on social, political, and economic developments likely to affect citizens' lives and values;

(2) function as a representative of and a watchdog for the public – reporting the actions of government and corporations and speaking for the public interest in order to hold the powerful accountable;

(3) engage in meaningful agenda-setting, identifying key issues of the day, including the political forces that have risen up around these issues and that may work to resolve them;
(4) function as platforms for informative and illuminating advocacy by spokespersons for diverse social causes and interests;
(5) operate as a channel for dialogue across a wide range of views and perspectives in society.

Of course many of these ethical ideals are not especially novel and, in fact, are part of journalism's long-standing traditions, professional codes, and even legal regulations. Nevertheless, they still retain their force as critical, inadequately realized, ethical standards for the news media in democracy. Given this ethical prescription, our question then becomes: how well did the journalism of the nineteenth- and twentieth-century fulfill its moral duties? Moreover, what guidance, what resources, did the public philosophies of "partisanship" and "objectivity" provide to journalism? Confronted by competing powerful political actors and by a mass public frequently intolerant of provocative ideas and controversial speakers, where did the press find the courage, authority, and insight to pursue its distinctive version of the truth? Where indeed can the press find such resources?

The resources and limitations of partisan journalism

From 1865 to 1896 political parties strode boldly across the political landscape, dominating the public arena. In election after election, the Democrats and the Republicans were recipients of the voters' ringing endorsements. These two organizations appeared as the only true and legitimate representatives of the people's will. Consequently, parties possessed an overwhelming mandate to define the contours and contents of public debate. From early in the century to late, the ritual combat of parties drowned out all other public voices, whether they be those of individual elected officials, independent intellectuals, the writers and sages at the daily paper, or the average American citizen.

The electorate, for its part, exuberantly identified with the spectacular battles between Democrats and Republicans. In openly casting their party's brightly colored ballot, or in seizing a flaming torch for an evening campaign march through town center, or in simply subscribing to a party daily, Americans repeatedly and publicly demonstrated their political commitments. Far from accepting our contemporary notion of politics as matter of private beliefs and individual interests, the nineteenth century saw communal public displays of political allegiances as central to the practice of citizenship. Empathic displays of political commitment secured one's own status in the local community as an upstanding citizen who deserved all the rights and respect incumbent upon an equal adult male. Parties and partisanship were seen as intrinsic to a well-functioning democracy.

In this sharply public and polarized political world, Detroit's daily sheets too did not shrink from parading their political biases and commitments. The authority of parties and the popular political culture of avid partisanship decisively affected the ideals of the late nineteenth-century press. The public sphere's broader cultural norms, and its distribution of power among different public–political voices, deeply molded the institution of journalism. In manifold ways, papers repeated, reinforced, and celebrated the assumptions of this overarching political culture.

Newspapers became explicit organs of particular political communities. Their mission: to articulate the unique perspective of their community; to operate as a forum for debates and dialogues within the group; and, more typically, to enhance the strategic interests of their party organization. To fulfill this last strategic task, the press labored vigorously to support the public predominance of parties – the parties' appearance as the sole natural and necessary form for representing competing political viewpoints in the public arena. In addition, journals worked to maximize and mobilize the hordes of party faithful. Towards this end, the press followed the parties' definition of the important political questions of the day. Democratic and Republican parties propounded issues that would split the available set of voters to their advantage. Party papers, in turn, devoted disproportionate attention to the problems and policies accented by the favored party. Indeed, under the aegis of their party protector, dailies were authorized to strongly pursue a partisan news agenda by choosing events for coverage according to their political relevance. Across multiple journalistic genres, papers elaborated the social import and likely consequences of policy decisions.

Of course, party speakers took pride of place in this publicity. As democratically anointed representatives of the citizenry, parties obtained uniquely privileged access to the public; party officials were deemed to possess an automatic right to directly address the democratic masses. Into these narratives, reporters – as partisans – were free to interject their own explicit judgments and evaluations in a manner that would seem entirely inappropriate to today's objective journalism.

Outside of the two parties, there seemed to exist no place from which the press could provide an independent perspective upon the daily affairs of the nation. The daily journals were seen as inevitably subject to the overwhelming gravitational pull of one party or the other in all matters of political import. And, indeed, by its formal public affiliation the press suggested that parties exhausted the spectrum of legitimate political representation and opinion.

This political universe forms a stark contrast to our own. Our contemporary political philosophy of individualism and nominalism skeptically denies the very possibility of one person or group adequately representing another's interests. Gilded Age parties instead were perceived as substantive entities, possessing a life of their own, worthy of popular devotion, and with a priority over the individual being represented. Journalistic "organs" here formed one more extension, one more public face to this sprawling, all-encompassing political creature.

The clear effect of the press's politicized reporting was to dramatize the issues at stake by repeatedly publicizing sharply opposed political positions. Every morning, readers partook of a helping of political ideology along with their breakfast. Every day, partisan journals served up a coherent, simplified, political worldview. The diverse events of the day were subsumed under a single overarching political narrative. The manifest consequence of this strongly partisan public world created by journalism and other public institutions was, as historians have noted, the nineteenth century's persistently high levels of electoral participation. The daily partisan paper spoke in emphatic, argumentative, and often personal tones. It addressed its audience as committed political participants and in some sense as one engaged citizen speaking to another. Journalistic discourse was far from being the ostensibly unified, authoritative, impersonal discourse of our era. Rather, it was a form of dialogue and debate no matter how narrow and limited.

But narrow it was – tinted and tainted by the overarching strategic concerns of politicians and party managers. Significant limitations marred press publicity and public debate in the partisan era. Thus we cannot simply laud parties of the time and their papers for their enhancement of popular political participation. Nineteenth-century newspapers imported the rigidities and exclusions of the parties' strategic agenda into the public sphere, and continually shored up the party's dominion over public discussion. Press and parties derided third parties. And they ignored alternative voices desperately seeking to attract the public's attention. The press slighted civil society's far broader array of viewpoints in favor of the agonistic contests of the Democrats and the Republicans. In the end, journalism was absorbed into the overly polarized, instrumental world of formal political organizations in their competition for state power.

Certainly, the close bonds between press and formal polity had dire consequences for the truthfulness and persuasiveness of news narratives. Many condemned the partisan press's instrumental use of the news, a use which ceaselessly corrupted the possibility of forthright expression of beliefs, opinions, and facts. Journalism fell into the maelstrom of endlessly subjective and manipulated representations, where all reliable reports of facts, indeed all claims of truth, were replaced by considerations of political success.[7]

Thus, the partisan press fell far short of the public sphere's classical ideals of open and unlimited rational debate among equal concerned participants. Not surprisingly, the newspaper industry attracted scores of critics. These ardent detractors resided not just among the elites afraid of an overly politicized mass politics, but also among the politically dispossessed. Workers and women, immigrants and minorities – all those denied equal opportunity for public expression – challenged the restrictions of the press and polity.

Transition

The twentieth-century press broke from this explicitly political formula for journalism. Its re-envisioning of journalism's ideals and practices depended, in turn, upon a transformation of American politics. Detroit journals found new reasons for marketing to the general populace a seemingly apolitical news commodity in two key events: the critical election of 1896 and Progressive reforms in the early 1900s.

The 1896 campaign, and the Fourth Party System's changed electoral rules, both described in chapter 5, displaced parties from their political centrality. Parties' social integrative capacity – their ability to define the political identities and loyalties of the populace – declined as governmental decision-making was increasingly privatized. As the power of parties in the public sphere faltered, the incentives and sanctions inducing newspaper partisanship declined sharply. This novel political context permitted newspapers to issue declarations of party independence. Freed from parties, newspapers were not, however, relieved of their burden of justifying the necessarily partial nature of their news reports. In an era in which newspaper competition was declining and journals no longer represented the opposed viewpoints of parties, yet still monopolized the means of formal public communication, newspapers required a novel legitimating basis. They needed new compelling reasons to justify their prominence in the public arena and to mask the arbitrariness of their reporting. This was the overall political and journalistic terrain that Detroit's publishers navigated by articulating their new ethic of objectivity and independence.

In the early 1900s, Progressive political reform captured the allegiance of numerous Michigan and Detroit journalists and politicians. Detroit publishers joined the reform movement and appropriated elements from Progressive ideology for their new professional ethic. Owners and managers Scripps, Booth, and Schemmerhorn readily subscribed to the Progressive program of a new, virtuously independent political stance for both citizens and journalists. They declared the press to be an impartial, expert recorder of the day's most important events. Detroit's journalists took over Progressive ideas of technical experts freed from the contamination of politics. The dailies were to represent no particular political interests, but rather, the general public good; their remuneration would come only from the profits to be gained by general service to the reading public, not partial political communities. As participants in the Progressive movements, newspapers recast the terms of American political journalism, even as they reconstructed the American public world.

On December 12, 1927, John Fitzgibbon, then in the twilight of his forty-year career as a political reporter, sketched the changes he had seen in Detroit journalism:

As far as I am aware, while there are now many Michigan newspapers . . . that consistently support candidates and policies of a given party, yet uniformly they print without bias the things said and done in campaign by both sides. Perhaps not 100 per cent bias-free, yet nevertheless untarnished by deliberate intent to distort. It means that the press of today reflects a spirit of political independence in striking contrast to the old two-fisted fighting organs.[8]

The abilities and disabilities of twentieth-century "objective" journalism

At the dawn of the new century, the press rejected this overly dramatic partisanship, returning to many of the classical ideals of the republican public sphere. Claims of reliable, factual information, impartiality, and an openness to civil society's diverse range of voices once again added luster to journalism's public performance. Progressive Era dailies rebelled not just against the Democrats or the Republicans, but against all external political interests and obligations. Journalism would float above the passions and furies of the public realm. It would mediate between government and the people, insuring that citizens received crucial facts purified of any manipulative efforts. The news would be an authoritative, impartial record of the day's momentous deeds, divorced from all social agendas and political considerations.

A new rhetorical guise assured readers that no political bias marred the straight gray columns of print; journalists became professional technicians, experts at gathering information and separating truths from half-truths, distortions, and outright lies. Reliable facts won pride of place over all political advocacy. Claims of public service supplanted past commitments to particular communities or private interests.

In principle, a new-found openness defined the press's reporting agenda. After all, in its comportment as an independent, differentiated institution, journalism should not provide automatic coverage to any group or individual because of ongoing political ties or interests. No longer chained to parties, newspapers were in principle accessible to civil society's full register of voices. Even the dominant narrative structure of the news – the famous "inverted pyramid" format with its summary lead paragraph – pointed to this independent and flexible posture of the press. Commencing with a bald summary of an incident, the narrative declared itself to be entirely dependent upon the chance occurrence of an important event, not the pronouncements of established authorities. Brute particular facts (the classical "who, why, what, when, and where" of journalism school), not overarching theories or social concerns, supposedly determined the make-up of the front page.

This ideal of openness, however, was seriously compromised. The daily paper of the twentieth century publicized only a highly circumscribed array of perspectives – corresponding to those views and voices most sanctioned by the institutions of political and social authority. How can one explain this limitation to our "free" press? First, the pose of the independent journalist found its legitimacy for narrating American social life not in a broader political standpoint or community, but in the facts. In its technocratic emphasis – the upholding of "truth" over "politics" – the press recognized little or no responsibility to enhance public deliberation across an array of viewpoints and perspectives.

Second, news workers began to perform their role as mere technicians who sift the evidence to discover the whys and wherefores of the day's events. Yet facts do not speak for themselves. Inevitably, subtle and usually unrecognized calculations enter into the journalists' determination of the details to note, the voices to attend to, and the story-lines to publicize. Instead of the explicit macro-narratives of parties, the reporters' judgments rested upon a flexible array of taken-for-granted social norms and cultural common-sense. The news thus became a fragmented mosaic of stories. In these necessarily selective, culturally constructed tales, which voices warranted the journalist's (and subsequently the reader's) full and undivided attention? Which sources appeared most trustworthy to working reporters and their superiors in the corporate hierarchy? Seeking hard facts and reliable information, the journalist chose those in positions of power and institutional authority. Such executives and officials were seen as most likely to possess authoritative information, to be legitimate spokespersons of their institution, whether governmental or private, and even to embody the ideals and identity of the nation.[9]

The press rapidly assimilated to the role of official interpreter and purveyor of governmental publicity.[10] The correspondent was less often governmental watchdog than lapdog. Such an embrace of power with its often corresponding access to insider knowledge was celebrated and taken as evidence of journalism's own elevated status. In this fashion, the press substituted the hegemony and support of elite political actors for the more threatening submersion in the debates and the impassioned disagreements of popular democracy.[11] By linking their fortunes to the elite, journalists gained a semblance of power and prestige, while keeping at a distance the supposedly ignorant, powerless, and irrational mass.[12] Furthermore, as official mediator between the legitimate center and the passive citizenry, the press could provide a series of enticing narratives depicting the dramas of the nation, as long as the formal polity retained a grasp on the hearts and minds of the populace.

Third and lastly, once the press severed its formal ties to legitimate political organizations, it lost its own mandate for forthright political expression. The nineteenth-century daily had been parasitic upon the parties' broader political authority in the public sphere. But twentieth-century journalism lacked (and continues to lack) this public mandate provided by the votes and the endorsement of a particular political public. Twentieth-century papers missed the sanctions for political voice secured through such democratic machinery as elections and public dialogue.

In their passion for rigorous objectivity, in their disavowal of any particular viewpoint, in their commitment to standing as external observers to the deceits and diatribes of public life, reporters lost their past capacity to interject their own evaluations and judgments; provide overarching interpretations; and explore controversial or, conversely, taken-for-granted social viewpoints. They lost the ability to independently set the news agenda. Indeed, as putatively impartial, the press possesses only a highly circumscribed authority for publicizing the views of the controversial, the provocative, or the marginal. If, in the face of criticisms and challenges, the press persisted in providing a public soapbox to such demagogues, charlatans, and outright subversives, then would this not reveal journalism's own illicit bias, its political agenda, its limited fidelity to its own standards of objectivity?

Especially after the Progressive movement's energies died out, the press renounced its reform pose as public watchdog. Already in 1906 President Theodore Roosevelt had coined the term "muckrake" to disparage and discipline the investigative tendencies of the independent press. Divorced from the support and authority provided by particular political publics and philosophies, the journalists found themselves isolated and weak, especially when confronting the hostile forces of public opinion or the powers that be. Lacking any justifications for an untoward display of partiality, and confronted by criticism, the print media typically retreated to a less exposed public posture. Indeed, in all contexts of controversy, the objective press provided an effaced, deferential narration of the views of legitimate authorities from formal political society.[13]

In this manner, the press duplicated the main movement of twentieth-century liberalism. Organizations such as political parties, trade unions, interest groups, and elected officials insulated themselves from the democratic demands of their members by utilizing institutionalized power, technocratic legitimations, successful economic performance, and anti-Communist repression. They retained power, but only at the price of destroying their own public authority and vitiating their democratic mandate.[14]

In the end, instead of sparing the press from criticism and sustaining it with the political resources to explore the pressing issues of the day, "objectivity" disabled journalism. Despite the unmistakable gains in reliable factual information and in openness, objectivity does not provide reporters with the political authority they need to accomplish their democratic mission. It does not protect news workers as they ask the hard questions and probe democracy's unpleasant issues. Rather, objectivity renders the press weak in the face of pressures from the market, the public, or the political elite.

Reconstituting a democratic mandate?

The question then becomes: from where can the press regain the resources and authority to fulfill its democratic mandate? Where can the news media find guidance as they navigate the chaos and pitfalls of a contentious public arena too often ruled by cynicism and conformity? The twentieth century's posture of independence from politics is illusory; the nineteenth century's alignment with politics was surely flawed.[15] Neither inside politics, nor outside – where can journalism stand in order to gain a critical perspective upon the workings of American democracy? The twentieth-century press's democratic inadequacies, its political weaknesses, its oft-remarked crisis of authority and credibility stem from journalism's detachment from the wellsprings of authority in modern democracy. The press needs to reforge its ties with the manifold voices, perspectives, concerns, and debates of civil society, outside the formal summits of political power. The press must reinsert itself into the public sphere, resituate itself within society's broad and inclusive political conversations.

It is in the public sphere that the populace forms a common conviction on the right and proper way to order social life. Detached from this communicatively generated consensus, the authority of the press in the long run becomes suspect. It grows susceptible to challenge, withers, and finds itself more and more dependent upon the reigning powers with their institutionalized resources of organization and money.[16] Only by actively consulting with the citizens, letting new voices enter into the media, and functioning as a sponsor of public debate and dialogue, will the press reestablish its authority to narrate the affairs of American society. Only in this fashion will the press reclaim an audience for its arguments and stories.

Not a detachment from the controversies of politics, but an avowed commitment to public–political discussion will generate a new legitimacy for journalism's mission. The media's allegiance, not to this or that political cause or party, but to the general value of democratic discussion, gives the press a stake, a defensible political perspective from which to mediate the public realm.[17] The press would not simply report on the day's events from the magisterial stance of a disinterested observer. Instead, the media would always maintain as their purpose the enhancement of the public's collective reasoning and enlightenment.

Redefining itself as a political medium, not just a scientific account, the press would undermine the grounds for its critics' perennial accusations of bias, illicit editorializing, and partisan agendas. The partisanship with which the press could then be accused would be only partiality for democracy. New criteria would come into play in evaluating the news media's accomplishment of this avowedly political mission. In turn, the press would become obliged to demonstrate its allegiance to these ideals of the public sphere – an expanded inclusive public participation, and the publicizing of speakers not just according to their prior social status or power, but according to their insights, how they address issues of public concern, and how they represent diverse social strands of the national fabric. In addition, journalism would acquire responsibility to take the words of speakers seriously by substantively engaging in their content as significant proposals for the direction of the commonweal. Policy initiatives could no longer be cynically dismissed as so much empty political rhetoric, as mere markers or chips in a grand political game.[18] Such an explicit allegiance to pluralistic public debate would reinforce the ideals of tolerance. The press would thus advance its own freedom to publicize views and voices outside of a narrowly defined political compass – a spectrum repeatedly narrowed by criticisms of "bias." The fulfillment of such critical standards would result in an expanded license or public trust for the press to independently determine how to best fulfill its journalistic duties.

The press regains its prestige and autonomy insofar as its coverage can be seen as guided by the demands of democratic discussion in general and as a response to the issues raised by citizens in particular. In alternative public forums, the concerns of the citizenry can achieve visibility, strength, and clarity through dialogue and mutual recognition. Such forums perform important sensitizing functions – bringing new questions and problems, novel perspective and possibilities to public attention.[19] These publicly articulated views furnish the news media with an alternative guide for ascertaining what is an important public issue requiring investigation. Through this process of consultation, the press obtains a distinct political mandate to detail American social life beyond the confines of the two-party consensus. In this context, the press can claim to be explicitly working to fulfill the public's desire to know and understand the social complexities and possible resolutions of the problems at hand. It avoids, therefore, all charges of self-serving bias and particular interests in its reporting. The press corps thus accrue the resources to resist the trivial, the sensational, the manipulative. They can say no to the publicity-aggrandizing strategies of politicians, corporate PR, or the free-lance efforts of individual celebrities, stars, and pundits.

Such a capacious press upholding an expanded public sphere would serve to awaken a public lapsed into cynicism and restore it to the national community. The press would, in de Tocqueville's words, recall the populace to the commonweal, away from its immersion in the private life with its sure, albeit limited, freedoms and solidarities. A more democratic press would offer new grounds for engagement to a citizenry which sees itself as marginal to the currently contrived debates of politicians and media professionals.

Contemporary Americans find themselves repelled by the haughty technocratic authority of the news media, with their dry narratives and privileging of elite voices, and are repulsed by the sterility of current political discourse with its scandals and vituperative attacks. The expanded dialogues of a rejuvenated press could offer multiple means for a citizenry to find new forms of participation and attachment to the US's communal discussions. A reformed press and public sphere would entice citizens with novel genres of rhetoric, innovative topics, alternative voices and representatives, and new forms of popular access.

In posing this ideal democratic model of the press, I recognize that my call to moral arms does not amount to a political project of change. More specifically, I see two distinct limits. First, to be accomplished, journalistic reform requires diverse social forces and pressures; all ideals, no matter how desirable, suffer the contingencies of history for their realization. Fortunately for this proposed ethics of journalism, a movement already exists working in its own fashion to remedy the deficiencies of the objective, corporate-controlled news media. I am referring to the various wings of the Public Journalism movement in the US. Here one can only note, not assess, the remarkable accomplishments achieved by this movement in a relatively short time span.[20] These proselytizers for reform seek to engage both the corporate rulers of journalism and working reporters in a program of change. They strive to transform journalism's professional vision and working practices in conformity with a broader, more democratic notion of the media's proper service to the community.

Second, a transfiguration of the institution of journalism depends indeed upon symbolic and material resources beyond the press itself. The news media, whatever their efforts towards expanding the reign of democracy, are not masters of their own destiny. The press of the twenty-first century remains, as in the past, entangled in and dependent upon the public sphere with its distribution of power and legitimacy amongst diverse public actors. The press cannot be seen as a completely autonomous entity. We should rather conceive of it as one infused by the ideas and energies of the public sphere, with its permanent contentions over who is a proper public speaker and what is appropriate public speech. A more democratic press will develop only in tandem with more encompassing social movements which can create and invigorate diverse forums for participatory deliberation and decision-making throughout American society.

NOTES

1 See Ettema and Glasser 1998.
2 See Carey 1989: introduction.
3 de Tocqueville 1945: V. 2, 119.
4 An exemplary guide to the limits and possibilities of democracy in our era is Habermas 1996: chs. 7–8. And see Bohman 1995: 422–7.
5 The debate between Dewey and Lippmann over the nature of contemporary democracy and the press revolved around two opposed notions of journal-

ism's role in public life – the press as a specialized instrument for the collection of data, and the press as a medium for the continuation of civil society's dispersed debates and dialogues. Cf. Carey 1989: 74–84.

6 Habermas 1996; Blumler and Gurevitch 1995; see also The [Hutchins] Commission of Freedom of the Press 1947.

7 Cf. Adams 1961 and Didion 1984.

8 Speech reported in the *News*, Dec. 30, 1927: 17. In 1926, Frank Thayer wrote: "The old political type of newspaper stressed its favorite party in both news and editorial columns, neglecting in large measure the activities of its opposition. In the best newspapers to-day, both major political parties are assured news space, even though the greater emphasis be given to one" (Thayer 1926: 91–2).

9 Cf. Sigal 1989. On the upper-middle-class's belief in the proper social authority of those who possess positions of social power and technical expertise see Lamont 1992: 40.

10 See the enumeration of cases of symbiotic collusion between journalists and governmental officials in Schudson forthcoming; Hallin 1994: ch. 9.

11 Prejudices of an ethnic, class, and status origin underwrote this limited range of the public sphere in two ways. For elites, the public is seen as divided into the disciplined cultural elites and the cultural masses. The former are proper public speakers and they provide disciplined, impartial, expert knowledge. The latter should be excluded from the public sphere, and in fact require supervision. Because of the masses' supposed lack of intellectual rigor, and their susceptibility to persuasion by manipulative appeals, it is necessary to limit their public exposure to demagogic voices. Implicitly a theory of mass society is part and parcel of this cultural cauldron. On the ethnic prejudices underwriting turn-of-the-century profes-sionalization projects see Collins 1979: 100.

12 In general, see the description of intellectuals' fears of impotence and isolation in Lasch 1965: ch. 6.

13 Once the news had been politically reconstructed in the early twentieth century, various economic devices reinforced the press's political conformity. The redefinition of its audience from a specialized to a general, mass audience obliged the paper to downplay divisive or offensive political coverage. Furthermore, the dependence of papers on advertising increased the press's susceptibility to political pressures for conformity. Advertising, of course, directly represented the voice and views of large economic interests but, in addition, advertisers can ill afford to be associated with any con-troversial journalism. See Barnouw's discussion of the pressures to eliminate all controversial political views or even serious drama from television in the 1950s (Barnouw 1978: 48–52, 101–21).

14 Rogin 1987: xvii–xviii, and chs. 2, 4; Montgomery 1979: ch. 7; Ginsberg and Shefter 1990: 10, 35, 77–86; and Lowi 1979. As Rogin argues, categories central to 1950s and 1960s political science analysis – "status politics" versus "pragmatic class politics" – were premised upon (and prescribed) the general demobilization of citizens from all forms of political participation, including even voting.

15 Elsewhere I present a more extended consideration of the press's proper

institutional realm in terms of the Habermasian division: market, political society, civil society. See Kaplan 1997.

16 Other "functional" media – power, money – replace the consent generated through unconstrained communicative dialogue. Cf. Habermas 1977.

17 Schudson 1995: ch. 10; Rosen 1992: 8–11.

18 Rosen 1992: 24–5.

19 See Fraser's "post-bourgeois" formulation of the public sphere in Fraser 1992; and Sheller 1996.

20 An important assessment of Public Journalism's accomplishments and philosophy is Glasser 1999.

METHODOLOGICAL APPENDIX

At the center of this book's argument is a systematic, longitudinal content analysis of the daily newspapers of Detroit from 1865 to 1920. I deemed such analysis necessary since to date no historian or sociologist has conducted adequate research on the timing and nature of changes in American journalism between the Civil War and World War One. The absence of such research has resulted in empirically flawed analyses based on episodic, impressionistic, or, worse, merely anecdotal evidence. Here I discuss some of the methodological issues entailed in my research choices.

The content analysis pursued here coded all the articles published on sampled days in Detroit's daily newspapers: the *Detroit Free Press*, the *Evening News*, the *Post*, the *Advertiser and Tribune*, the *Union*, the *Times*, and the *Journal*. In 1867, at the start of this study, Detroit was the site of four daily papers. At times, the total increased to five journals, but it diminished to three in 1919. Why code the entire population of dailies of a single city? Any narrow sampling of papers risks producing an unrepresentative portrait of American newspapers, thus introducing arbitrary bias into one's research.[1] Furthermore, as John Nerone argues, sampling abstracts journals from their web of entangling ties.[2] Studying *all* the dailies of a city highlights the interactive ecology of the urban newspaper trade with its market niches, its conflicts and competitions, and its symbiotic journalistic relations.

Why Detroit? Detroit has the merit of political representativeness. This growing midwestern city demonstrated the "main dynamics" of American politics in the late nineteenth and early twentieth centuries. While party organization was stronger in the Northeast and weaker in the newer, western states, the main national trend throughout the Gilded Age was hardy party organizations in significant competition.[3] Detroit's Democrats and Republicans maintained formidable party organizations in close electoral competition throughout the late 1800s. In the twentieth century, following the critical elections of 1894–96 and the subsequent party transformations, Detroit again conformed to the majority pattern. The Republicans became entrenched in the state as the dominant party. Furthermore, in the early 1900s, Detroit and Michigan suffered the political turmoil and reform typical of the Progressive Era.[4] Besides its representative nature, Detroit was a sufficiently large city to possess a press that displayed the full range of partisan and factional divisions typical to the nineteenth-century city. At the same time, this growing industrial metropolis was small enough to make the coding of the existing population of daily journals a reasonable proposition.

American political life exhibits a cyclical nature following the periodic schedule of elections. Consequently, the coverage of political news displays strong differences between election season and non-election times. To avoid any confusion such cycles might have introduced into my search for long-term changes, I constructed a stratified sample of newspapers. The sample included a newspaper edition from each presidential election campaign and an edition from the preceding non-election year. A copy of the October 15 issue of each daily was analyzed for the presidential election years, 1868–1916. And from the preceding year I analyzed a copy of the February 15th edition of all journals, 1867–1919. In the end, approximately 10,000 news stories were coded.[5]

Newspapers are necessarily selective and consequently "biased" political creatures. "Objectivity" is not possible. Partiality is an enduring feature of the press. In contrast to this relatively constant "bias" of the press, I defined "partisanship" more restrictively as a newspaper's *continuous*, ongoing *display* of allegiances to a *specific* formal political organization, most particularly to a party. This second more limited notion of partisanship helps capture ways in which American journalism has fundamentally changed over time. [6]

Partisan political preference in this limited sense operates through two main forms, which I label "manifest" and "covert" (or "selective") bias.[7] In manifest bias, reporters introduce their own *explicit judgments* for or against a party into the narrative. The literary theory of "enunciation" helps us formalize the elements that should be coded as manifest in contrast to covert displays of bias. Enunciation refers to all those literary traits of a written text that draw our attention to the author as a particular person actively organizing the narrative report and openly speaking as an "I" to a "you," the reader. Enunciation occurs through a variety of grammatical features. These include:

the personal pronouns of the first and second persons; the demonstrative pronouns [this, those, etc.]; the adverbs and adjectives that Bally calls relatives (here, now, yesterday . . .); and the verb tenses organized around the present, that is, the time of enunciation . . . and the performative verbs . . .

But especially germane for consideration of open and unabashed judgments by the author are:

certain strata of the lexicon in which there appear evaluative and emotive terms (terms containing semantic features that imply a judgment or a particular attitude on the part of the speaker)[8]

Explicit judgments, however, do not exhaust the operation of political bias in late nineteenth and early twentieth-century journalism. There also occurred "covert bias," where the news report appeared to be impartial. The narrator abstained from voicing any personal judgments and evaluations. This latent bias functioned in two distinct forms: the *discriminating choice of speakers* and the *selective reporting of topics*. In the first case, newspapers overwhelmingly quoted speakers and reported accomplishments from their favored party while steadfastly ignoring the opposition. The bias was masked as the neutral, factual reporting of significant words and deeds. However, at a certain point (given the gross inequalities in coverage) this supposedly covert, relatively unpronounced bias became an evident and expected dimension of partisanship.

In the second form of covert bias, the journal provided selective coverage to social events that implicitly supported the policy positions of the favored party. Here, readers themselves needed to draw the proper political conclusions from the news. For example, in the 1896 election, Republican papers repeatedly published the statements of business leaders who predicted dire consequences for the nation's economy if the Democratic candidate, William Jennings Bryan, was elected. Adequate coding of this last dimension of covert bias – a newspaper's selective attention to events – depends upon understanding of the articulated policy divisions between the two parties. In the technical language of content analysis, this is the "context unit."[9]

The editorial pages of the partisan journal often clarified these "context units" (to both the reader and the researcher) by elaborating the policy differences that divided the two parties. Furthermore, the editorials often drew attention to the news stories and made explicit the implicit partisan assumptions guiding the paper's news choices.

NOTES

1 Numerous studies choose individual big city dailies for study. But selecting papers such as the *New York Times* neglects the fact that such journals are only one type out of the entire panoply of American journals. The *Times* in the period of my study was distinctly an upper-class, conservative, Democrat, expensive, prestige daily, entirely different from other journals inhabiting New York City.
2 Nerone 1993.
3 Shefter 1983: 459–83.
4 Burnham 1982: ch. 1.
   Detroit also fits in with a general class of exponentially growing cities in the years 1880–1920. Spanning the Midwest and the Northeast, these manufacturing cities propelled the US's climb to world leadership in industrial output. Detroit, like Buffalo, Cleveland, Chicago, St. Louis, Pittsburgh, etc. fueled American economic growth with a burgeoning population of immigrants, largely drawn from the south and east of Europe. The most sophisticated

study of Detroit's economy, spatial geography, and ethnic and class make-up is Zunz 1982. Oestereicher insightfully explores the ethnic and class character of Detroit and its labor movement in Oestereicher 1986.

5 All articles published for the selected dates were coded for their political bias and their length was measured. The constructed measure of "percent bias" is the percentage of the papers' space devoted to these two types of partisanship.

6 In the contemporary era, US press selectivity typically does not systematically elevate one political party over the other. More usual is the selection of "legitimate" mainstream political speakers over citizens, the marginal, and "illegitimate" political speakers.

7 In general, compare the coding procedures in Merrill 1965 and Shaw 1967. Shaw, however, focuses exclusively on manifest bias. He writes:

> A biased news story was any which had as a referent a presidential or vice-presidential candidate and which contained value statements in such a way the overall impression created upon today's reader was a positive or negative feeling toward that referent. An unbiased news story did not create this positive or negative feeling, regardless of whether or not such value statements including adjectives, adverbs, nouns or verbs phrases or statements were used.

8 Todorov 1979: 324. And see the application of considerations of enunciation to contemporary television news in Morse 1985.

   The specific coding criteria was to count as overtly biased any article with three or more statements of partisan evaluation by the reporter. If the article was under three inches long then it was overtly biased with two or more statements of preference. In any case, articles tended to cluster around one end of the coding spectrum or the other – either explicitly evaluative or totally non-evaluative.

9 Krippendorf 1980: 59–60.

References

ARCHIVAL PAPERS

George G. Booth Papers. Burton Historical Collection, Detroit Public Library. Cranbrook Archives, Bloomfield Hills, MI.
George B. Catlin Papers. Burton Historical Collection, Detroit Public Library.
Joseph Greusel Papers. Burton Historical Collection, Detroit Public Library.
Senator James McMillan Business Papers. Burton Historical Collection, Detroit Public Library.
James E. Scripps Papers. Cranbrook Archives, Bloomfield Hills, MI.

BOOKS AND ARTICLES

Aldrich, A. J. 1884. "Relation of the Newspaper to Politics." *Proceedings of the Michigan Press Association*, June 24. Detroit Public Library, Burton Historical Collection.
Alexander, Jeffrey. 1981. "The Mass Media in Systemic, Historical and Comparative Perspective." In Elihu Katz and Tamas Szecisko (eds.) *Mass Media and Social Change*. Beverly Hills: Sage.
Allen, Robert C. (ed.) 1987. *Channels of Discourse: Television and Contemporary Criticism*. Chapel Hill: University of North Carolina Press.
Amburgey, Terry, Marjo-Riitta Lehtisalo, and Dawn Kelly. 1988. "Suppression and Failure in the Party Press." In Glenn Carroll (ed.) *Ecological Models of Organizations*. Cambridge: Ballinger.
Anderson, Kristi, and Stuart Thorson. 1989. "Public Discourse or Strategic Game: Changes in Our Conceptions of Elections." *Studies in American Political Development* V. 3.
Angelo, Frank. 1981. *On Guard: A History of the Detroit Free Press*. Detroit: Detroit Free Press.
Anon. 1993. "Croatia Clamps Down on Opposition." *San Francisco Chronicle*, May 13: A8.
Applegate, Thomas. 1907. *Michigan Historical Collections*, V. 6: *History of the Press of Michigan*. Michigan Pioneer and Historical Society. Lansing, MI.
Arato, Andrew. 1981. "Civil Society Against the State." *Telos*, no. 47 (Spring).
Arendt, Hannah. 1959. *The Human Condition*. Chicago: University of Chicago Press.
Ayer & son, N. W. 1880–1930. *American Newspaper Annual*.

Baehr Jr., Harry. 1972. *The New York Tribune Since the Civil War*. New York: Octagon.

Bagdikian, Ben. 1987. *The Media Monopoly*. Boston: Beacon.

Baker, Jean. 1983. *Affairs of Party: The Political Culture of Northern Democrats in Mid-Nineteenth Century*. Ithaca: Cornell University Press.

Bailey, Kenneth D. 1982. *Methods of Social Research*, 2nd edition. New York: Free Press.

Baldasty, Gerald. 1991. "The Nineteenth-Century Origins of Modern American Journalism." *Proceedings of the American Antiquarian Society* V. 100, part 2.

1992. *The Commercialization of News in the Nineteenth Century*. Madison: University of Wisconsin Press.

1993. "The Role of Competition in Defining the News: E. W. Scripps and Working Class Papers." Paper presented to the Western Journalism Historians Conference, Berkeley (February 25–26).

Baldasty, Gerald, and Jeffrey Rutenbeck. 1988. "Money, Politics and Newspapers: The Business Environment of Press Partisanship in the Late 19th Century." *Journalism History* V. 15, no. 2–3.

Barnouw, Erik. 1978. *The Sponsor: Notes on a Modern Potentate*. New York: Oxford University Press.

Barraclough, Geoffrey. 1967. *An Introduction to Contemporary History*. New York: Penguin.

Barros, Robert. 1986. "The Left and Democracy: Recent Debates in Latin America." *Telos* no. 68 (Summer).

Barsamian, David. 1992. *Stenographers to Power*. Monroe, ME: Common Courage.

Baughman, James. 1992. *The Republic of Mass Culture*. Baltimore: John Hopkins.

Baum, Dale. 1984. *The Civil War Party System: The Case of Massachusetts, 1848–1876*. Chapel Hill: University of North Carolina Press.

Bellah, Robert, Richard Madsen, William M. Sullivan, Steven Tipton, and Ann Swidler. 1985. *Habits of the Heart*. Berkeley: University of California Press.

Bender, Thomas. 1987. *New York Intellect*. New York: Alfred Knopf.

Bensel, Richard. 1986. *Sectionalism and American Political Development: 1880–1980*. Madison: University of Wisconsin Press.

Benveniste, Emile. 1971. *Problems in General Linguistics*, trans. by M. Meek. Coral Gables, FL: University of Miami.

Berger, Suzanne. (ed.) 1982. *Organizing Interests in Western Europe*. Cambridge: Cambridge University Press.

Bingay, Malcolm. 1949. *Of Me I Sing*. New York: Bobbs-Merrill.

Blodgett, Geoffrey. 1976. "A New Look at the Gilded Age: Politics in a Cultural Context." In Daniel W. Howe (ed.) *Victorian America*. University of Pennsylvania Press.

Blumler, Jay G. and Michael Gurevitch. 1995. *The Crisis of Public Communication*. New York: Routledge.

Bobbio, Norberto. 1987. *The Future of Democracy*. Minneapolis: University of Minnesota Press.

Bohman, James. 1995. "Review of Bernhard Peters, *Die Integration moderner Gesellschaften*." *Constellations* V. 1, no. 3 (January).

Bolt, Robert. 1970. *Donald Dickinson*. Grand Rapids, MI: William B. Eerdmans.

Boorstin, Daniel. 1961. *The Image*. New York: Harper and Row.

Booth, George. 1918. "Spirit and Purpose of the Ideal Newspaper." *Editor and Publisher* V. 50, no. 38 (March 2).

Bourdieu, Pierre. 1985. "The Social Space and the Genesis of Groups." *Social Science Information* V. 24, no. 2.

1986. "An Antinomy in the Notion of Collective Protest." In Alejandro Foxley et al. (eds.) *Development, Democracy and the Art of Trespassing*. Baltimore: John Hopkins University Press.

1991. *Language and Symbolic Power*. Cambridge, MA: Harvard University Press.

Bow, James. 1989a. "George Gough Booth: Artisan as Publisher." Paper presented to the Michigan Academy of Sciences, Arts and Letters (March 17).

1989b. "George G. Booth and His Vision of the American Worker, 1888–1910: The Empire Building Years of Detroit's Artisan-Publisher." (Ms., November.)

1992. "The Detroit Evening News: Nonpartisan, Reform Journalism in the 1870s, 1876–77." Paper presented to the *AJHA Annual Convention*, Lawrence, Kansas (October 3).

Breed, Warren. 1955. "Social Control in the Newsroom: A Functional Analysis." *Social Forces* V. 33 (May).

Bridges, Amy. 1984. *A City in the Republic: Antebellum New York and the Origins of Machine Politics*. Ithaca: Cornell University Press.

Britt, Albert. 1960. *Ellen Browning Scripps: Journalist and Idealist*. Oxford: Oxford University Press.

Brooks, Peter. 1985. *The Melodramatic Imagination: Balzac, Henry James, Melodrama and the Mode of Excess*. New York: Columbia University Press.

Bruce, Robert V. 1959. *1877: Year of Violence*. Indianapolis: Bobbs-Merrill.

Bryan, William J. 1896. *The First Battle: A Story of the Campaign of 1896*. Chicago: W. B. Conkey.

Bryce, James. 1909. *The American Commonwealth* V. 2. New York: Macmillan.

Buck, Paul H. 1937. *The Road to Reunion*. Boston: Little, Brown and Co.

Burawoy, Michael. 1989. "Marxism without Micro-Foundations." *Socialist Review* no. 89/2.

Bureau of the Census. 1972. *Census of Population* V. 1. Washington, D.C., May.

Burgess-Jackson, Kenneth. 1990. "Democracy Versus Republicanism: Detroit Press Reaction to the Reconstruction Act of 1867." *Southern Studies* V. 1, no. 4 (Winter).

Burin, Frederic, and Kurt Shell. (eds.) 1969. *Politics, Law, and Social Change: Selected Essays of Otto Kirchheimer*. New York: Columbia University Press.

Burnham, Walter D. 1970. *Critical Elections and the Mainsprings of American Politics*. New York: W. W. Morton.

1981. "The System of 1896: An Analysis." In Paul Kleppner (ed.) *The Evolution of American Electoral Systems*. Westport: Greenwood.

1982. *The Current Crisis in American Politics*. New York: Oxford University Press.

1986. "Periodicization Schemes and 'Party Systems': The 'System of 1896' as a Case in Point." *Social Science History* V. 10, no. 3 (Fall).

1987. "Voting." In A. James Reichley (ed.) *Elections American Style*. Washington, DC: Brookings Institute.

Campbell, Brewster, and Edgar Guest. 1948. "William E. Quinby." In Earl Babst and Lewis Vander Velde (eds.) *Michigan and the Cleveland Era*. Ann Arbor: University of Michigan Press.

Carey, James W. 1974. "The Problem of Journalism History." *Journalism History* V. 1, no. 1 (Spring).

1986. "Why and How? The Dark Continent of American Journalism." In Michael Schudson and Robert K. Manoff (eds.) *Reading the News*. New York: Pantheon.

1989. *Communication as Culture*. Boston: Unwin Hyman.

Carroll, Glenn. 1984. "Concentration and Specialization: Dynamics of Niche Width in Populations of Organizations." *Organizational Behavior and Industrial Relations Working Paper*, no. 2. University of California, Berkeley.

Catlin, George B. 1926a. "Little Journeys in Journalism: Michael J. Dee." *Michigan Historical Magazine* V. 10, no. 1.

1926b. "Little Journeys in Journalism: Wilbur F. Storey." *Michigan History Magazine* V. 10, no. 4.

1926c. *The Story of Detroit*. Detroit: Evening News Association.

1945. "Adventures in Journalism: Detroit Newspapers Since 1850." *Michigan History Magazine* V. 29, no. 3 (July–September).

Caves, Richard. 1977. *American Industry: Structure, Conduct, Performance*. Englewood Cliffs, NJ: Prentice-Hall (fourth edition).

Chandler, Alfred D. 1980. *The Visible Hand: The Managerial Revolution in American Business*. Cambridge: Belknap.

Clark, Anna. 1990. "Queen Caroline and the Sexual Politics of Popular Culture in London, 1820." *Representations* no. 31 (Summer).

Clarke, Stuart Alan. 1991. "Fear of a Black Planet." *Socialist Review* V. 91 no. 3–4 (July).

Clemens, Elizabeth. 1993. "Organizational Repertoires and Institutional Change: Women's Groups and the Transformation of U. S. Politics, 1890–1920." *American Journal of Sociology* V. 98 (Jan.).

Cohen, Jean L. 1983. "Rethinking Social Movements." *Berkeley Journal of Sociology* V. 23.

1996. "The Public Sphere, the Media, and Civil Society." In Monroe Price and Andras Sajo (eds.) *Rights of Access to the Media*. Boston: Kluwer Law International.

Cohen, Jean L. and Andrew Arato. 1989. "Politics and the Reconstruction of the Concept of Civil Society." In Thomas McCarthy et al. (eds.) *Zwischenbetrachtungen: Im Prozess der Aufklaerung*. Frankfurt: Suhrkamp Verlag.

1992. *Civil Society and Political Theory*. Cambridge, MA: MIT Press.

Collins, Randall. 1979. *The Credential Society*. New York: Academic Press.

Cornwell, Elmer E., Jr. 1959. "Presidential News: The Expanding Public Image." *Journalism Quarterly* (Summer).

Couvares, Francis. 1984. *The Remaking of Pittsburgh: Class and Culture in an Industrializing City, 1877–1919*. Albany: State University of New York Press.

Croly, Herbert. 1953. "The Campaign of 1896." In George Whicher (ed.) *William Jennings Bryan and the Campaign of 1896*. Boston: D. C. Heath.

Crouthamel, James L. 1989. *Bennett's New York Herald and the Rise of the Popular Press*. Syracuse: Syracuse University Press.

Curl, Donald. 1980. *Murat Halstead and the Cincinnati Commercial*. Boca Raton: University Presses of Florida.

Currie, Harold. 1968. "A Socialist Edits the Detroit Times." *Michigan History Magazine* V. 52, no. 1 (Spring).

Darnton, Robert. 1984. *The Great Cat Massacre*. New York: Basic.

Denning, Michael. 1987. *Mechanics Accents: Dime Novels and Working-Class Culture in America*. New York: Verso.

Dicken-Garcia, Hazel. 1989. *Journalistic Standards in Nineteenth-Century America*. Madison: University of Wisconsin Press.

Dilla, Harriette. 1912. *The Politics of Michigan, 1865–1878*. New York: Columbia University.

Dunbar, Willis, and William Shade. 1972. "The Black Man Gains the Vote: The Centennial of 'Impartial Suffrage' in Michigan." *Michigan History* V. 56, no. 1.

Durkheim, Emile. 1965. *The Elementary Forms of Religious Life*. New York: Free Press.

Dyer, Carol Stewart. 1989. "Political Patronage of the Wisconsin Press, 1849–1860: New Perspectives on the Economics of Patronage." *Journalism Monographs* no. 109 (February).

Edsall, Thomas B., and Mary D. Edsall. 1991. "When the Official Subject is Presidential Politics, Taxes, Welfare, Crime, Rights or Values . . . the Real Subject is Race." *Atlantic Monthly* (May).

Ely, John, and Volker Heins. 1989. "Interview with Helmut Wiesenthal." *Capitalism, Nature, Socialism* no. 3 (November).

Emery, Edwin. 1972. *The Press and America*. Englewood Cliffs, NJ: Prentice-Hall.

Epstein, Edward. 1973. *News From Nowhere*. New York: Vintage.

Ettema, James S., and Theodore L. Glasser. 1998. *Custodians of Conscience: Investigative Journalism and Public Virtue*. New York: Columbia University Press.

Falasca Zamponi, Simonetta. 1992. "The Aesthetics of Politics: Symbol, Power and Narrative in Mussolini's Fascist Italy." *Theory, Culture and Society* V. 9.

    1997. *Fascist Spectacle: The Aesthetics of Power in Mussolini's Italy*. Berkeley: University of California Press.

Feher, Ferenc. 1986. "Remarks on the Postmodern Intermezzo." *Theory, Culture and Society* V. 3, no. 2.

Ferman, Louis. 1963. *Death of a Newspaper: The Story of the Detroit Times*. Kalamazoo: W. E. Upjohn Institute for Employment Research.

Fine, Sidney. 1956. *Laissez-Faire and the General-Welfare State*. Ann Arbor: University of Michigan Press.

Fischer, Claude S., Michael Hout, Martin Sanchez Jankowski, Ann Swidler, Kim Voss, and Samuel Lucas. 1996. *Inequality by Design*. Princeton: Princeton University Press.

Fisher, Philip. 1988. "Democratic Social Space." *Representations* no. 24 (Fall).

Fiske, John. 1989. *Understanding Popular Culture*. New York: Routledge.

Fleishman, Joel (ed.) 1982. *The Future of American Political Parties.* Englewood Cliffs, NJ: Prentice-Hall.

Folkerts, Jean. 1985. "Functions of the Reform Press." *Journalism History* V. 12, no. 1.

Foner, Eric. 1970. *Free Soil, Free Labor, Free Men.* New York: Oxford University Press.

1988. *Reconstruction: America's Unfinished Revolution, 1863–1873.* New York: Harper and Row.

Foucault, Michel. 1979. *Discipline and Punish.* New York: Vintage.

Fraser, Nancy. 1992. "Rethinking the Public Sphere: A Contribution to the Critique of Actually Existing Democracy." In Craig Calhoun (ed.) *Habermas and the Public Sphere.* Cambridge, MA: MIT Press.

Fredrickson, George. 1965. *The Inner Civil War: Northern Intellectuals and the Crisis of the Union.* New York: Harper and Row.

1981. *White Supremacy.* New York: Oxford University Press.

Gais,Thomas, Mark Peterson and Jack Walker. 1984. "Interest Groups, Iron Triangles and Representative Institutions in American National Government." *British Journal of Political Science* V. 14.

Gardner, Gilson. 1932. *Lusty Scripps: The Life of E. W. Scripps.* New York: Vanguard.

Gebhardt, Eike, and Andrew Arato. (eds.) 1978. *The Essential Frankfurt School Reader.* New York: Urizen.

Geertz, Clifford. 1973. *The Interpretation of Cultures.* New York: Basic.

George, Sister Mary Karl. 1969. *Zachariah Chandler: A Political Biography.* East Lansing: Michigan State University Press.

Gienapp, William. 1982. "'Politics Seem To Enter into Everything': Political Culture in the North, 1840–1860." In Stephen Maizlish (ed.) *Essays on American Ante-bellum Politics, 1840–1860.* Arlington: Texas A and M University Press.

Gillman, Susan. 1989. *Dark Twins.* Chicago: University of Chicago Press.

Ginsberg, Benjamin. 1986. *The Captive Public: How Mass Opinion Promotes State Power.* New York: Basic.

Ginsberg, Benjamin, and Martin Shefter. 1990. *Politics by Other Means.* New York: Basic.

Gitlin, Todd. 1980. *The Whole World Is Watching: Mass Media in the Making and Unmaking of the New Left.* Berkeley: University of California Press, 1980.

Glasser, Theodore L. (ed.) 1999. *The Idea of Public Journalism.* New York: Guilford.

Godkin, Edwin L. 1898. *Unforeseen Tendencies of Democracy.* Westminster: Archibald Constable.

Goldfarb, Jeffrey. 1982. *On Cultural Freedom: An Exploration of Public Life in Poland and America.* Chicago: University of Chicago Press.

1991. *The Cynical Society.* Chicago: University of Chicago Press.

Goldner, Fred. 1991. "Opinion Expression and Formation in the Context of Polarized Groups." In *International Journal Of Public Opinion Research* V. 3, no. 3.

Goodwyn, Lawrence. 1978. *The Populist Moment.* New York: Oxford University Press.

Griffith, Sally. 1984. "Mass Media Come to the Small Town: The Emporia Gazette in the 1920s." In Catherine Covert and John Stevens (eds.) *Mass Media Between the Wars.* Syracuse: Syracuse University Press.

1989. *Home Town News: William Allen White and the Emporia Gazette.* New York: Oxford University Press.

Gutman, Herbert. 1963. "The Workers' Search for Power." In H. Wayne Morgan (ed.) *The Gilded Age.* Syracuse: Syracuse University Press.

1977. *Work, Culture and Society in Industrializing America.* New York: Vintage.

Haber, Samuel. 1964. *Efficiency and Uplift: Scientific Management in the Progressive Era, 1908–1920.* Chicago: University of Chicago Press.

Habermas, Jürgen. 1970. *Towards a Rational Society,* trans. by J. Shapiro Boston: Beacon.

1974. "The Public Sphere: An Encyclopedia Article." *New German Critique* no. 3 (Fall).

1977. "Hannah Arendt's Communications Concept of Power." *Social Research* V. 44, no. 1 (Spring).

1986. "The New Obscurity." *Philosophy and Social Criticism* V. 11, no. 2 (Winter).

1989. *The Structural Transformation of the Public Sphere,* trans. by T. Burger Cambridge, MA: MIT Press.

1996. *Between Facts and Norms: Contributions to a Discourse Theory of Law and Democracy.* Cambridge, MA: MIT Press.

Hallin, Daniel. 1985. "The American News Media: A Critical Theory Perspective." In John Forester (ed.) *Critical Theory and Public Life.* Cambridge, MA: MIT Press.

1986a. "Cartography, Community and the Cold War." In Michael Schudson and Robert Karl Manoff (eds.) *Reading the News.* New York: Pantheon.

1986b. *The Uncensored War: The Media and Vietnam.* Berkeley: University of California Press.

1994. *We Keep America on Top of the World.* New York: Routledge.

Hallin, Daniel, and Paolo Mancini. 1984. "Speaking of the President: Political Structure and Representational Form in U.S. and Italian Television News." *Theory and Society* V. 13, no. 6.

Hays, Samuel. 1964. "The Politics of Reform in Municipal Government in the Progressive Era." *Pacific Northwest Quarterly* V. 55 (October).

Hertsgaard, Mark. 1988. *On Bended Knee: The Press and the Reagan Presidency.* New York: Schocken.

Heyda, Marie. 1970. "Senator James McMillan and the Flowering of the Spoils System." *Michigan History Magazine* V. 54, no. 3 (Fall).

Hirsch, Paul. 1977. "Occupational, Organizational and Institutional Models in Mass Media Research: Toward an Integrated Framework." In Peter Miller, Paul Hirsch and F. Gerald Kline (eds.) *Strategies for Communication Research.* Beverly Hills: Sage.

Hofstadter, Richard. 1955. *The Age of Reform.* New York: Vintage.

1967. *The Paranoid Style in American Politics and Other Essays.* New York: Vintage.

1973. *The American Political Tradition.* New York: Vintage.

Holden, Edward. 1918. "Carl Schurz in Michigan." *Michigan History Magazine* V. 2, no. 1.

1927. "Little Journeys in Journalism: Recollections of Some Prominent Members of the Free Press Staff." *Michigan History Magazine* V. 11, no. 3.

Holli, Melvin. 1969. *Reform in Detroit: Hazen S. Pingree and Urban Politics.* New York: Oxford University Press.

(ed.) 1976. *Detroit.* New York: New Viewpoints.

Honneth, Axel. 1987. "Critical Theory." In Anthony Giddens and Jonathan Turner (eds.) *Social Theory Today.* Cambridge: Polity.

1995. *The Fragmented World of the Social* (ed. Charles W. Wright). Albany: SUNY Press.

Horkheimer, Max. 1973. "The Authoritarian State." *Telos* no. 15 (Spring).

Howard, June. 1985. *Form and History in American Literary Naturalism.* Chapel Hill: University of North Carolina Press.

Howells, William D. 1957. *A Modern Instance.* Boston: Houghton Mifflin.

Hoyer, Svennik. 1982. "Recent Research on the Press in Norway." *Scandinavian Journal of History* V. 7.

Hoyer, Svennik, Stig Hadenius and Lennart Weibull. 1975. *The Politics and Economics of the Press: A Developmental Perspective.* Beverly Hills: Sage.

Hughes, Helen MacGill. 1971. "From Politics to Human Interest." In James Shorter, Jr. (ed.) *The Social Fabric of the Metropolis.* Chicago: University of Chicago Press.

The [Hutchins] Commission of Freedom of the Press. 1947. *A Free and Responsible Press.* Chicago: University of Chicago Press.

Iyengar, Shanto. 1991. *Is Anyone Responsible? How Television Frames Political Issues.* Chicago: University of Chicago.

Jensen, Richard. 1969. "Armies, Admen and Crusaders: Types of Presidential Election Campaigns." *History Teacher* (January).

1971. *The Winning of the Midwest.* Chicago: University of Chicago Press.

Johnson, Terence. 1972. *Professions and Power.* London: McMillan.

Josephson, Matthew. 1953. "The Bryan Campaign." In George Whicher (ed.) *William Jennings Bryan and the Campaign of 1896.* Boston: D. C. Heath.

Kaplan, Amy. 1988. *The Social Construction of American Realism.* Chicago: University of Chicago Press.

1990. "Romancing the Empire: The Embodiment of American Masculinity in the Popular Historical Novel of the 1890s." *American Literary History* V. 2, no. 4 (Winter).

Kaplan, Richard. 1995. "The Economics of Popular Journalism in the Gilded Age." *Journalism History* V. 21, no. 2 (Summer).

1997. "The American Press and Political Community: Reporting in Detroit, 1865–1920." *Media, Culture and Society* V. 19, no. 3. (July).

1998. "Power, Objectivity and the Press: A Neo-Institutionalist Theory of the Origins of Contemporary Press Ethics." Paper presented to annual Social Science History Association convention.

Kasson, John F. 1976. *Civilizing the Machine: Technology and Republican Values in America, 1776–1900.* New York: Grossman.

Katzman, David. 1973. *Before the Ghetto: Black Detroit in the Nineteenth Century.* Chicago: University of Illinois Press.

Katznelson, Ira. 1989. "'The Burdens of Urban History': Comment." *Studies in American Political Development* V. 3.

Keller, Morton. 1977. *Affairs of State: Public Life in Late Nineteenth-Century America*. Cambridge, MA: Harvard University Press.

Kernell, Samuel. 1986. *Going Public: New Strategies of Presidential Leadership*. Washington, DC: Congressional Quarterly Press.

Key Jr., V. O. 1954. "The Direct Primary and Party Structure: A Study of State Legislative Nominations." *The American Political Science Review* V. 48, no. 1 (March).

Kirchheimer, Otto. 1969. "The Transformation of the Western European Party System." In Frederic Burin and Kurt Shell (eds.) *Politics, Law, and Social Change*. New York: Columbia University Press.

Kleiman, Jeffrey. 1986. "The Rule From Above: Businessmen, Bankers, and the Drive to Organize in Grand Rapids, 1890–1906." *Michigan History Magazine* V. 12, no. 2 (Fall).

Klein, Joe. 1986. "Our Man in Managua." *Esquire* (November).

Kleppner, Paul. 1980. "Coalitional and Party Transformation in the 1890s." In Seymour M. Lipset (ed.) *Party Coalitions in the 1980s*. San Francisco: Institute for Contemporary Studies.

1982. *Who Voted? The Dynamics of Electoral Turnout, 1870–1980*. New York: Praeger.

1987. *Change and Continuity in Electoral Politics, 1893–1928*. New York: Greenwood.

1989. "Government, Parties, and Voters in Pittsburgh." In Samuel Hays (ed.) *City at the Point: Essays on the Social History of Pittsburgh*. Pittsburgh: University of Pittsburgh Press.

Knight, Peter. 1968. "'Competition' in the U.S. Daily Newspaper Industry, 1865–68." *Journalism Quarterly*, V. 45 (Autumn).

Krippendorf, Klaus. 1980. *Content Analysis*. Beverly Hills: Sage.

Lamont, Michele. 1992. *Money, Morals and Manner: The Culture of the French and the American Upper-Middle Class*. Chicago: University of Chicago Press.

Lasch, Christopher. 1965. *The New Radicalism in America, 1889–1963*. New York: Vintage.

1967. *The Agony of the American Left*. New York: Alfred A. Knopf.

Leab, Daniel J. 1970. *A Union of Individuals: The Formation of the American Newspaper Guild, 1933–1936*. New York: Columbia University Press.

Leach, Eugene. 1986. "Mastering the Crowd: Collective Behavior and Mass Society in American Social Thought, 1917–1939." *American Studies* V. 27, no. 1 (Spring).

Leach, William. 1993. *Land of Desire: Merchants, Power and the Rise of New American Culture*. New York: Vintage.

Lee, Alfred M. 1947. *The Daily Newspaper in America*. New York: MacMillan.

Lee, James Melvin. 1917. *History of American Journalism*. New York: Garden City.

Lee III, Orville.1988. "Observations on Anthropological Thinking about the Culture Concept: Clifford Geertz and Pierre Bourdieu." *Berkeley Journal of Sociology* V. 33.

Lefort, Claude. 1988. *Democracy and Political Theory.* Minneapolis: University of Minnesota Press.

Leiss, William, Stephen Kline, and Sut Jhally. 1990. *Social Communication in Advertising.* New York: Routledge.

Leonard, Thomas. 1986. *The Power of the Press: The Birth of American Political Reporting.* New York: Oxford University Press.

1995. *News for All: America's Coming-of-Age with the Press.* New York: Oxford University Press.

Lester, Marilyn. 1974. "News as a Practical Accomplishment." Dissertation, University of California, Santa Barbara.

Levine, Lawrence. 1984. "William Shakespeare and the American People: A Study in Cultural Transformation." *American Historical Review* V. 89, no. 1 (February).

Liebes, Tamar. 1988. "Cultural Differences in the Retelling of Television Fiction." *Critical Studies in Mass Communication,* V. 5, no. 4 (December).

Lippmann, Walter. 1965. *Public Opinion.* New York, Free Press.

Lippmann, Walter, and Charles Merz. 1920. "A Test of the News." *The New Republic* V. 23 (August 4).

Lipset, Seymour M., and Stein Rokkan. (eds.) 1967. *Party Systems and Voter Alignments.* New York: Free Press.

Livingstone, William. 1904. *The Republican Party.* New York: G. P. Putnam.

Lodge, John C. (with the collaboration of M. M. Quaife) 1949. *I Remember Detroit.* Detroit: Wayne State University.

Lowi, Theodore. 1979. *The End of Liberalism.* New York: W. W. Norton.

Luhmann, Niklas. 1974. "Sociology of Political Systems." In K. Von Beyme (ed.) *German Political Studies* V. 1. London: Sage.

Lukes, Steve. 1974. *Power: a Radical View.* London: MacMillan.

Lutz, William W. 1973. "James E. Scripps Founds the Detroit News." *Detroit In Perspective* V. 1 no. 3 (September).

Lynd, Robert, and Halen Merrell Lynd. 1959 [1929]. *Middletown: A Study in Modern American Culture.* New York: Harcourt, Brace and Jovanovich.

Maier, Charles. 1981. "'Fictitious Bonds . . . of wealth and law': On the Theory and Practice of Interest Representation." In Suzanne Berger (ed.) *Organizing Interests in Western Europe.* Cambridge University Press.

Manca, Luigi. 1989. "Journalism, Advocacy and a Communicative Model for Democracy." In Marc Raboy and Peter Bruck (eds.) *Communication for and Against Democracy.* New York: Black Rose.

Mancini, Paolo. 1991. "The Public Sphere and the Use of News in a 'Coalition' System of Government." In Peter Dahlgren and Colin Sparks (eds.) *Communication and Citizenship.* New York: Routledge.

Marx, Karl. 1972. "On the Jewish Question." In Robert C. Tucker (ed.) *The Marx-Engels Reader.* New York: W. W. Norton.

McCabe, Charles R. 1951. *Damned Old Crank: A Self-Portrait of E. W. Scripps.* New York: Harper.

McConnell, Grant. 1966. *Private Power and American Democracy.* New York: Vintage.

McCormick, Richard L. 1981. *From Realignment to Reform: Political Change in New York State, 1893–1910.* Ithaca: Cornell University Press.

1986. *The Party Period and Public Policy.* New York: Oxford University Press.

McDonald, Terrence J. 1989. "The Burdens of Urban History: The Theory of the State in Recent American Social History." *Studies in American Political Development* V. 3.

McGerr, Michael E. 1986. *The Decline of Popular Politics: The American North, 1865–1928.* New York: Oxford University Press.

McKern, Joseph. 1977. "The Limits of Progressive Journalism History." *Journalism History* V. 4, no. 3 (Fall).

McPherson, James. (ed.) 1969. *Anti-Negro Riots of the North, 1863.* New York: Arno.

McRae, Milton A. 1924. *Forty Years in Newspaperdom.* New York: Bretano.

Mead, George Herbert. 1962. *Mind, Self and Society.* Chicago: Chicago University Press.

Melder, Keith. 1992. *Hail to the Candidate: Presidential Campaigns from Banners to Broadcasts.* Washington: Smithsonian Institution.

Merrill, John. 1965. "How Time Stereotyped Three U.S. Presidents." *Journalism Quarterly* V. 42.

Michels, Robert. 1962. *Political Parties.* New York: Crowell-Collier.

Mills, C. Wright. 1957. *The Power Elite.* New York: Oxford University Press.

Miroff, Bruce. 1982. "Monopolizing the Public Space: The President as a Problem for Democratic Politics." In Thomas E. Cronin (ed.) *Rethinking the Presidency.* Boston: Little, Brown.

Mohr, James C. 1976. "Introduction." In James C. Mohr (ed.) *Radical Republicans in the North.* Baltimore: Johns Hopkins University Press.

Molotch, Harvey. 1979. "Media and Movements." In Mayer Zald and John McCarthy (eds.) *The Dynamics of Social Movements.* Cambridge, MA: Winthrop.

Molotch, Harvey, and Marilyn Lester. 1974. "Accidents, Scandals and Routines: Resources of Insurgent Methodology." In Gaye Tuchman (ed.) *The TV Establishment.* Englewood Cliffs, NJ: Prentice-Hall.

Mommsen, Wolfgang. 1981. "Max Weber and Roberto Michels." *Archives Europeennes de Sociologie* V. 22.

Montgomery, David. 1979. *Workers' Control in America.* Cambridge: Cambridge University Press.

1981. *Beyond Equality: Labor and the Radical Republicans, 1862–1872.* Chicago: University of Illinois Press.

Moran, J. Bell. 1949. *The Moran Family: Two Hundred Years in Detroit.* Detroit: Alved of Detroit.

Morse, Margaret. 1985. "Talk, Talk, Talk." *Screen* V.26, no. 2 (March–April).

Mott, Frank. 1963. *American Journalism: 1890–1900.* New York: Macmillan. 3rd ed.

Munson, Eve S., and Catherine A. Warren. (eds.) 1997. *James Carey: A Critical Reader.* Minneapolis: University of Minnesota Press.

Nerone, John. 1987. "The Mythology of the Penny Press." *Critical Studies in Mass Communication* V. 4, no. 4.

1993. "A Local History of the Early U.S. Press: Cincinnati, 1793–1848." In William Solomon and Robert McChesney (eds.) *Ruthless Criticism.* Minneapolis: University of Minnesota Press.

(ed.) 1995. *Last Rights: Revisiting Four Theories of the Press.* Urbana: University of Illinois Press.

Nord, David P. 1984. "The Business Values of American Newspapers: The 19th Century Watershed in Chicago." *Journalism Quarterly* V. 61, no. 2 (Summer).

Norris, James D. 1990. *Advertising and the Transformation of American Society, 1865–1920.* New York: Greenwood.

Oestereicher, Richard. 1986. *Solidarity and Fragmentation: Working People and Class Consciousness in Detroit, 1875–1900.* Urbana: University of Illinois Press.

——— 1988. "Urban Working-Class Political Behavior and Theories of American Electoral Behavior, 1870–1940." *Journal of American History* V. 74, no. 4 (March).

Offe, Claus. 1976. "Political Authority and Class Structure." In Paul Connerton (ed.) *Critical Sociology.* London: Penguin.

——— 1984. *Contradictions of the Welfare State.* Cambridge, MA: MIT Press.

Ohmann, Richard. 1981. "Where Did Mass Culture Come From? The Case of Magazines." *Berkshire Review* no. 16.

O'Reilly, Kenneth. 1979. "'M. Quad' and Brother Gardner: Negro Dialect and Caricature in Nineteenth Century Detroit." *Detroit In Perspective* V. 3, no. 2 (Winter).

Orren, Gary. 1982. "The Changing Styles of American Party Politics." In Joel Fleishman (ed.) *The Future of American Political Parties.* Englewood Cliffs, NJ: Prentice-Hall.

Park, Robert E. 1960. The Natural History of the Newspaper." In Wilbur Schramm (ed.) *Mass Communications.* Chicago: University of Illinois Press (2nd edition).

Parsons, Talcott. 1969. *Politics and Social Structure.* New York: Free Press.

Peterson, Richard. 1979. "Revitalizing the Culture Concept." *Annual Review of Sociology* V. 5.

Pilgrim, Tim A. 1991. "How Newspapers Came to Carry the Shining Shield of Natural Monopoly." Paper presented at the *AEJMC Convention,* Boston, August.

Pingree, Hazen S. 1895. *Facts and Opinions or, Dangers that Beset Us.* Detroit: F. B. Dickerson.

Pizzorno, Alessandro. 1981. "Interests and Parties in Pluralism." In Suzanne Berger (ed.) *Organizing Interests In Western Europe.* Cambridge: Cambridge University Press.

——— 1993. "Il Sistema della Corruzione e la Corruzione del Sistema." Paper presented to the conference *Deconstructing Italy,* San Francisco, Spring.

Plotke, David. 1997. "Representation is Democracy." *Constellations* V. 4, no. 1 (April).

Poggi, Gianfranco. 1978. *The Development of the Modern State.* Stanford: Stanford University Press.

Porter, Kirk, and Donald B. Johnson. (eds.) 1966. *National Party Platforms, 1840–1960.* Urbana: University of Illinois Press.

Pound, Arthur. 1948. "Donald Dickinson." In Earl D. Babst and Lewis G. Vander Velde (eds.) *Michigan and the Cleveland Era.* Ann Arbor: University of Michigan Press.

1964. *The Only Thing Worth Finding: The Life and Legacies of George Gough Booth*. Detroit: Wayne State University Press.

Presbrey, Frank. 1929. *The History and Development of Advertising*. Garden City: Doubleday, Doran.

Przeworski, Adam. 1985. *Capitalism and Social Democracy*. Cambridge: Cambridge University Press.

Quad, M. (Charles B. Lewis) 1875. *Quad's Odds*. Detroit, R. D. S. Tyler.

1882. *Brother Gardner's Lime-Kiln Club*. Chicago: Belford, Clarke.

Rimmerman, Craig. 1991. "The 'Post-Modern' Presidency: A New Presidential Epoch?" *Western Political Quarterly* V. 44, no. 1 (March).

Rodgers, Daniel. 1982. "In Search of Progressivism." *Reviews in American History* V. 10.

1987. *Contested Truths: Keywords in American Politics Since Independence*. New York: Basic.

Roediger, David. 1991. *Wages of Whiteness: Race and the Making of the American Working Class*. New York: Verso.

Rogin, Michael. 1967. *The Intellectuals and McCarthy: The Radical Specter*. Cambridge, MA: MIT Press.

1971. "Max Weber and Woodrow Wilson: The Iron Cage in Germany and America." *Polity* V. 3, no. 4 (Summer).

1987. *Ronald Reagan, the Movie and Other Episodes in Political Demonology*. Berkeley: University of California Press.

1991. *Fathers and Children: Andrew Jackson and the Subjugation of the American Indian*. New Brunswick: Transaction Publishers (second edition).

Rogin, Michael, and John Shover. 1970. *Political Change in California*. Westport, CT: Greenwood.

Rosen, Jay. 1992. "Politics, Vision and the Press." In Suzanne Charle (ed.) *The New News v. the Old News: The Press and Politics in the 1990s*. New York: Twentieth Century Fund.

Ross, Edward A. 1918. "The Suppression of Important News." In Willard Bleyer (ed.) *The Profession of Journalism*. Boston: Atlantic Monthly.

Rothman, David. 1974. "The Structure of State Politics." In Felice A. Bonadio (ed.) *Political Parties in American History, 1828–1890* V. 2. New York: Putnam.

Rowell, George, & Co. 1870–78. *American Newspaper Directory*. New York.

Rubin, Richard. 1981. *Press, Party and Presidency*. New York: W. W. Norton.

Ryan, Mary. 1990. *Women in Public: Between Banners and Ballots, 1825–1880*. Baltimore: John Hopkins University Press.

Sabel, Charles, and Michael Piore. 1984. *The Second Industrial Divide*. New York: Basic.

Sabel, Charles, and Jonathon Zeitlin. 1985. "Historical Alternatives to Mass Production: Politics, Markets and Technology in Nineteenth-Century Industrialization." *Past and Present* no. 108 (August).

Salcetti, Marianne. 1995. "The Emergence of the Reporter." In Hanno Hardt and Bonnie Brennen (eds.) *Newsworkers*. Minneapolis: University of Minnesota Press.

Sarasohn, David. 1989. *The Party of Reform: Democrats in the Progressive Era*. Jackson: University Press of Mississippi.

Sarasohn, Stephen, and Vera Sarasohn. 1957. *Political Party Patterns in Michigan.* Detroit: Wayne State University Press.

Saretzki, Thomas. 1988. "Collective Action Vs. Functionalism?: Some Remarks Concerning Hans Joas' Critique." *Praxis International* V. 8, no. 1 (April).

Sarfatti Larson, Magali. 1977. *The Rise of Professionalism: A Sociological Analysis.* Berkeley: University of California Press.

Saxton, Alexander. 1971. *The Indispensable Enemy: Labor and the Anti-Chinese Movement in California.* Berkeley: University of California Press.

——— 1975. "Blackface Minstrelsy and Jacksonian Ideology." *American Quarterly* V. 27 (March).

——— 1990. *The Rise and Fall of the White Republic: Class, Politics and Mass Culture in Nineteenth-Century America.* New York: Verso.

Schattschneider, E. E. 1975. *The Semisovereign People: A Realist's View of Democracy in America.* Hinsdale, IL: Dryden.

Schiller, Dan. 1981. *Objectivity and the News: The Public and the Rise of Commercial Journalism.* Philadelphia: University of Pennsylvania Press.

Schmitz, Neil. 1989. "Naturalism Undone." *American Literary History* V. 1, no. 4 (Winter).

Schudson, Michael. 1978. *Discovering the News.* New York: Basic.

——— 1982. "The Politics of Narrative Form." *Daedalus* V. 111 no. 4 (Fall).

——— 1984a. "Making Journalism Safe for Democracy." *The Quill* V. 72, no. 10 (November).

——— 1984b. *Advertising, the Uneasy Persuasion.* New York: Basic.

——— 1986a. "Deadlines, Datelines and History." In Michael Schudson and Robert Karl Manoff (eds.) *Reading the News.* New York: Pantheon.

——— 1986b. "The Menu of Media Research." In Sandra Ball-Rokeach and Muriel Cantor (eds.) *Media, Audiences and Social Structure.* Beverly Hills: Sage.

——— 1990. *Origins of the Ideology of Objectivity in the Professions.* New York: Garland.

——— 1991. "The Sociology of News Production Revisited." In James Curran and Michael Gurevich (eds.) *Mass Media and Society.* New York: Edward Arnold.

——— 1994. "Review of *The Commercialization of the News in the Nineteenth Century.*" *Journal of American History* V. 81, no. 1 (June).

——— 1995. *The Power of News.* Cambridge, MA: Harvard University Press.

——— 1998. *The Good Citizen: A History of American Civic Life.* New York: Free Press.

——— forthcoming. "Persistence of Vision: The Partisan Press, 1880–1950." In Janice Radway and Carl Kaestle (eds.) *History of the Book,* V. 4. Cambridge: Cambridge University Press.

Schumpeter, Joseph. 1950. *Capitalism, Socialism and Democracy.* New York: Harper and Row.

Schwarzlose, Richard A. 1990. *The Nation's Newsbrokers,* V. 2. Evanston: Northwestern University Press.

Scott, Walter Dill. 1921 [1908] *The Psychology of Advertising.* Boston: Small, Maynard.

Scripps, Edward W. 1966. *I Protest: Selected Disquisitions of E. W. Scripps,* edited and introduced by Oliver Knight. Madison: University of Wisconsin Press.

Scripps, James E. 1879. "Some Elements of Success in Journalism." In *Proceedings of the Michigan Press Association,* 12th Annual Meeting.

1900. "Wilbur F. Storey, Detroit's First Great Journalist." *Detroit News-Tribune*, Sept. 16: 14.

Seitz, Don C. 1916. *Training for the Newspaper Trade*. Philadelphia: J. B. Lippincott.

Seymour-Ure, Colin. 1968. *The Press, Politics and the Public*. London: Methuen.

Shaw, Donald L. 1967. "News Bias and the Telegraph: A Study of Historical Change." *Journalism Quarterly* V. 44, no. 1 (Spring).

Shefter, Martin. 1983. "Regional Receptivity to Reform: The Legacy of the Progressive Era." *Political Science Quarterly* V. 98, no. 3 (Fall).

Sheller, Mimi. 1996. "Democracy after Slavery: Post-Emancipation Publics in Haiti and Jamaica." Dissertation, New School for Social Research.

Sigal, Leon V. 1986. "Who? Sources Make the News." In Michael Schudson and Robert Manoff (eds.) *Reading the News*. New York: Vintage.

Skocpol, Theda. 1992. *Protecting Soldiers and Mothers*. Cambridge, MA: Harvard University Press.

Skocpol, Theda, and John Ikenberry. 1983. "The Political Formation of the American Welfare State." *Comparative Social Research*, V. 6.

Skowronek, Stephen. 1981. *Building a New American State: The Expansion of National Administrative Capacities, 1877–1920*. Cambridge: Cambridge University Press.

Slotkin, Richard. 1985. *The Fatal Environment: The Myth of the Frontier in the Age of Industrialization, 1800–1890*. New York: Atheneum.

Smith, Culver H. 1977. *The Press, Politics and Patronage*. Athens: University of Georgia Press.

Smith, David C. 1964. "Wood Pulp and Newspapers, 1867–1900." *Business History Review* V. 38, no. 3.

Smythe, Ted Curits. 1980. "The Reporter, 1880–1900: Working Conditions and their Influence on the News." *Journalism History* V. 7, no. 1 (Spring).

Stark, George. 1943. "Schermerhorn of the Times." *Michigan History Magazine* V. 27, no. 3 (Summer).

Stensaas, Harlan. 1986–87. "Development of the Objectivity Ethic in U.S. Daily Newspapers." *Journal of Mass Media Ethics* V. 2, no. 1 (Fall/Winter).

Stocking, William. 1915. "Prominent Newspaper Men in Michigan." *Michigan Pioneer and Historical Collections* V. 39. (Reprinted in George Fuller (ed.), *Historic Michigan*, Nortical Historic Association; V. 2.)

Stone, Melville. 1883. "The Model Newspaper." *Michigan State Publisher Proceedings*, March 29–30 (Detroit Public Library, Burton Historical Collection).

Sundquist, Eric J. 1988. "Mark Twain and Homer Plessy." *Representations* no. 24 (Fall).

1993. *To Wake the Nations: Race in the Making of American Literature*. Cambridge, MA: Harvard University Press.

Susman, Warren. 1984. *Culture as History*. New York: Pantheon.

Swanberg, W. A. 1961. *Citizen Hearst*. New York: Scribner.

1967. *Pulitzer*. New York: Scribner.

Swidler, Ann. 1986. "Culture in Action: Symbols and Strategies." *American Sociological Review* V. 51 (April).

Thayer, Frank. 1926. *Newspaper Management*. New York: D. Appleton.

Thorndike, Clarence. (ed.) 1958. *Thorndike-Barnhart Comprehensive Desk Dictionary.* Garden City: Doubleday.

Tilly, Charles. 1984. *Big Structures, Large Processes, Huge Comparisons.* New York: Russell Sage Foundation.

Tocqueville, Alexis de. 1945. *Democracy in America,* Vs. 1–2, trans. by H. Reeves. New York: Vintage.

Todorov, Tzvetan. 1979. "Enunciation." In Tzvetan Todorov and Oswald Ducrot (eds.) *Encyclopedic Dictionary of the Sciences of Language,* trans. by C. Porter. Baltimore: John Hopkins University Press.

Tompkins, David. 1969. "Profile of a Progressive Editor." *Michigan History Magazine* V. 53, no. 2 (Summer).

Touraine, Alain. 1981. *The Voice and the Eye.* Cambridge: Cambridge University Press.

Tuchman, Gaye. 1972. "Objectivity as Strategic Ritual: An Examination of Newsmen's Notions of Objectivity." *American Journal of Sociology* V. 77, no. 4.

1978a. *Making News: A Study in the Construction of Reality.* New York: Free Press.

1978b. "Professionalism as an Agent of Legitimation." *Journal of Communications* V. 28 (Spring).

1978c. "The News Net." *Social Research* V. 45, no. 3 (Summer).

Tulis, Jeffrey. 1987. *The Rhetorical Presidency.* Princeton: Princeton University Press.

Udell, Jon. 1978. *Economics of the American Press.* New York: Hasting House.

U.S. Bureau of the Census, Historical Statistics tables D-735, D-738, D-740.

Utley, Henry M. 1906. *Michigan as a State,* V. 4. New York: Americana Press.

Vajda, Mihaly. 1978. *Fascism as a Mass Movement.* New York: St. Martin's Press.

VanderMeer, Philip. 1989. "Political Crisis and Third Parties: The Gold Democrats of Michigan" *Michigan Historical Review* V. 15, no. 2.

Villard, Oswald G. 1918. "Press Tendencies and Dangers." In Willard Bleyer (ed.) *The Profession of Journalism.* Boston: Atlantic Monthly.

Wacquant, Loic. 1987. "Symbolic Violence and the Making of the French Agriculturalist: An Enquiry into Pierre Bourdieu's Sociology." *Australian and New Zealand Journal of Sociology* V. 23, no. 1 (March).

Walker, Jack. 1977. "Setting the Agenda in the U.S. Senate: A Theory of Problem Selection." *British Journal of Political Science* V. 7.

Wattenberg, Martin. 1986. *The Decline of American Parties, 1952–1984.* Cambridge: Harvard University Press.

Weaver, Paul. 1974. "The Politics of a News Story." In Harry M. Clor (ed.) *The Mass Media and Modern Democracy.* Chicago: Rand McNally College.

1994. *News and the Culture of Lying.* New York: Free Press.

Westbrook, Robert. 1983. "Politics as Consumption: Managing the Modern American Electorate." In Richard W. Fox and T. J. Jackson Lears (eds.) *The Culture of Consumption.* New York: Pantheon.

White, Hayden. 1987. *The Content of the Form.* Baltimore: John Hopkins University Press.

White, William Allen. 1946. *The Autobiography of William Allen White.* New York: MacMillan.

White, Z. L. 1888. "Western Journalism." *Harper's Magazine* V. 77 (October).

Wiebe, Robert. 1967. *The Search for Order, 1877–1920*. New York: Hill and Wang.

Wilentz, Sean. 1982. "On Class and Politics in Jacksonian America." *Reviews in American History* (December).

1984. *Chants Democratic*. New York: Oxford University Press.

Woodward, C. Vann. 1966. *Reunion and Reaction: The Compromise of 1877 and the End of Reconstruction*. Boston: Little, Brown.

Woodward, C. Vann, John Blum, Bruce Catton, Edmund S. Morgan, Arthur Schlesinger Jr., and Kenneth Stamp. 1968. *The National Experience*, Part 2. New York: Harcourt, Brace and World. Second edition.

Wuthnow, Robert. 1987. *Meaning and Moral Order: Explorations in Cultural Analysis*. Berkeley: University of California Press.

Yellowitz, Irwin. 1965. *Labor and the Progressive Movement in New York State, 1897–1916*. Ithaca: Cornell University Press.

Young, John R. 1915. *Journalism in California*. San Francisco: Chronicle.

Ziff, Larzer. 1966. *The American 1890s*. New York: Viking.

Zunz, Oliver. 1982. *The Changing Face of Inequality: Urbanization, Industrial Development and Immigrants in Detroit, 1880–1920*. Chicago: University of Chicago Press.

Index

advertising, 9, 17, 19 n25, 58, 104, 106,
  117, 120–3, 124, 126–9, 198 n13
African-Americans, *see* Democratic Party
  issues and Republican Party issues
agenda, 15, 26, 29, 36, 41, 42, 43, 45, 47,
  53 n78, 151, 188
  see also party issues, partisan journalism
Alexander, Jeffrey, 169, 182 n111
anti-draft riots, 35–6, 51 n40
Arendt, Hannah, 49 n12
Associated Press, 92, 173

Baehr, Harry, 106, 112, 123
Baker, Jean, 33, 36, 38, 43, 45, 46, 82, 83,
  94, 95
Baldasty, Gerald 8–10, 68 n4, 72, 99 n16
Booth, George G., 104, 110, 112–13, 116,
  119, 121, 151, 163–69, 181 n99, 191
Bourdieu, Pierre, 18 n24, 26, 81–3, 100
  n34
Bow, James, 113, 181 n99
Bryan, William J., 66, 116, 140, 143–47
Bryce, James, 43, 92
Burnham, Walter D., 13, 75, 150, 160, 179
  n71

capital investment, 8, 58, 122, 124, 126,
  129
Chandler, Zachariah, 41–2, 62, 64
circulation, 105, 110–11, 114–15, 123
  and universal inclusion, 104, 105, 107,
  108, 111–12, 114–15, 129
  see also working-class and newspapers
civic journalism, 197
commercialization, 8–10, 17, 105
competition, 55, 57, 58, 59, 60, 64, 104,
  111, 122–4, 125–7, 168
consolidation, 57, 65, 104, 111, 123–4,
  125–7
construction of the news, political–cultural,
  18 n5, 48 n11, 167, 185, 192
consumer society, 17, 56, 108, 118, 122,

124–5, 128, 131 n23, 131 n24, 180
  n90
corporations, political influence of, 73, 83,
  95–7
critical elections and democracy, 74–5
cynicism, 141, 161–3

Democratic Party issues, 29–39, 42
  African-American franchise, 30, 32, 33,
    36
  African-Americans, 29, 30–9, 43–7, 54
    n 99
  corruption, 29–30, 38
  crime, 34–5
  despotism, 29–30, 36–7
  see also agenda
Detroit, 32, 35, 157–60, 200, 203 n4
dialect, 44, 47, 53 n84

economic models
  ascetic, 107, 110, 114, 118, 121, 122
  dynamic, 106, 107, 118, 123, 126
election of 1872, 58, 61, 75
election of 1896, 16, 66–7, 116, 140,
  142–7, 148
  see also ending of partisanship
election of 1904, 151–6, 172
election of 1908, 171–5
Emery, Edwin, 110, 123
exchanged news, 34, 40

Ferris, Woodbridge, 152–5, 156
Foucault, Michel, 49 n12

Godkin, E. L., 109, 128, 132 n25
Greeley, Horace, 23, 27, 58–61

Habermas, Jürgen, 5–6, 11, 18 n15, 186,
  197 n4
Hallin, Daniel, 18 n2, 183 n121
Hearst, William R., 105, 106, 112, 113,
  115, 126, 127, 135 n66, 140

221